MARTINŮ

MARTINŮ
Brian Large

Duckworth

First published in 1975 by
Gerald Duckworth & Co Ltd
The Old Piano Factory
43 Gloucester Crescent, London NW1

ISBN 0 7156 0770 7

Printed in Great Britain by
Bristol Typesetting Co Ltd
Barton Manor, St Philips, Bristol

In memory of SFS, good friend and teacher

Contents

List of Illustrations

Preface

The Czech composer Bohuslav Martinů was a curiously elusive artist. Fifteen years after his death his name is still sometimes confused with that of Giovanni Battista Martini and his music mistaken for that of his contemporary Frank Martin. This curious state of affairs has developed despite the fact that Martinů has been the subject of numerous articles and studies over the last thirty years. As early as 1937 Pierre-Octave Ferroud published in *The Chesterian* (Vol. XVII No. 122) an essay on Martinů's musical personality under the title 'A Great Musician Today', and two years later, in June 1939, the *New York Times* printed an article on Martinů's output by the Czech diplomat Miloš Šafránek. This was followed by another Šafránek article in *Music Quarterly* (Vol. XXIX No. 3) in July 1943 and by *The Book of Modern Composers* (1942) in which Paul Nettl summarised the composer's career. But in all of these and notably in *Bohuslav Martinů – The Man and his Music,* written by Šafránek in Czech in 1943, translated into English by Božena Linhartová and published in London in 1946, the writers have stressed the romantic-sounding circumstances surrounding Martinů's life at the expense of good musical criticism. Of course, it was only to be expected that Martinů's birthplace, the Polička Church Tower, would lead some commentators to draw parallels with Alfred de Vigny's poem *La Tour d'ivoire* – or at least Sainte-Beuve's interpretation of it. But in reality there was no question of Martinů taking refuge in any metaphorical ivory tower in order to escape life around him as some biographers would have us believe. Early on he conquered the disadvantages of a peasant upbringing in rural Bohemia and developed into a forceful musical personality during the 1920s and 30s mainly by dint of hard work, determination and technical boldness. Unfortunately critics have so far failed to appreciate the way Martinů's style, albeit erratically, was maturing during the 1940s and 1950s and how much he contributed to Czech music at this time.

It was only after the composer's death in 1959 that Miloš Šafránek was moved to take to his pen again and produce his 'authorised' biography, called *Martinů – His Life and Works.* This appeared in Czech in 1961 and in English translation the following year. While the author was able to revise and reconsider some of his earlier opinions he again stressed the biographical aspects of the man's life at the expense of the music. Here Šafránek, the friend, remembers Martinů as he had known him, many years before; but there is no attempt to appraise the composer's art. For informed critical comment one must turn to the Czech writings of Jaroslav Mihule who has recently done much for the Martinů cause in Prague. Unfortunately his research has been restricted to Czechoslovakia; but I am grateful to him for much friendly advice and help, as I am to Zdeněk Zouhar who edited an excellent collection of memoirs called *Sborník vzpomínek a studií* (Brno 1957) which has proved a useful area of reference.

While Drs. Mihule and Zouhar have carried out a considerable amount of Martinů research in Czechoslovakia and their findings have been published in Prague and Brno, little has appeared elsewhere. Admittedly Harry Halbreich published his comprehensive *Werkverzeichnis Dokumentation und Biographie* in 1968 but this is valuable more for its catalogue of works than for its understanding of the composer's style. Martinů's life was rich and full and in preparing this, the first full-length English study of the composer, I have tried to give an insight into Martinů's works with the help of letters, documents and the personal recollections of those who knew the composer well. I have not attempted to make a systematic analysis of Martinů's 390 compositions, though each is listed and cross-referenced. To have done so would have imposed certain tensions on the reader and extended the book to unreasonable lengths. Instead I have concentrated on the composer's more important scores, placing them against the background and times in which they were written. Thus, I have directed the reader to the twenty or thirty works in Martinů's catalogue that in my opinion have lasting significance and will repay study and repeated hearings. I have also tried to list the recognisable features of Martinů's style, to point to the formative influences behind the music, to assess his musical personality and to place him amongst his contemporaries.

A book of this nature would not have been possible without the help of a number of devoted enthusiasts in Czechoslovakia and France and throughout my studies I have been fortunate in having the friendship and advice of the composer's widow, Charlotte Martinů. Her memories, letters and diaries have been a constant source of information. These documents, together with a number of unpublished manuscripts, have been placed at my disposal and here I must record the debt I owe her. I would also like to acknowledge my thanks for permission to use freely throughout this work extracts from Madame Martinů's unpublished memoirs. Dr. F. Popelka at the Martinů Museum provided welcoming facilities in Polička and much encouragement for my research into the juvenilia, and Maruška Pražanová, the old Martinů family friend in

Polička, offered hospitality and a wealth of personal papers originating from the composer's late brother and sister. Paul Sacher, Marcel Mihalovici, Rudolf Firkušný, Rafael Kubelík and Jan Novák have all contributed one way or another. Zdenka Podhajský has provided valuable help in documentation, and Katherine Wilkinson has prepared the typescript with painstaking thoroughness. Dr. V. Dam (Supraphon, Prague) and his friends in the Czech Music Information Centre (Brno and Prague) have generously supplied scores not available in the West and Dr. John Tyrrell has furnished information and penetrating criticism concerning the opera *The Three Wishes* which he had the good fortune to see in Brno before me.

Brian Large
London September 1973

Introduction

It is a commonplace that artists, like the Saints, are willing to flout the values of the world. Indifferent to wealth and comfort, to recognition and sympathetic understanding, some composers have worked persistently to produce works which had but the slightest chance of public performance during the writer's life. Posterity profits from scores which did nothing for the composer financially; and yet is one to suppose that the man who worked in poverty and obscurity, often sacrificing not only himself, but family and friends, merely failed to achieve the success that he had aimed at? The musician is sometimes indifferent to recognition and fame and more often than not has no regard for his efforts once they have been committed to paper. Such composers call to mind Bernard Shaw's attempt at explaining *Joan of Arc* :

That there are forces at work which use individuals for purposes far transcending the purpose of keeping those individuals alive . . . is established by the fact that men will, in the pursuit of knowledge and of social readjustments for which they will not be a penny the better, and are indeed often many pence the worse, face poverty, infamy, exile, dreadful hardships and death. Even the selfish pursuit of personal power does not nerve men to the efforts and sacrifices which are eagerly made in pursuit of extensions of our power over nature, though these extensions may not touch the personal life of the seeker at any point. There is no more mystery about the appetite for food : both are known as facts . . . the difference between them being that the appetite for food is necessary to the life of the hungry man and is, therefore, a personal appetite, whereas the other is an appetite for evolution, and, therefore, a super-personal need.

However one regards Shaw's thoughts about the *élan vital,* it is possible to recognise the truth in his description of a certain type of artist. To this class Bohuslav Martinů belonged. Without doubt he was a dedicated composer. In the business of writing music which made no concession to public taste, which brought little material reward, and the only purpose of which was to satisfy the composer's imperious demands for self-expression, Martinů overcame the disadvantages of a humble birth, his shyness and diffidence, his slowness in ordinary academic pursuits, and his linguistic difficulties; and so displayed that sort of facility which is one of the marks of genius.

It is the purpose of this book to describe the course of the composer's life, to examine the characteristics of his style through a discussion of his works and to assess the degree of his originality.

1 Polička: 1890-1907

I've always kept a picture postcard of Polička as seen from our tower-like home in my room. This view, and many others, are so firmly planted in the memory that I know them all to the last detail. On one side there's the lake, on the other the cemetery and village stretching further and further into the distance. To the north there's flat, unwooded country, and below, the town itself, everything in miniature, with tiny houses and tiny people moving, creating a kind of shifting pattern. And above, boundless space where the sky kept changing as regularly as nature did below. Expanses of winter snow changed into russet fields, green patches and blue forests. The harsh atmosphere of winter began to melt away: the fields grew into a sea of golden grain and life moved from the town to the country where people became part of nature's pattern along with trees, streams and birds. And at night there were storms and fires and I don't know what else . . . These are impressions of home, my home, indelible and unforgettable.

Thus wrote Bohuslav Martinů at the age of forty-four when recalling Polička, his birthplace, a quiet country town five hundred metres above sea level in the Bohemian-Moravian highlands. Here, in the north-easterly tip of Bohemia, the countryside is not typically highland in character but pleasantly hilly with a thickly-wooded landscape steeped in tradition. To this region, known locally as the Vysočina, Martinů was bound as strongly as a child is tied to its mother. And to the Vysočina and to Polička he kept returning all his life, in his writings if not in person. But it was not only in words that Martinů recalled his home; above all it was in music that he gave expression to the experiences and impressions evoked by it. Though Martinů's life's course took him from Polička to Prague, to Paris, on to America and back to Europe, neither foreign surroundings nor international fame could wipe out the memories of youth and home. Talent is sometimes nurtured by environment, and there are few people to whom this applied in greater measure than Bohuslav Martinů. His affection was fastened to one geographical spot – Polička.

Local records show that Polička (literally 'little fields') had been the home of the Martinů family since the fifteenth century when in 1432, one Martin, a settler from Italy and smith by trade, was made Parish Councillor and later Mayor. In 1460 and 1483 the name appeared in connexion with Councillor Martin, a potter, and thereafter it can be traced down to the nineteenth century when Bohuslav's ancestors, weavers, cutlers, brick-layers and carpenters, had seen Polička develop into a flourishing trading centre.

Polička is a town with a centuries-old tradition. It was founded by the Royal decree of Přemysl Otakar II in 1265 on the site of a market village originating from a royal guardpost on one of the main trade routes linking Moravia with Bohemia. Peopled by Czech free-men and colonists from Silesia, Bavaria and Thuringia, Polička grew up as an agricultural centre where an important weaving industry was practised. In 1307 Rudolf I gave his consort, Queen Elizabeth, the lease of several communities of which Polička was one; thus it became a royal dowager town paying taxes direct to the Bohemian Queen. In 1421, during the Hussite Wars, Jan Žižka occupied Polička and only after the Thirty Years War did it slowly recover from his campaigns. During the eighteenth century it grew prosperous, but in 1845 a destructive fire, Polička's second, rased to the ground the whole of the town's inner ward, thus effacing Polička's original classical chessboard character and many of its superb Baroque buildings. In the forty-five years which separated the great fire from Martinů's birth in 1890 Polička was gradually rebuilt, not totally, but piecemeal, so that its ramparts and bastions, reminders of the time when Polička was a strongly fortified medieval town, were joined to new buildings in higgledy-piggledy fashion. With six hundred dwellings and a population of four-and-a-half thousand to safeguard, the free-men and Mayor of Polička had a Town Keeper appointed by special decree whose duty it was to guard against fire by day and night. The look-out was to be the highest vantage point in Polička – the rebuilt Church of Sv. Jakob (St. James), in the tower of which had been constructed a small living-room above the belfry and clock mechanism. So it was on September 12, 1889, that the local cobbler, the thirty-six-year-old Ferdinand Martinů, seeking to better his poor circumstances with an additional source of income, moved to the top of the tower with his wife and two children.

For his fire-watching duties Ferdinand Martinů was paid three gulden a week. (In case of emergency he had to sound the alarm, point a red lantern in the direction of the blaze and shout its whereabouts through a loud hailer to the people at the foot of the tower.) He was also responsible for winding the church clock, ringing the hours and tolling the bells for service – a labour which brought him an extra twelve gulden a year. In addition to free accommodation, he was allowed a supply of eight cubic metres of hard wood from the Polička forests and twenty gulden towards light. With the emoluments from his work being so small he was obliged to continue his shoemaking, but could expect few passers-by to mount the one-hundred-and-ninety-three steps to his workshop just for a fitting. Indeed, access from the street was almost as hazardous as an expedition to Prague at this time.

1. *and* 2. Martinů's birthplace, the church of St. James, Polička.

3. *and* 4. The Martinůs' living-room at the top of St. James's church tower, Polička.

From the heavy iron doorway at the foot of the tower, forty-four stone stairs spiralled past the organ-loft to the triforium. A second flight, fifty-six steeper stairs, provided access to a storage area where wood and potatoes were kept and where the primitive hand-operated rope-lift, which hoisted provisions from ground-level, stopped. From here everything had to be carried up by hand. Twenty-eight dimly-lit wooden steps led to a door and to the draughty bell-platform with its immense beams and cross-pieces – the home of bats and pigeons. Now the ascent became perilous. A narrow wooden staircase wound past the incessant hammerlike ticking of the clock to a final landing. Twenty-two steps later the intrepid climber came to daylight and the thirty-inch-wide balcony running round the tower, enclosing a three-foot stone parapet secured by gablets. Two final steps led into the Martinů's home itself – an oblong room, light and airy with windows on three sides, which served as living, working and sleeping quarters for the entire family. In summer meals were prepared in a small ante-room on one side, but from November (when the snows came) until April, this was used for storing fuel and drinking water drawn from a pump at ground level and carried up in a bucket.

Today, the tower, now a museum, is much as it was when the Martinůs lived there. The climb to the top is just as exhausting, the view from the balcony just as exhilarating. In the living-room, now neat and orderly, are relics of the Martinů household, pieces of furniture, functional if scant. This is no fine ancestral home but a parlour-cum-workshop with Ferdinand Martinů's bench, his hammers and leather cutters, his primitive sewing machine standing alongside the family bed, and a crudely carved table. Here, too, are his fire-watcher's loud-hailer and lantern, and on one of the walls hangs a diploma from the Polička fire brigade recognising Martinů's membership of the local rescue force. Next to it are pictures of St. Anne, of the Virgin Mary and of a Guardian Angel – reminders that the Martinůs were practising Catholics – and nearby are portraits of Jan Hus and leaders of the Sokol gymnast movement. Prominently displayed over a bookcase is a certificate recording that Martinů and his wife were members of the Polička Singing Club for the year 1886. But despite an atmosphere coloured by reminders of the Martinůs' residence, it is hard to believe that six people lived and worked in this one room – a room measuring little more than sixteen feet by eleven – and that they did so for nearly thirteen years.

The Martinůs were simple country folk and extremely hard-working. Ferdinand, son of Jan Martinů, a weaver and brick-layer, was a generous kind-hearted man. In his easy-going way he dabbled in forecasting the

B

3

weather and derived as much pleasure from keeping budgerigars (twelve cages of them) as he did from growing flowers in window boxes and displaying them on all sides of the tower. His greatest love, however, was for the Polička theatre, where for many years he had been a member of the amateur dramatic society and in his spare time had participated both as player and prompter. His wife, Karolina, daughter of František Klimeš, a cabinet-maker and free-man of Polička 'within the walls', was made of much sterner stuff. She was the real head of the family, a forceful, well-built woman who could turn her hand to any strenuous work in order to make good the deficiencies in the family budget. She was strict to the point of severity, had little time for social diversions, and spent most of her hours either embroidering or laundering the shirts of the Polička well-to-do.

Sharing the tower with them were their two children, František (b. 1880) and Marie (b. 1882). Two other children, Antonín (b. 1884) and Jaroslav (b. 1886) had died in infancy, and an illegitimate son, Karel Klimeš, born to Karolina in 1872, had previously moved to Prague to make room for Marie and František. Somehow room was made for two lodgers – Karel Stodola, an elderly shoemaker, known as *děda* (grandfather), who slept behind the tower clock, and Stanislav Hnát, an apprentice. A frequent visitor was the old Polička washerwoman Mrs. Štěpánková, who brought laundry for Karolina to iron and helped with chores when she was overworked, as in the autumn of 1890, the time when she was expecting her sixth child. On 8 December, Karolina gave birth to another son. His arrival was greeted by the pealing of bells for the feast of the Immaculate Conception, a sign, according to Lucie Kříklavová, the local midwife, that a great man had just been born. Six days later he was christened Bohuslav Jan.

Bohuslav was a frail child. He was always ailing and had to be carried everywhere. Consequently he rarely left the tower and was brought up in a prison-like atmosphere, isolated and ignorant of Polička and the human world below. Like Leo Tolstoy, who as a child was brought up in a similarly close family environment, Bohuslav found it hard to believe that other people existed apart from his parents. But his energetic father was far too busy to play with him and from his domineering mother he gained little love or warmth. Left to his own devices Bohuslav would spend hours peering through the star-shaped apertures in the parapet onto the world below with its kaleidoscope of tiny fields cultivated with neatness and devotion by the Polička farmers. As he grew stronger he began to play with a rocking horse and on rainy days would spend hours cutting soldiers out of old newspapers. Later he ventured into the tower itself where he came in touch with the mechanical

4

world – the world of bell, hammer and church clock whose elaborate mechanism and rhythmical ticking played counterpoint to the strains of the church organ wafting through the rafters below. From time to time he also heard his mother sing, for a musical vein in her could sometimes soften her natural hardness; but the greatest musical stimulus came from old Stodola who livened up his odd jobs by singing a variety of folk songs and nursery rhymes. Stodola, who originated from the neighbouring village of Borová, may well have been the first to arouse Bohuslav's interest in music, and was certainly responsible for encouraging him to beat a small drum with such force that he soon acquired a reputation among the locals (though whether as a performer or as a nuisance is not clear). Later the drum was replaced by two pieces of wood which served for fiddle and bow, and on fine days Bohuslav could be seen processing around the balcony, scraping away to Stodola's singing.

Apart from this Bohuslav's life was particularly sheltered. He was nervous and shy, as is hardly surprising for one who spent the first six years of his life almost entirely within the tower. He rarely descended to the street so he rarely met the people of Polička.

Since I was so long isolated on the tower and as cut off from the outside world as if I had lived in a lighthouse, I could do nothing but engrave the views from the top of the tower in my memory. From each side of the balcony the outlook was different, and a wide expanse of space covered everything . . . This space, I think, was the greatest impression of my childhood. Before everything else it penetrated my consciousness and it was only later that I became aware of people. In my early days people seemed like little dots, shifting I knew not where nor why, figures working in an unknown fashion . . . building houses like boxes, moving like ants. This picture, I remember, was always changing and was dominated by space. When you consider that I lived more or less in isolation except for spatial phenomena, it perhaps explains why I viewed everything differently.

Clearly Bohuslav looked down on Polička with a false perspective and for him humanity assumed significance only when it involved groups of people, such as wedding or funeral processions, winding slowly to and from the church, or masses like the occasional military manoeuvre which looked like a game of animated toy soldiers with cannon, horses and men. Little wonder that, when at the age of six the boy was carried down to start school, he felt different from his fellows. A child reared in less than two hundred square feet of floor space, one-hundred-and-ninety-three steps above the ground could scarcely escape being tongue-tied, even frightened; and it was long before Bohuslav could fully realise the identity of the Lilliputian world, which he had observed

5

from the tower, and the Brobdingnagian existence which now towered above him at street level.

The Polička school was much like those in other small towns on the Bohemian-Moravian border at the close of the last century. It provided a rudimentary education on strict Austrian lines, but little else. For those who had distinguished themselves, the gymnasium in the neighbouring town of Vysoké Mýto offered a more advanced curriculum. Bohuslav, however, did not distinguish himself. He seems to have been especially weak in mathematics and drawing and to have lacked the ability of making friends easily. He was shy and withdrawn, and is remembered as a quietly-spoken dreamer invariably engrossed in a world of his own. Away from school he would spend hours dreaming in the woods around Medlov and Cykovec, relishing the spicy aroma of the soil. As he grew stronger Bohuslav developed a love for walking and sometimes would climb through dandelion fields to the hillside village of Tři Studně ('Three Wells') or, nearer home, to Šibenice Hill – the former haunt of brigands and the place of gallows. From there the blue-hazed Vyso-čina opened before him with bright mornings, velvet evenings and an atmosphere smelling of summer clover. Clearly Bohuslav preferred to observe life rather than to participate in it, and many of his observations were acute; for much that he saw of local folk custom in the surrounding countryside left indelible impressions which were to furnish ideas for choral and theatrical works in years to come. The Vysočina was, and is, an area rich in folk-lore and Bohuslav immersed himself in the colourful folk festivals which he saw being celebrated every year – the Burning of Judas in Holy Week, the Burning of Witches at the end of April, the Opening of the Wells in May, the procession of children from the Shrine of St. Antony around Polička's outer walls at Corpus Christi and similar pageants for the feasts of St. Wenceslas and St. Bartholomew. But most memorable were the Christmas ceremonies when Bethlehem Shepherds and an Angel accompanied the Three Kings around the town distributing gifts to the children and poor.

With Bohuslav's descent to earth something else entered his life. The two pieces of wood which had served as fiddle and bow on the tower were now replaced by a three-quarter-sized violin bought at the annual Polička Fair and a proper start was made to playing. Twice a week Bohuslav went for lessons at the local tailor's house in a side street near the church. Here Josef Černovský, who kept a cow in his backyard, taught in his spare time. By all accounts he was a good musician: he could play several stringed instruments and had a knowl-edge of the clarinet and flute as well. Beginners worked their way through a string tutor prepared by Jan Malát and lessons were taken in groups of five at a cost of four hellers per head. Bohuslav's progress was rapid. What he failed to be able to say in words he seemed to make up for in music; and recognising the boy's talent, Černovský quickly promoted him to a student quartet and later to the Polička string orchestra. He also encouraged him to compose, though in all probability these compositions, such as they were, can have been little more than improvisations. However, Bohuslav regarded Černovský affectionately and later paid his memory this compliment.

When I look back there is no one who can replace him. Even though he had no diploma or anything like that, he had a love of music and art of which he himself was possibly unaware. It was he who showed me the way to appreciate both music and art. His lessons were extraordinary. He was the first to acknowledge my gifts and the first to encourage me.

Bohuslav's interest in music did little to break down his shyness. If anything it added to it, for his diligent hours of practice isolated him even from his class-mates. However, his playing did bring variety to life in the tower and broke the monotony of long winter evenings when there was little else for the family to do but strip feathers or ply some craft. In Polička winter arrives with the strides of a giant, and even today the town falls into a deep sleep between November and March. These were the months for reading and though the Martinůs were far too poor to buy books they borrowed every kind of historical novel, passing them from hand to hand as if they were a circulating library. In this way Bohuslav discovered the world of V. B. Třebizský and Alois Jirásek and the humorous plays of František Rubeš and Václav Klicpera. Next to music, reading became his greatest passion.

About the same time that music entered Bohuslav's life the boy also became acquainted with the theatre – not in any formal or social sense, but backstage; for as a prompter to the Polička Players Ferdinand Martinů often took his eight-year-old son to rehearsals. In the tiny, darkened theatre with its poor facilities Bohuslav entered a land of make-believe, of dreams and of fantasies. Here he was initiated into the mysteries of the actor's world and began to appreciate the techniques of stagecraft. Though Polička had a long stage tradition dating back to 1819 and had been one of the first Bohemian towns to acquire a permanent theatre, the repertoire rarely ventured beyond the usual run of conversational comedies of Klicpera and Šubrt. From time to time, however, a travelling company would bring a Smetana opera or an Offenbach operetta to Polička and this event would quite turn Bohuslav's head. Almost certainly the roots of his enthusiasm for and appreciation of dramatic art are to be found in these childhood experiences; and it is hardly surprising that he was later to create twenty-eight works (operas and ballets) for the stage.

So to Bohuslav's two great interests – music and reading – a third was now added. But by this time music had become an obsession. When he was not practising the violin, he would sit in a corner composing on home-made manuscript paper, with the stave lines drawn by hand since Karolina Martinů was far too careful to waste money on such luxuries. The earliest of Bohuslav's compositions to have survived is a string quartet called *Tři jezdci* (*The Three Riders*) dating from 1902 and inspired by the programmatic ballad of Jaroslav Vrchlický which describes how three Czech nobles bring to their homeland the tragic news of the burning of Jan Hus. (Fifty years before, the same subject had moved Smetana to write his ballad for male voices, though the text of his *Three Riders* was provided by Jiří Jahn.) Bohuslav's quartet is a simple three-movement essay in D major covering nine sides of manuscript paper, with the viola part notated in the treble clef, and even if the musical invention is childlike the string writing is certainly playable.

With Bohuslav's constant music-making and three growing children around him Ferdinand Martinů found it increasingly hard to carry on as a shoemaker. Clearly the time had come for the Martinůs to find different accommodation and in 1902, after thirteen years in the tower, the family moved to a small terraced house next to the Polička Savings Bank near the rampart gate. Here Ferdinand Martinů, now fifty, took up the post of watchman in the Bank and became odd-job man in the Mayor's office nearby. The Martinůs were to stay at Svépomuc 24 for the next nineteen years, and from this house passers-by could hear Bohuslav's violin more clearly. He still had occasional lessons from Černovský but spent most of his hours practising chamber music in the attic with the brothers Antonín and Stanislav Růzha. In 1905 a barber, Josef Vintr, settled in Polička where he took a lively interest in the Youth Band and became leader of the town's amateur orchestra. After a few months Bohuslav went to him for tuition and with Vintr as partner he rapidly mastered Mazas's six *Grand Duos* (Op. 41), Bériot's three *Duos Concertants* (Op. 57) and Viotti's three *Serenades* (Op. 23). In the summer of 1905 Bohuslav became leader of the Polička String Quartet and on 19 August made his debut as a soloist at an inn in the nearby village of Borová. Karolina Martinů tells us about this event in her memoirs :

At first people laughed when they saw a little boy had been invited to entertain them, and because he was so small the landlord had to bring a barrel for him to stand on. But when Bohuš began to play, everyone listened with rapt attention and afterwards congratulated him and me also.

Bohuslav's talents were fast becoming known throughout the town and an appearance at the Polička Fencing Club confirmed the earlier impression. But lessons with Vintr did not last long. Karolina Martinů maintains that her son soon outshone his teacher and for a while continued to play without supervision.

In 1906 the time was fast approaching when a decision had to be made about Bohuslav's future. Few opportunities presented themselves to those seeking employment in the Vysočina. Bohuslav's wide reading and feelings for literature were little to the point when a manual job or trade came into question, and his slender abilities in most academic subjects precluded a professional career; yet he showed a genuine talent for music and for the violin in particular, and in the spring of 1906 several Polička worthies managed to persuade the boy's parents to consider sending him to Prague if a place could be found at the Conservatoire. Adolf Vaníček, the local schoolmaster, promised to make the necessary introductions and to support his application, provided funds could be raised. Following a recital sponsored by the *Fajfka (Pipe)* Society, held on 29 June 1906, in the Polička Assembly Rooms where Bohuslav played Bériot's *Scénes de ballet* and Wieniawski's Concerto in D minor, the local newspaper *Jitřenka (Morning Star)* made the following appeal :

We have before us a gifted and promising youth. All that is required is for some generous benefactor or rich organisation to take notice of this needy young fellow and assist him to find a place at the Conservatoire in Prague where, we venture to maintain, he could bring his patron and Polička great honour. Let all who can help him!

Gradually donations were collected for Bohuslav's trip to the capital and by August sufficient had been raised to send him and his mother to Prague. Karolina Martinů records the details of this excursion in her Diary.

Prague was completely new to us but nevertheless we succeeded in finding Václav Štěpan, who kept a brewery in the Vinohrady district. Bohuš took with him his score of *The Three Riders* and, after having examined it, Mr. Štěpán told us to return the following day when we would be able to meet Milan Zuna, the conductor, whose orchestra rehearsed regularly in the brewery. So we did as we were instructed and the next day came to the brewery where the orchestra was playing a movement from Smetana's *Má vlast*. Bohuš had never heard anything like it and was electrified. Afterwards he showed his composition to Mr. Zuna, who was as much impressed by this as he was by my son's playing. He recommended us to see Jan Mařák, a teacher at the Conservatoire who, after hearing Bohuš play, told me that there was something in the boy and that it must be brought out. It was decided that Bohuš should go to the Conservatoire to sit the entrance examination, and after some days we went where we had been directed. I was so afraid I could hardly breathe, for there were many candidates and few places. Mr. Zuna accompanied us and eventually we came before Professor Knittl, the Director, who was so impressed by Bohuš's composition that at first he doubted whether the score was my son's own work, and asked who had helped him to write *The Three Riders*. After Bohuš had played the violin we heard that he had been offered a place, provided he could pass the medical examination (which he did) and if we could put up eighty gulden towards his fees and for his name to be registered.

Back in Polička there was much celebration on the boy's behalf. Many speculated that Bohuslav would become a second Jan Kubelík, who several years before had started his career as a virtuoso violinist, but others were more sceptical – among them the boy's hesitating parents who were far from able to meet the costs of sending him to Prague. Once again Adolf Vaníček rallied public support. On 20 August 1906, a petition signed by sixteen influential townsfolk was delivered to the Polička Council appealing for charitable assistance.

In this small and modest figure we are confronted with the rare talent of a future master of violin music. God has endowed his frame with a real artistic gift which may carry him forward to his desired goal, or may even bring him endless grief . . . The gift of music is a gift of God and is given not for His use alone, but for the spiritual enjoyment of the people. It is undoubtedly the duty of the public to make up to this poor lad what his good and well-conducted father is unable, through poverty, to give him . . . We therefore appeal to the Council to be of assistance in training the boy by giving him a grant; for only assistance in the form of a local scholarship can give Bohuslav Martinů the necessary security he needs.

Adolf Vaníček's appeal did not go unheard and within weeks Ferdinand Martinů was given a hundred gulden which represented the annual contribution of the Polička Council towards Bohuslav's training in Prague. Assistance, too, came from the bookseller, Mr. Kanka, who agreed to make a small allowance for the boy's board and lodgings. So it was that in January 1907, the seventeen-year-old youth set out for Prague; and while the people of Polička looked forward to seeing him develop into their own celebrity, Bohuslav nursed no such ambition. He was about to begin a new life – a life which was to be as strange and as alien to him as Polička had been after six years of isolation in the tower. For Martinů the world was now opening out.

2 *Prague: 1907-23*

There were moments when I was without bearings, when I could not speak, when all I could do was gaze in wonder.

So wrote Bohuslav Martinů in 1907, the year he came to Prague. And just as Kafka had fallen under the city's spell a few years before so, too, did Martinů, though he can hardly have imagined that the move from Polička to Prague would be so great, or that student life would be so liberating. He had lived in a tower : he had moved down to a town. Now he said farewell to the countryside and crossed the hills to see the opulence and beauty of a great city. The experience must have been overwhelming. Martinů was never to forget his first impression of Prague, the view across the Vltava – Smetana's river – to the old town.

This panorama soon gave way to others and after years of provincialism it is little wonder Martinů was exhilarated by his new surroundings. With two opera houses (German and Czech), flourishing concert and recital programmes, exhibitions and well-stocked libraries, Martinů found himself in a cultural wonderland and far too pre-occupied to see the city as it really was. It is not that he was insensitive to Prague's architectural beauties, cradled in history as it was and crowned with the splendour of its cathedral and castle : he was much too absorbed by his new environment to take in the stifling atmosphere that was symptomatic of life under the drab and economically unstable Hapsburg Monarchy, or to pay much attention to the currents of political unrest which were disturbing the capital in 1907. Though 1907 saw T. G. Masaryk leading the People's Party, campaigns for universal suffrage, schemes to set up great Pan-Slav congresses and attempts by the German Burgher element to establish a German State Language on the same footing as Czech, Martinů was oblivious to everything except music and the arts. For him 1907 was the year of discovery – the year when Ema Destinnová, Karel Burian and Otakar Mařák were the stars at the Opera, when Karel Kovařovic was in charge of the National Theatre, when Eduard Vojan was appearing there in a cycle of Shakespearian tragedies; it was the time when Josef Suk and Vítězslav Novák were championing the cause of new Czech music, when the National Theatre Orchestra, the Czech Quartet and Czech Society for Chamber Music were establishing themselves as first class ensembles and laying the foundations of Czech interpretation; it was the period when paintings of Daumier, Cézanne and Van Gogh were being exhibited in Prague, when the Czech people were beginning to appreciate the work of Auguste Rodin, Eduard Munch and members of the Impressionist school; but above all it was the year when Martinů heard for the first time symphonies and operas by Dvořák as well as Verdi's *La Traviata, Il Trovatore* and *Aïda* and a generous amount of Wagner whose *Der fliegende Holländer, Tannhäuser* and *Lohengrin* were staple diet at the German Theatre. To a curious and emotionally receptive youth such as Martinů, Prague offered as much in the way of culture as any other European city at the time. Understandably he was excited and sometimes confused by what he heard. Music in Prague was in a state of flux. Dvořák had died in 1904 and the national revival movement as embodied in his music and that of Smetana was fast subsiding. The tradition of the classical symphony had somehow lost its former impetus and the neo-Romantic school as seen in the music of Fibich was dying. In 1907 Prague was submerged by various cross-currents of European music, and people were keen to hear new German scores by Richard Strauss and Max Reger, to discover French Impressionism with the music of Debussy and to sample Italian verismo in the operas of Leoncavallo, Mascagni and Puccini. In Prague as in other capitals the music of Wagner, Tchaikovsky and Brahms was waning in popularity as a new musical generation of composers struggled to assert themselves.

Despite the period of transition in which he found himself Martinů spent a great deal of time in the National Theatre and even longer outside it queuing for tickets. If he liked an opera or a play he would go to see it time and again. In this way he came to terms with the basic operatic repertoire and at the Rudolfinum and Smetana Hall began to know the symphonies of Mendelssohn and Schumann (none of which made much impression on him) and some by Bruckner and Mahler. To the works of Beethoven he seems to have been indiffrent at this time, but for the tone poems of Richard Strauss he had boundless admiration. However, the composer whose music made the greatest impact on the seventeen-year-old student was Debussy, and in *Pelléas et Mélisande,* first performed in Prague in German in 1908, Martinů discovered a score that was to affect him deeply. To be confronted with the wealth of Prague's musical life after his previous sheltered existence made it especially difficult for Martinů to readjust himself, and when it came to academic studies at the Conservatoire he was faced with more serious problems.

The Prague Conservatoire of 1907 was maintained on the same principles which governed the Austrian educational system. Students were obliged to follow a rigid curriculum and were subject to strict regulations forbidding them to participate in any kind of public activity. The newly-appointed Director, Jindřich Kàan, ruled his Institution with a rod of iron and was feared by students as much for his adherence to discipline as for his criticism of musical standards. At first Martinů's work went well. He practised diligently and attended classes regularly, but after a while, possibly as a result of his years of freedom in Polička, he found it difficult to conform to the timetable of lectures and instruction. There were rhythm and memory classes, individual lessons three times a week and group instruction for theory and aural training. The course was demanding and after a short while it became clear to Martinů's violin teacher, Štěpán Suchý, that his charge was not ideally suited to the concentrated work required for one wishing to make a career on the concert platform. According to Jan Mařák's *Hudební revue*, Suchý taught with passion and severity. His pupils had to acquire their technique by dint of laborious exercises, and in performance he would tolerate nothing less than perfect. To Martinů this was anathema. He soon tired of practising endless scales and arpeggios and spent a lot of his time playing in amateur orchestras. He would, in fact, play anything anywhere to escape the treadmill of the Conservatoire's hidebound routines. As a result of accepting an engagement in Čáslav, he and fifteen fellow students were expelled for appearing in public without special permission of the Director. Appeals were made and eventually Jindřich Kàan reluctantly re-instated those concerned, but they remained in disfavour, especially Martinů who, at the annual examination, failed to attain the required grading and was obliged to stay down.

Martinů's second year at the Conservatoire saw little improvement in either his work or his attitude towards it. He had a strong need for personal freedom and something in him, perhaps those early images of vast, unrestricting space, revolted against the narrowness of the Conservatoire rules. His standard of attainment fell lower than before. As he went his own way, he began to acquire a habit that was to help him greatly in his creative life – walking through the streets, browsing through second-hand book shops. He had always been an omnivorous reader, but now he began to discover the Russian classics of Gogol, Tolstoy and Dostoyevsky, and the impressions made on him by Przerwa-Tetmajer, Przybyszewsky and Strindberg were to affect him deeply. However, his second year in Prague brought him a close and inseparable friendship with a student violinist, Stanislav Novák, who was Martinů's senior by a month. Novák had come to the Conservatoire full of plans and with sufficient determination to see them through (he lived to become leader of the Czech Philharmonic Orchestra and founder of the Frank Quartet). He was talented and conscientious and was drawn to the 'black sheep' Martinů by his greater knowledge of music and literature. They passed their student days together, shared a room in a house on the Kampa (an island on the Vltava), partnered each other in violin sonatas and in four-handed piano arrangements of classical symphonies. For three years they helped one another to make the difficulties and poverty of student life more bearable. They were inseparable at concerts, at the opera, and on holidays. But in class they could not have been further apart. While Novák shot ahead, Martinů remained as disinclined to work as ever and in the July examinations of 1908, his failure to gain a satisfactory mark resulted in him being transferred to Jindřich Bastař, who, as leader of the Vinohrady Theatre Orchestra, impressed himself on Martinů more for his huge moustache and steel-framed spectacles than for the quality of his instruction. Bastař's lack of understanding of his eighteen-year-old student was not conducive to good work or happy relations. He failed to realise that Martinů could come to music only through feeling and contemplation. For Bastař feeling was not enough. He considered Martinů indolent. Tensions grew and in the summer examinations of 1909 Martinů fared worse than before. The Conservatoire Report (preserved in the Polička Museum) records his behaviour as 'less than satisfactory' and his aptitude to work as 'erratic and inconsistent'. Only for his knowledge of harmony, form and analysis did he attain an acceptable marking. Most surprising of all was his grading for violin playing, which reads 'incompetent'. Clearly Martinů could no longer continue in the Violin School; but what his teachers there and benefactors in Polička failed to realise was that he wanted to compose and no amount of violin tuition could substitute for it. In Polička it was decided to give him one more chance and after the summer vacation he retuned to Prague, not to the Violin Class however, but to the Organ School.

Founded in 1830 for the training of organists and choral conductors, the Organ School was the only institution in Prague where composition was taught. Dvořák and Janáček had been pupils there as had Josef Suk, Vítězslav Novák and Oskar Nedbal. Hopeful that at last he would be initiated into the mysteries of the composer's craft, Martinů began to apply himself more painstakingly to his studies; but it was not simply a case of transferring from the violin to composition. He was placed with Vítězslav Novák's former teacher Karel Stecker for compulsory theory lessons and with Ondřej Horník, choirmaster at the Prague Church of SS. Cyril and Methodius, for organ instruction. As for tuition in composition, for Martinů there was none. He had no desire to become a church organist and even less to graduate as a choirmaster. He simply wanted to compose and had, in fact, been doing so in his modest, self-taught way for years. He already had several scores to his credit apart from *The Three Riders,* having completed in 1907 a five-movement suite for strings and flute called *Posvícení (Candlemass* or *Village Wake),* and in 1910 an *Elegy* for violin and piano for Stanislav Novák. It was not long before Martinů became disillusioned with his course at the Organ School, and continued absence and unpunctual attendance produced poor marks in the December examinations. By summer his standard of organ playing was so unsatisfactory that on 4 June, 1910, he had to be expelled from the Royal and Imperial State Conservatoire of Bohemia for 'incorrigible negligence.'

Martinů's stay at the Organ School had been short and ineffective and his return to Polička was marked by bitter reproaches from the town worthies who understandably felt he had squandered every opportunity. Somehow his benefactors failed to grasp that Martinů was not cut out to become a second Kubelík and that his way of thinking and artistic outlook were totally incompatible with the teaching methods of the day. To the people of Polička, Martinů had changed unexpectedly. He was no longer the well-ordered, promising talent of three years before but apparently a lazy, ne'er-do-well with neither resolve nor sense of direction. However, through his parents' generosity he was able to return to Prague where he hoped to widen his experience and devote himself to composition; but once in the city he continued much as before, immersed in the various streams of European music which met and competed with each other in the musical whirlpool that was Prague between 1909 and 1912. A number of composers led by Otakar Zich, Otakar Ostrčil, Josef Suk and Vítězslav Novák were striving to win recognition for the specific sound of Czech music in the mass of first Czech performances that were being given in the National and German Theatres. In these years Martinů not only heard Ostrčil's *Kunálovy oči* and Zich's *Malířský nápad* but discovered Leoncavallo's *Zazà,* Pfitzner's *Die Rose vom Liebergarten,* Humperdinck's *Königskinder,* Wolf-Ferrari's *Susanna's Secret* and *Jewels of the Madonna* and Strauss's *Elektra, Der Rosenkavalier* and *Feuersnot.* In the Rudolfinum and Smetana Hall Schoenberg's *Verklärte Nacht, Pierrot Lunaire* and *Pelléas et Mélisande* were on the programme along with works by Stravinsky and the young and little known Béla Bartók. But in the concert hall, as in the opera house, it was the music of Debussy which most coloured Martinů's approach to composition and, though at twenty he could barely expect to contribute anything to Prague's musical life himself, he could at least try to express himself, if only to satisfy an innate urge for composition which had been driving him ever since he left Polička. At this time his ears rang with the echoes of many styles. He was hearing a great deal of music and possibly too much of other people's compositions to find time to develop his own creative consciousness. Consequently, his style was derived from the music he heard around him, and occasionally his youthful efforts move from Debussy-like Impressionism to Straussian chromaticism within the space of a few bars. However, before the end of 1910 Martinů was to produce no fewer than twenty-five works, including sixteen songs to various texts by Hálek, Sládek, Heyduk and Edgar Allan Poe, a set of five Waltzes for piano and another group of five piano pieces called *Pohádka a zlatovlásce (Tales of the Golden Fleece)*, as well as a *Romance* for violin and piano, a Concerto for the same combination, and three symphonic poems.

After reading *Les Travailleurs de la mer*, Martinů was moved to write an orchestral fantasy on the pictures evoked by Victor Hugo's novel. Unfortunately, this progressed no further than the fourth page of a sketch. More absorbing was his work on a second tone poem, inspired by Maurice Maeterlinck's puppet play *La Mort de Tintagiles*. This Martinů completed and sub-titled 'Prologue', but in spite of obvious stylistic imitations of Debussy's *La Mer* the score is rambling – it runs to eighty-seven pages of manuscript – and is distinguished more by its youthful exuberance than by its musical invention. The same applies to a third orchestral work, dramatically called *Anděl smrti (The Angel of Death)*, based on the novel by the Polish lyric writer Przerwa-Tetmajer. Composed hastily in a mood of despair following an unhappy love affair, the hundred-and-ten-page manuscript attempts to describe how the sculptor Rdzawicz, jilted in love, carves his greatest work – his own tomb. The immature Martinů was passionately identifying himself with Przerwa-Tetmajer's hero, but here the parallel stops; for instead of creating a work comparable to Rdzawicz's tomb, Martinů almost digs his own grave. The musical expression is exaggerated and overloaded, the instrumentation clumsy and sometimes unplayable. Throughout the idiom leans heavily on Debussy's, and like his scores, Martinů's manuscript is well salted with instructions, though from time to time these suffer from an excess of enthusiasm. (Within the space of a few bars the orchestra is asked to play *pppp, crescendo furioso, feroce con fuoco, ffff* and then *appassionato religioso*.) Clearly the musical worth of these pieces is slight, and none displays the creative characteristics of the future Martinů; but they did provide the composer with a chance to learn his craft. After all, he was self-taught and there was no one to whom he could turn for help in tackling the technical problems of composition. What these pieces do display is Martinů's will to compose and his ability to work with unflagging persistence at a prob-

lem, even though he was ill-equipped to solve it at this stage. From
Stanislav Novák's *Memoirs* we know that Martinů would often get up as
early as five in the morning to work at his desk and nothing, it seems,
could distract him, least of all the question of earning a living.

For months his parents had been concerned for the welfare of their
son and had urged him to think in terms of teaching as a career. Possibly
to pacify his anxious father, Martinů had enrolled for the State Teaching Examination in the spring of 1911, but with twelve new works to his
credit and his head teeming with ideas for future compositions, he devoted
little time to preparing the syllabus. He lived in a world of his own and
failed to take the examination seriously. That he was confident of
success is clear from a letter written to Mr. Kanka, the Polička bookseller, in December 1911.

The examination is fixed for Monday the 11th at two o'clock. I am not
afraid even though I expect Director Kàan to pull me to pieces. They will
test me in violin playing, history and pedagogy. I am not to be examined in
piano playing, and since I am on bad terms with the Director it is better if
I take the piano tests when I am more prepared. How wonderful it would
be if I could pass this exam, but I don't want to spoil my chances by poor
marks for piano playing. Recently I asked Josef Suk's opinion of my
compositions. He says I should have proper instruction and promises to
recommend me to Novák. How I long for this! – then possibly some of
my pieces will be published. Everything will go well, I assure you; and if you
come to Prague you shall see how brave I'll be.

In spite of his bravery Martinů failed every part of the examination. In
each subject, including violin playing, he was awarded the lowest grading *Nedostatečně* (*Deficient*) and only for his knowledge of teaching did
he gain a satisfactory mark. Just to make matters worse the report was
signed by the very man with whom he most wanted to study – the
composer Vítězslav Novák. Duly shaken, Martinů sent details of his
latest catastrophe to Mr. Kanka.

I have failed! This I did not expect. I am so unhappy I don't know what
to do. I suppose I will find a job somewhere, but what will they think at
home? Please speak to my parents for me and tell mother gently – I'm
afraid to write to her myself. I did do some practice and don't think I
played that badly. Yet he, Kàan, dared to fail me! As far as he's concerned I might just as well have a block of wood for a head! Why, he does
not even know what music is!! I've given my life and everything to music
and such a person as he ignores my efforts. Yes, I'm bitter. What can I do
against them? Do you know, the candidate who was before me played a
Grade III concerto miserably and passed and I was given the most difficult
concerto in the book and did not perform it that badly; yet they make out
I'm lazy. What sort of person am I according to this report? I begin to

think I know nothing about music at all. They have spoiled everything for me, but I am not to be easily beaten. I'll go through with it and show them what's what!

During 1912 Martinů devoted himself more seriously to the syllabus, and on 10 December presented himself for examination, this time just scraping through. Though his teaching certificate somewhat placated his anxious parents, whose concern for their son had been made more acute by Stanislav Novák's graduation from the Prague Conservatoire with a Certificate of Maturity, Martinů had no real intention of making teaching his career. He regarded his diploma much as others would an insurance policy: it was there in case he could not make a success of music. And as if to ensure his very success Martinů flung himself into the midst of Prague's musical activity, attending concerts and opera as often as he could afford. But by 1912 Czech musical life was changing. It was being troubled by a peculiar kind of uncertainty, in fact by a shattering of its former confidence. This malaise was not limited to music, but was gradually being felt throughout Czech culture, then in the grip of an intellectual disorientation. It stemmed no doubt from the depressing economic situation of the Austro-Hungarian Empire, which was near bankruptcy, and the political passivity of the Czech leaders, who were to bring the nation near to ruin. The shadow of war was approaching and pressing heavily on all spheres of social activity. Furthermore there were a number of scandalous musical affairs: the so-called Smetana/Dvořák controversy boiled up in full force again, Vítězslav Novák's musical personality was being questioned, the compositions of Josef Suk were suddenly thought to be second-rate, Josef Foerster was being ignored, the music of Otakar Ostrčil was out of fashion and Leoš Janáček was being kept at bay in Brno.

However, this period of musical crisis did not affect Martinů adversely; on the contrary it may well have prompted him to make a more positive mark for himself as a composer. In 1912 he produced over thirty pieces which, if they show little else, display his facility for turning out music in a variety of forms in a short space of time. Seven piano pieces based on Hans Andersen fairy tales demonstrate the speed with which he could compose – the set was tossed off in the first week of January, with one item completed every day. Uneven and flawed most of these pieces may be, but, among the songs with their growing feeling for poetry, the violin and chamber pieces with their flourish and ring of youth, and the sketches for the first movement of a symphony, there are a number of very good scores.

The song cycle with instrumental accompaniment called *Niponari* shows him trying to break away from the run-of-the-mill pieces he

5. Martinů's parents.   6. Martinů aged three.

7. Martinů aged five.   8. Martinů aged seven.

9. Černovský's student orchestra. Martinů is second from left, front row.

had so far attempted. *Niponari* is a collection of seven lyric songs for female voice on oriental texts in which each song is accompanied by a different instrumental combination. 'The Blue Hour' is scored for flute, cor anglais, harp, solo violin, four violas and four cellos; 'Old Age' for solo viola, harp, cor anglais and five violins; 'Remembrance' for flute, violin and harp; 'Day Dreams' for three flutes and three violins; 'Footprints in the Snow' introduces piano and celeste to harp and strings; 'Looking Backwards' balances flutes against four each of violins, violas, and cellos, and the last song 'By the Sacred Lake' omits violas and cellos altogether. Though *Niponari* was written under the influence of Puccini's *Madam Butterfly* it is Martinů's exotic and highly-coloured instrumentation which is the most striking feature of the cycle. The imaginative low flute trills against harp harmonics and string tremelos in the first song, and the use of glisssandos on harp with soft gong sonorities in the final piece all point to Martinů's growing sensitiveness to timbre. Whereas in songs like *První láska (First Love)*, *Slzy (Tears)*, *Růže (The Rose)* and *Lucie* the vocal lines are bound to angular piano accompaniments, in *Niponari* they emerge flexible and free of harmonic cliché. Here and there Martinů reflects the mood of his Japanese lyrics by gently introducing the pentatonic scale, and in 'Remembrance' there is a good attempt at canonic imitation. 'Old Age', possibly the most memorable of the seven pieces, uses harp ostinatos over sustained pedals to suggest the pendulum-like imagery of Kinfsuna's verse.

After completing *Niponari* Martinů turned to the melodrama, a form established in Bohemia by Jiří Benda in the eighteenth century, from which time it had flourished in the hands of Josef Nešvera and reached a climax in the dramatic work of Zdeněk Fibich in the period 1880–1895. Almost certainly Martinů had seen Fibich's *Hippodamia* triology at the National Theatre, and may even have heard his concert melodramas during his student days. It is likely then that his own contributions to the form were modelled upon Fibich's or the more contemporary scores of Ostrčil. *Večer (Evening)* based on Albert Samain's poem *Le Séraphin des soirs passe le long des fleurs* is designed for speaker with harp accompaniment. In *Vážka (The Dragonfly)* to a poem by Henri d'Orange and *Tanečnice z Jávy (Dancers from Java)* to verses by Arthur Symonds, the speaker is supported by violin, viola, piano and harp; and it is interesting to note that these are possibly the first pieces where Martinů combined these last two instruments – a feature of scoring looking forward to the symphonies written between 1942 and 1946. All three melodramas date from 1913 and show Martinů expressing himself in Debussy-like idiom that makes for a nice mixture of Bohemian student and French master.

C

From the same year dates Martinů's acquaintance with Diaghilev's Ballet Russe, when the Company gave a number of guest performances at the Prague German Theatre, with Fokine, Karsavina and Nijinsky as principals and Pierre Monteux conducting. Under the impression of Stravinsky's *The Firebird* and *Petrushka* and‑ Debussy's *Prélude à l'après-midi d'un faune* and *Jeux*, Martinů now began to sketch his first music for dancing. For the Czechs, nationalistic in feeling and closely attached to the countryside, dance meant folk dance, the *furiant, hulan* and *skočná*. Almost alone among Czech composers, Janáček had attempted in 1891 to create Czech ballet in his *Rákoš Rákoczy*, but this did little more than transport folk dance from the countryside to the theatre. When in 1913 Martinů came to approach the genre he found himself breaking new ground; for such scores as Karel Kovařovice's *Hašiš* (1881) with its Délibes-like grace, Karel Bendl's *Česká svatba (Czech Wedding)* (1895) with its combination of folk dance and song, or Oskar Nedbal's ballet-pantomime *Pohádka o Honzovi (Fairytale about Johnny)* could not provide the material that was needed to pioneer a new form of ballet. Undaunted, Martinů began to sketch *Noc (Night)*, a 'meloplastic scene in one Act', to a scenario by Alois Kohout, which shows a striking similarity in subject and style to the ballet created from Debussy's *Prélude à l'après-midi d'un faune*. An Old Faun is discovered in a rocky bay playing a syrinx. It is evening and he is watched by an entranced Nymph. As the Old Faun plays, the echoes of his music are mysteriously altered, and under the charm the Nymph begins to dance. A group of young fauns partner her and one succeeds in seducing her and carrying her away. As the moon rises the young fauns disappear leaving the Old Faun to play his syrinx and accept his lonely destiny. The ballet, all one thousand, four hundred and eighty-one bars of it, has never been performed and is scored for a huge orchestra with triple woodwind, three harps and a large percussion section. Throughout, Martinů's instrumentation is closely modelled on the Impressionistic expression of Debussy's tone poem with muted horns, hazy string tremelos, harp glissandos and sensuous phrases for flutes, oboes and cor anglais; and the introduction of a wordless chorus for female voices behind the scene suggests Martinů's awareness of Debussy's 'Sirènes' from the orchestral *Nocturnes*. Apart from this the score is more interesting for its detailed instructions for staging and lighting. These suggest that at twenty-three the composer had a considerable sense of the theatre – something notable in a first stage work.

Inspired by the dancing of Olga Gzowska, principal ballerina at the National Theatre, Martinů began a second 'meloplastic scene' which he called *Tance se závoji (Dances with a Veil)*. How far this was modelled on the 'Dance of the Seven Veils' from Strauss's *Salome* we shall never know; for Martinů's sketch and score are lost and it was not until 1916 that he completed his next ballet which he entitled *Stín (The Shadow)*. Like *Noc, Stín* is based on a scenario of Kohout and was intended as part of a triology of one-act ballets. (A dramatisation of Böcklin's painting 'Villa by the Sea' was to have formed the third part, but this never materialised.) In *Stín,* Kohout and Martinů broke away from the *corps de ballet* scheme of their earlier collaboration and devised a series of dances for solo ballerina who plays with a ball, a skipping rope and finally with her own shadow. Here Martinů tempered his former instrumental extravagance and produced a score for chamber orchestra with added piano and off-stage soprano. In this work he matches the clarity of sound with a directness of melody that seems to have a folk-song source. But despite this simplification, Martinů forgot to take into account the physical capabilities of the solo ballerina who is required to dance with her shadow, mostly in waltz or polka tempos, for two thousand bars, before dancing herself to death for another five hundred and sixty-three. Perhaps this was reason enough for the National Theatre to reject the score in 1920, since when it has lain forgotten and unperformed.

At the outbreak of war in 1914, Martinů returned to Polička where he hoped to delay, if not evade, conscription into the Austrian Army. It was not long, however, before he was pressed into uniform, and from the start the stupidities of military life appalled him; but fortunately he only had to endure a week or so, having been granted exemption from military service on medical grounds. Now settled in Polička with his parents and sister, who had set herself up as a dress-maker, Martinů earned a living by teaching the violin in the municipal school, whose regular teacher had been called up. While Martinů found this arduous and greatly missed the musical life of Prague, he contented himself with reading and composing, though at this period the fruits of his efforts seem to have been more experimental than anything else. He produced a great deal of piano music, most of it simple and inspired by the *thé-dansant* or salon pieces of the day. However, a *Nocturne, Three Lyric Pieces* (from 1915) and *Ruyana* (from 1916) suggest that the influence of Debussy's *Préludes* was still with him; and *Five Polkas* (1916), a *Furiant* and a *Burlesque* (1917) show Martinů writing within the framework of Smetana's *Czech Dances*. With these pieces Martinů continued to work out his apprenticeship but, in the suite called *Sníh (Snow)* and a collection entitled *Loutky (Puppets)*, he began to break away from his earlier forms in favour of delicately etched miniatures, as much remarkable for their tidy and effective presentation as for their harmonic vocabulary and engaging musical ideas. The three volumes which make up *Loutky* describe some aspect of puppet life – 'The Sick Puppet', 'Puppets' Ball' and 'Pierrot's Dance' are typical titles, yet despite these saccharine labels the pieces themselves are simple and charming. Although the set dates from well before Martinů's maturity, there is no denying its attractions and many of the items would make a welcome addition to the repertoire of young performers for whom *Loutky* was surely intended.

More adventurous was a projected cycle of symphonic dances of which only the title page of the second, a *Nocturne* with a *fin-de-siècle* sub-title 'Les Roses dans la Nuit', and the fourth, a *Ballad* after Böcklin's 'Villa by the Sea', have survived. It is worth noting that here again the piano is introduced in the symphony orchestra, a mark of style of the later Martinů. The piano also plays a prominent rôle in the F sharp minor *Nocturne* of 1915, which reveals a confidence in orchestral technique and in the organisation of a tone poem on a large scale. But the score is more remarkable for the way the opening looks forward to the mature composer of the Violin Concerto written thirty years later.

By far the most original work to be composed at this time (1917) was the choral-ballet *Koleda* (*Christmas Carol*). Unfortunately the score is lost but, from letters of the period and Martinů's copy of the libretto, it seems that *Koleda* was based on a series of old Czech Christmas customs and divided into four parts with twenty-six scenes comprising songs, folk dances, instrumental interludes and spoken recitatives. Possibly Martinů had in mind a form of entertainment similar to the ones used by Škroup in *Fidlovačka* or Bendl in *Czech Wedding*. But whereas Bendl had fashioned his choral-ballet around a Bohemian wedding ceremony and padded it with reference to local folk customs, Martinů based his scenario on a more universal theme – the Christmas story – into which he incorporated a number of traditional carols and poems describing the birth of Christ. The Prologue and first Part announce the Christmas message. Part II deals with the Nativity, Part III depicts the Adoration of the Magi, and the final Part devoted to a setting of Jan Neruda's *Christmas Eve Romance,* ends with a collection of Czech carols including the well known *Narodil se Kristus Pán* (*Christ is born today*) sung by the entire cast. From the scenario, which Martinů devised himself, the ballet seems to have been inspired by a number of folk customs associated with the Vysočina and as such initiated a genre that was to be developed in the composer's later dramatic works.

Koleda was followed by a period devoted to the production of chamber music. Two string quartets from the year 1917–18 show Martinů composing very much on traditional lines, and an unnumbered and incomplete quartet in E flat minor confirms that his working method was modelled on the quartet style of Dvořák. The so-called Quartet No. 1, possibly his third or fourth attempt at the medium, is technically much more assured and shows Martinů to have the measure of the form well and truly in his grasp. Again Dvořák is the influence behind the outer movements, but in the central Andante there is more than a hint of Debussy's String Quartet with extensive use of the bowed tremelo, trill and sustained pedal notes. Despite its derivative stylistic qualities, the Quartet displays Martinů's fondness for a process of developing tonality (the first movement begins in E minor and ends in E flat, the second opens in B major and closes in F sharp, and the finale starts in A flat and stops in F major) – a mark of style which anticipates the symphonies by thirty years.

For Martinů the war years spent in Polička were uneventful. He taught privately, founded a student group similar to the one he himself had once belonged to and made simple arrangements of pieces by Mozart, Grieg and Tchaikovsky for string orchestra. From time to time he was even persuaded to play the violin in public, but now he excited little attention from the people of Polička. Martinů was always hankering after Prague, and despite his difficulties in making ends meet he managed to keep in touch with Stanislav Novák, who had joined the ranks of the first violins of the Czech Philharmonic. Through him Martinů was invited to join the orchestra too, but on a part-time basis. During the war the Philharmonic experienced great difficulty in maintaining its former strength and, consequently, extra players were needed. Martinů was always ready to augment the back desks of second violins and was often more rewarded by the musical experience of playing in a large orchestra than by the few crowns he received for a rehearsal and evening performance. Towards the end of 1917 he began to appear more regularly with the Philharmonic and from the inside began to appreciate how a symphony orchestra functioned. More important, he was learning how certain instrumental sonorities were achieved. Martinů found the Czech Philharmonic a vital training ground; for the orchestra, though financially insecure, was ambitious, and the conductor, Vilém Zemánek, was no ordinary Kapellmeister but a man of vision who brought Mahler from Vienna to conduct his own works, and Vassily Safonov from Moscow to give concerts of music by Tchaikovsky, Mussorgsky and Skryabin. Under the batons of Artur Nikisch and Felix Weingartner the standard of playing was raised and the repertoire extended to include the tone poems of Liszt and Strauss, and symphonies by Bruckner and Sibelius as well as contemporary Czech scores of Foerster, Kovařovic, Novák, Nedbal and Ostrčil.

Meanwhile Martinů continued to compose, and one of the more

interesting scores of the period is the patriotic cantata *Česká rapsódie* (*Czech Rhapsody*), inspired, as was Janáček's chorus for male voices *Česká legie* (*Czech Legion*), by a growing feeling for political and cultural independence which culminated in the setting up of the first Czech Republic on 28 October 1918. *Czech Rhapsody* is dedicated to the author Alois Jirásek and as a work stands out from Martinů's juvenilia. In some respects it occupies a position in his catalogue similar to that held by Dvořák's *Hymnus – The Heirs of the White Mountain*. Both are patriotic works and date from the period when their composers were about thirty years of age. But whereas Dvořák's *Hymnus* is a lament by the Czechs for the independence lost in the Battle of the White Mountain (1620) and a call for loyalty and valour in the fight for freedom, Martinů's is a declaration of faith in the new Republic and a paean of praise for the newly-found independence won after nearly three hundred years of domination. Celebrating the founding of the new nation, Martinů appropriately speaks with a new force, passionately and ardently nationalist, here and there suggesting the patriotic idiom of Smetana's *Česká píseň* (*Song of the Czechs*). The text, compiled by the composer himself, is a setting of part of Psalm 23 (*The Lord is my Shepherd*) and a collection of secular words and verses from old Bohemian chorales. The cantata, which Martinů later considered amateurish, opens with a portentous and solemn introduction that may well have been prompted by the popular Czech hymn *Bože cos račil*. Later there is a direct quotation from another hymn *Svatý Václav* (*St. Wenceslas*) which Josef Suk had put to good use in his *Meditations on a Bohemian Chorale* for string orchestra in 1914. The choir repeat this initial material and thereafter Martinů continues the process of interspersing lines of text with alternating orchestral sections, much in the manner of a Bach Chorale Fantasia. Except for the opening the choir is instructed to sing *ff* throughout and page after page of choral writing gives way only to a final unison setting of the St. Wenceslas chorale. No one can question Martinů's enthusiasm in this youthful song of thanksgiving, but one longs for the introduction of the simplest of contrapuntal lines. In January 1919, ten weeks after the Austro-Hungarian Empire had collapsed, the cantata was premièred by the Czech Philharmonic in the Smetana Hall. For the composer, who at twenty-nine had so far experienced little recognition for his music, the performance must have been a valuable and encouraging stimulus. With a repeat performance on 24 January, attended by the President of the Republic, Martinů officially entered the ranks of Prague's acknowledged composers. Thereafter his name was quickly forgotten and was not to be heard in this connexion for another four years.

Back in Polička, Martinů followed *Czech Rhapsody,* his one-hundred-and-eleventh composition, with a cycle of songs for soprano and large orchestra called *Kouzelné noci (Magic Nights)* to verses by the Chinese poets Li-Tai-Po and Tschang-Jo-Su. The verses were taken from Hans Bethge's anthology of lyric poetry *The Chinese Flute,* which had appeared in a German translation in 1908 and had moved Mahler to write *Das Lied von der Erde.* Almost certainly Martinů had Mahler's model in mind when composing his own songs for, like *Das Lied von der Erde,* the pieces in *Magic Nights* alternate between moods of abject pessimism and brittle splendour. Close comparison reveals Martinů's collection to be little more than a pale reflection of Mahler's masterly cycle. There was no question of performing *Magic Nights* but, undeterred, Martinů began a lengthy four-movement Sonata for violin and piano, the first of five for this medium. Then came his *Malá taneční svita (Small Dance Suite)* for large orchestra – a lusty and highly-coloured divertimento – which goes through the motions of a waltz, a tender folk song, a lively scherzo and a Smetana-like polka, but exhausts the ear with its insistence on square dance-rhythms.

Martinů – now in his thirtieth year and a striking figure – was however an ordinary citizen without means, connexions or permanent position. He had a hundred and fourteen compositions to his name but apart from *Czech Rhapsody* few had been heard. No wonder people in Polička felt he had fulfilled little of the early promise with which he had seemed so well endowed. Nevertheless, through the good offices of Stanislav Novák, Martinů was recommended to join the augmented National Theatre Orchestra which was to make an official tour to London, Paris and Geneva in the spring of 1919. Though the excursion was to be of short duration, for Martinů it was to be of paramount importance: in Paris he was to be thrust into the centre of Western culture. The experience was shattering, the impact far-reaching. He longed to discover the city's secrets and soak up the atmosphere with which he had fallen in love. But however much Paris attracted him, there could be no sudden elopement. Martinů was obliged to travel back to Czechoslovakia, but he did so with the resolve to return to France soon, and for a longer period. Four years were to pass before he was to fulfil this ambition.

These four years were spent with the Czech Philharmonic, which after the war was reorganised on a more permanent and financially secure footing. For Martinů the pulse of musical life now quickened as he became a regular member of the second violin section. From his place at the third desk he was to learn far more about music than at any other period in his life. Under Václav Talich, the thirty-six-year-old

Musical Director, the standard of orchestral playing was raised to a new level, and with his determination to break away from the German repertoire with its preponderance of symphonies by Beethoven and Brahms, new music by Debussy, Ravel, Dukas and Roussel was introduced. Through arduous rehearsals and performances Martinů gradually found the music of the Impressionist composers coursing in his veins, and between rehearsals he would sit in the Philharmonic's library studying scores to broaden his own musical horizon. Somehow he found time to compose, and during his years with the orchestra (1920–3) he produced sixteen works which range from attractive piano pieces, like *Jaro v zahradě* (*Spring in the Garden*) and *Motýli a rajky* (*The Butterflies and the Birds of Paradise*), to two full length ballets, *Istar* and *Kdo je na světě nejmocnější?* (*Who is the Most Powerful in the World?*) and an orchestral suite called *Míjející půlnoc* (*Vanishing Midnight*). Of the three movements, 'Satyrs in the Cypress Grove', 'Blue Hour' and 'Shadows', only the second has survived, but this alone points to Martinů's greater response to instrumental timbre. Here he begins to use orchestral colouring with such skill that after its first performance (by Talich and the Czech Philharmonic on 18 February 1923) he came to be regarded as a 'French' composer – a label which was to dog him when his ballet, *Istar*, was premièred on 11 September 1924.

For nearly four years Martinů had struggled to complete this vast three-act score and with it he hoped to emerge as a composer of importance. Though the music is accomplished and deals well with its exotic subject – a variation of the Orpheus legend with colourful excursions to the Underworld – at its best *Istar* is little more than effective programme music to a scenario by the Czech mystic Julius Zeyer, who based his poem on a Sumerian myth about Istar's journey to Hell to rescue and immortalise her lover, Tammuz. From a letter to Otakar Ostrčil dated 15 October 1921, it seems Martinů had set out to write his score in anything but orthodox fashion.

My idea was to compose a symphonic poem for dancing, but in a dance form quite different from any in which the classical ballets are conceived. Hence I adapted the libretto myself in order to achieve proportions of form and opportunities for gradations in musical expression. I have departed from a strict correspondence of the dance to the rhythm and carried this through to the expression which is embodied in the melody and character of the individual scenes.

But the score is unorthodox only inasmuch as Martinů composed not one symphonic poem but three, one for each act. These are bound by two motifs: one for Istar representing good, the other for Irkalla, Queen of the Underworld, who personifies evil. Instead of formalised dance sequences Martinů writes a continuous stream of music which treats the motifs like a recurring thread in a series of variations. These allow him to exploit moods that develop from grief to joy and paint orchestral colours which move from darkness to light. The orchestral forces are large and the score calls for a well-stocked array of percussion, whose rôle is not merely decorative, but an integral part of the music. Every stage picture or passing image is differentiated in the orchestra with sensuous, plaintive melodies on flute, oboe or cor anglais and sonorous wind chords coloured by the metallic shimmer of cymbal, gong and harp. To these precisely imagined timbres Martinů adds a women's chorus at the close of Act III, and the way he uses it suggests his indebtedness to Ravel's *Daphnis et Chloë*. With such varied forces Martinů produces a wealth of exotic effects. The string writing, with occasional eight-part divisions, produces a variety of oriental sounds which delight the ear when they do not tire it; but Martinů's kaleidoscope of sound has its shortcomings, and it is at moments when he is most enthusiastic that his complex textures break down and the climaxes lose their true effect. Nevertheless, *Istar* is important in documenting the course of Martinů's development as a composer; but by the time of its Prague première at the National Theatre he had already outgrown its Impressionistic idiom. In 1922 he produced *Who is the Most Powerful in the World?*, a deliberate reaction to his earlier ballet, and here he evolved a score in contemporary dance forms based on a fairy tale. It is little wonder that after the first performance in Brno (31 January 1925), where it was coupled with Janáček's *Cunning Little Vixen*, Talich was moved to remark of Martinů's style: 'It's not a step – it's a jump ahead!' The score abounds in touches of parody and moments of gentle humour, for Martinů's intention was little more than entertainment. He suggested as much himself in the programme to the first performance. 'I did not avoid writing a Straussian waltz, a Meyerbeerian march or even a simple polka when the situation needed it. At the end the little mouse dances a Boston. Why shouldn't she? She only wants to be admired!' The delightful animal ballet tells how two parent mice decide to marry their attractive daughter not to the Mouse Prince but to him who is the most powerful in the world. The quest to find this being leads them to offer their daughter in turn to the sun, the cloud, the wind, and finally to the wall; but when the wall tumbles over as neighbouring mice burrow under it, the parents realise that mice are the most powerful beings in the world and that their daughter must marry the Mouse Prince after all. The ballet ends with a sequence of dances to celebrate their wedding.

Unlike the heavily chromatic idiom of *Istar, Who is the Most Powerful in the World?* is essentially diatonic. Martinů seems to have consciously simplified his style and is here writing with a light, airy, quality which matches the charming naïvety of the fairy tale. He expresses the characteristic of each dance with a rhythmic or melodic motif and appropriates to each a different instrument, as Prokofiev was to do more than a decade later in *Peter and the Wolf*. Of course Martinů had previously used a system of motifs in *Istar*, but with less force and flexibility. There they never acquired the freedom they assume in the mouse ballet, where the cloud is represented by a solo tuba, the sun by a piano, the little mouse by a cello, and he who is he most powerful in the world by a xylophone. Though large, the orchestral forces are used sparingly, with greater contrast between instrumental sections and lengthy cadenzas for harp, percussion and solo piano. Martinů's score is a busy one with pointed rhythms and catchy phrases taken from the Shimmy, the Charleston and the Foxtrot (he had actually written his first piece in popular dance style as early as 1919 when he produced the *Kitten's Foxtrot* for piano) and there is even a parody of the waltz sequence from Strauss's *Der Rosenkavalier* in the final scene. Martinů's mouse ballet is a happy score and shows him enjoying a youthful fling. In one sense it is transitory work in which the former Impressionistic style is giving way to something new, not yet defined, though the welcome influence of jazz and a greater insistence on rhythm at the expense of colour are discernible. With *Who is the Most Powerful in the World?* Martinů was leaving behind the romantic subjects of his earlier works – the fauns in Arcadian landscapes and nymphs in cypress groves. New experiences and discoveries, notably the music of Josef Suk, were changing his ideas. His years in the Czech Philharmonic had brought Martinů closer to Suk's *Zrání, Praga* and *Asrael* symphony.

Now full of admiration for the delicate lyricism and technical mastery of these works, Martinů enrolled himself in Suk's Composition Master Class at the Conservatoire. But for all his admiration of Suk's scores, Martinů's studies did not progress well. The twelve years which separated his first and second courses had made little difference in his attitude to disciplined work and, dilatory as ever, he failed to complete even the compulsory exercise – an overture called *Vesna (Spring)*. The fact that studies with Suk were cut short, however, was due to a number of external circumstances. The unexpected death of seventy-year-old Ferdinand Martinů in Polička touched his son deeply. Martinů had always been closer to his father than to his mother and, as if some strong family bond had been severed, he now decided to leave Czechoslovakia. Neither the publication of some of his piano pieces from the *Loutky* collection, nor negotiations for the première of *Istar* at the National Theatre could keep him. Ever since his visit to Paris in 1919, Martinů had longed to return, and when in 1923 he was awarded a small grant by the Ministry of Education for study abroad there seemed nothing to hold him. Paris, the centre of the musical world, complex and attractive, seemed to beckon him. At the time he had no intention of staying there for more than three months; he little realised that he was altering the course of his career and that he was leaving his native land. Martinů's migration Westward had begun.

3 Paris: 1923-30

I went to France not to seek my salvation but to confirm my opinions. What I sought most on French soil was not Debussy, nor Impressionism, nor, in fact, musical expression, but the real foundations on which Western culture rests and which, in my opinion, conform much more to our proper natural character than a maze of conjectures and problems.

After spending seventeen years in Paris, Martinů was as much captivated by the capital as he had been when he arrived in October 1923. Possibly something of the feeling of isolation and strangeness which he had experienced on leaving the Polička tower to attend school, and which had affected him on going to Prague, returned during his first days in Paris, for he was cut off by not knowing the language and found it hard to come to grips with his new environment. Post-war Paris was full of artistic expatriates and it was a time of serious creativity. Disturbed, and often surprised, by the experiments he found around him, Martinů took some time to settle down and his principal occupation seems to have been strolling around the city at all hours of the day and night noticing the different modes of Parisian life, watching the activity and soaking up the city's many moods. Martinů was still an observer. Although he intended to stay in France only a few months he found himself so enchanted by Paris and all she stood for that he could not bear to tear himself away. He had reached the city with a suitcase and a few savings, almost no knowledge of French and no clear idea of how he was to subsist. He had neither connexions nor friends, and indeed it remains a puzzle how he survived.

Martinů was thirty-two. He was tall and slim, with prominent features and soft blue eyes. His receding hair revealed a massive forehead which tended to increase the impression of commanding height that he carried with him. He had spent most of his life dedicated to music and, apart from a short spell as a teacher, had not taken up any other activity. But he had not made his fortune. He had never attempted to cut a figure in society; he was shy, almost a recluse; he blushed easily and was relaxed only with intimate friends, many of whom were humble, unremarkable people. Martinů's tastes were plain, even ordinary. He was fond of animals, he loved the country, he was simple and unsophisticated, and he took an unashamed delight in good eating when he could afford to. His clothes were well-worn, almost to the point of shabbiness; but there was no affectation in him – the poverty-stricken state in which he existed was the result, purely and simply, of indifference. He was completely indifferent to wealth, to comfort and security, and without this indifference he would not have wandered through Paris as he did, with no apparent sense of direction. It was not long however before his savings were exhausted, yet somehow he managed to live in conditions of real poverty until July 1924 when he was obliged to return to Polička. By a stroke of luck his application for an allowance towards further study in France was granted by the Ministry of Culture and on 9 September he set out for Paris with four hundred crowns in his pocket and the promise of fifteen hundred francs to be collected from the Legation.

Martinů's return to the 'miraculous city', as he called it, put him into the main stream of cultural thought; for Paris in the 1920s was not only the home of contemporary music, but of contemporary painting and literature. Composers, artists and poets from all parts of the world were drawn to Montparnasse and Montmartre. Here a strong reaction to late nineteenth-century Romantic thinking and to the Romantic's search for the exotic caused a certain confusion of ideas and gave rise to many strange and superficial novelties. Picasso, the *Fauves* and the Cubists were revolutionising the visual arts. The Futurists were becoming intoxicated with speed and mechanical beauty and Diaghilev's Ballet Russe was giving a renewed vision of line, angle and movement. In the field of music Paris had taken the neo-classicists to its heart. Stravinsky was a prominent figure; but there were also Bartók, Falla, Milhaud, Honegger, Auric, Hindemith, Prokofiev, Malipiero, Kodály and Poulenc, whose names appeared from time to time on programmes for the Concerts Koussevitzky, and whose music was applauded by a smart Parisian society for whom music was as much a game as anything else.

Understandably Martinů was anxious to know all that was new and fashionable, and the music of these composers attracted and confused him, as it did the many young musicians who had come expressly to study with Nadia Boulanger at the recently founded American Conservatoire at Fontainebleau. At first Martinů was struck by the wealth and richness of Parisian musical life and he was more than a little taken aback to discover that musical Impressionism was so much out of vogue with its haziness and vaguely evocative sense of poetry which no longer satisfied even those who were best able to express such moods in music. After his death in 1918, Debussy's music was seldom heard in Paris. Music was in a state of transition. With Jean Cocteau as their propagandist and intellectual cover, *Les Six* were turning out frivolous, gay, scandalous pieces, with pretty pastel shades and charming volubility.

They were discovering new ways of combining negro rhythms and tunes from Parisian night-life in irreverent, frothy products in an attempt to escape from the horrors of the years 1914-1918, and from the burden of commitment to the cause of war. Alongside *Les Six,* Erik Satie, *excentrique extraordinaire*, with only a year to live, was creating a series of idiosyncratic visions in a number of musical styles drawn from the cafés, the circus and the music-hall – producing ballets like *Les Aventures de Mercure* and *Relâche*, pantomimes such as *Jack-in-the-Box* and music-hall numbers for *La Belle Excentrique*. 'Hot Jazz' arrived with Louis Armstrong and Bessie Smith. Ragtime, also blown from the other side of the Atlantic, was being welcomed in the piano compositions of Jean Wièner; and in the hands of Darius Milhaud jazz, Harlem-style, found powerful expression in *La Création du monde*, as did Brazilian airs and Tango and Rumba rhythms in his cabaret fantasy *Le Boeuf sur le toit*. Nineteenth-century musical seriousness was out of fashion. Now the purpose of music was simply to amuse and the rôle of the composer was to provide a supply of titillating and witty creations – preferably short. This was the time when facility was considered more important than invention, when it was necessary for a composer only to write in order to have his talent proclaimed and his music printed. But in spite of these trends, for Martinů it was a period of assimilation. His reaction to his new environment and to the Parisian, rather than French, music he was hearing appeared only gradually. His powers of adapting himself quickly to new surroundings and situations had never been great and in Paris were strained to their limits. Much that he heard in the way of *avant-garde* music he disliked or failed to understand, and he remained sceptical and unconvinced when it came to the compositional techniques being explored by Schoenberg and the Viennese school. However, it was impossible for him to remain insensitive to current musical thought for long. Up to this time his outlook had been allied to musical Impressionism, but in 1924 it suddenly changed – a change that was largely due to the music of Igor Stravinsky, who had moved from Switzerland to set up headquarters in Paris. Martinů, reeling under the impact of *L'Histoire du soldat* and the recently-premièred *Les Noces*, decided to adopt his idiom. Dominated by Stravinsky's strikingly original approach to harmony, with its bi- and polytonal clashes, and by his linear conception of music with its return to a primitive form of polyphony, he responded with a ten-minute Rondo for large orchestra called *Half-time*. Written in ten days, *Half-time* marks a turning point in his career. It is an unexpected work and with it everything that had preceded it seemed to have lost its value. The old world of twilight landscapes is replaced by an excited crowd at a soccer match, and in harsh, uncompromising terms Martinů describes the tense atmosphere as supporters wait to see who scores the next goal. *Half-time*'s everyday subject, presented in contemporary language, not unnaturally surprised and shocked those who heard the first performance in Prague in December 1924. Siding with the catcalls which drowned the cheers, the Czech press unanimously damned it. Critics accused Martinů of plagiarising Stravinsky and an examination of the score shows how justified they were. Martinů's main interest is rhythmic rather than melodic and the fragmentary rondo theme which dominates the work immediately invites comparison with Petrushka's motif in Stravinsky's score. Furthermore, there is the kind of conflict of tonality that Stravinsky produces at the opening of his ballet. Stravinsky's influence prevails and one of Martinů's episodes is clearly modelled on the Russian Easter Hymn from *Petrushka*'s opening tableau. Elsewhere harsh ostinatos, motoric rhythms and aggressive, stabbing chords reveal Martinů's acquaintance with *Le Sacre du printemps*. Obviously *Half-time* is a derivative work, and to substitute a Stravinsky influence for that of Debussy is no great step in the direction of independence or originality. Nevertheless *Half-time* is a signal for the future and the score displays certain characteristics which were to become part of the mature Martinů technique. In the rhythmic flexibility, freedom from the barline, preference for small rhythmic fragments stemming from a single motif and worked into the texture through a process of continuous development, there is more than a glimpse of the mature Martinů. As yet there is no trace of folk music or jazz. These were elements he was to assimiliate only gradually in the course of his time in Paris.

Paris provided Martinů not only with a broader musical horizon, but with a group of friends, most of them, like himself, who were geographically rather than temperamentally Bohemian. Somehow they were drawn together by their Czech origin, the significance of which they only began to appreciate when separated from their homeland. This was the Paris of the Great Depression. There was little money to be earned from composition alone, so Martinů picked up whatever he could by playing for dance groups here and there. Afterwards he would return weary and depressed to the lodgings he shared with the Czech painter, Jan Zrzavý who, like himself, had come to Paris to search for new artistic values. Together they turned a couple of rooms in the rue le Chapelais into an artists' colony. They had no money and their discomfort was extreme. In summer they sweltered and in winter they froze. The Paris of the *haute cuisine* was a long way off as they took it in turns to cook in one day enough for the week. But such hardship was not reflected in the music Martinů wrote at this time and having acquired an old upright piano he began to compose with a zest that had been missing for months. A String Trio (marked No. 1) and a Quartet for clarinet, horn, cello and side-drum explore some of the rhythmic possibilities exploited in Stravinsky's *L'Histoire du soldat* – a work Martinů much admired. Now, in 1925, a number of songs and chamber pieces appeared, mostly experimental, mostly in a variety of styles, yet important in that they show how the composer's idiom was evolving. The Concertino for cello and small instrumental group (piccolo, flute, oboes, clarinets, bassoon, horn, trumpet, trombone, piano and percussion) is a one-movement rhapsody in which a number of motifs undergo processes of transformation in the form of continuous variation. The music is firmly anchored around C and the solo part is basically diatonic in the sense that the composer knows what key he is pretending to be in, though the busy instrumental strands often result in a clash of meaningless dissonance. The cello part is crisp with nervous energy and throughout Martinů plays naturally with syncopated and changing rhythms. Bars of 7/8 alternate with bars of 5/8 and 3/8 but the ear tends to tire of this rhythmic juggling, especially when it is emphasised by a prominent side-drum beat.

The Concertino was followed by a Nonet, intended for soloists in the Czech Philharmonic but never completed, two volumes of *Children's Songs* (*Dětské písničky*), a group of *Chinese Songs* (*Čínské písně*) and a set of piano pieces called *Bajky* (*Fables*). Although the five fables are slight in length and value, they do display the composer's strengthening artistic grasp and his ability to translate feelings into musical terms. None of these pieces make demands on the player's technique and generally each is arranged in two parts. Throughout, Martinů works with diatonic material but there is an insistent use of consecutive sevenths in 'On the Farm', of consecutive seconds in 'The Poor Rabbit', and of consecutive fourths in 'The Monkeys'. In 'The Angry Bear' a more percussive note is sounded and Martinů's tendency to develop the lower register of the keyboard makes a departure from the orthodox piano writing to be found in *Puppets. Fables* was followed by another suite for piano called *Film en miniature* – a set that could well have been prompted by the Charlie Chaplin film shorts of which Martinů was a warm admirer. Here again the piano writing is simple and direct; but with the composer's modest ability at the keyboard one questions how it could be otherwise. After all, he was for the most part self-taught. His hands were large and he often experienced difficulty in playing anything but chords; his technique was limited and his interest in piano music sporadic. He rarely played the piano for

10. The Prague Conservatoire.

11. Martinů in 1906.

12. Martinů in 1909.

13. The Czech Philharmonic Orchestra in 1920. Martinů is arrowed.

14. Martinů with Stanislav Novák.

15. Martinů in 1912.

pleasure and was not known to play even his own compositions in public. In later years he invited the concert pianist Rudolf Firkušný to accompany him to publishing houses in order to give an impression of his scores; and when it came to preparing a piano reduction of a stage work Martinů was obliged to ask the pianist Karel Šolc to re-arrange vocal scores for him. But because Martinů was not the possessor of an advanced keyboard technique himself it must not be assumed that his piano music is undemanding. The Piano Concerto No. 1 and Concertino for Piano (left hand) show how complex his keyboard writing could be.

For all its merits the Concertino, written for Otakar Hollman in 1926, does not bear comparison with Janáček's *Capriccio* composed for the same soloist at roughly the same time. Martinů's is a backward-looking score belonging to the warm, Romantic, nineteenth-century school with a style of piano writing that suggests Blumenfeld's *Étude* for the left hand (Op. 38) or watered-down Liszt. Although Martinů's responses stay within the measure of the music, the keyboard part, with arpeggiated figuration, cantabile melodies, scale passages and rapid octave work, makes it a more grateful work to the performer than the First Piano Concerto, written a year earlier. Though this is a more interesting score, little of the keyboard writing falls naturally under the hand. The solo part includes numerous chord clusters and octave patterns, often in rapid tempi with darting passage work calling for considerable agility. Here Martinů rarely uses the piano as an instrument for producing cantabile effects. Instead he creates a number of dry, harpsichord-like textures belonging more to the neo-classicist than the Romantic idioms. The Concerto lacks intellectual rigour, and interest is again rhythmic rather than melodic, with irregular phrase-lengths and complex syncopations that tend to break down the rigidity of the barline. Throughout his three movements Martinů uses the solo piano as a vehicle for experimenting with sonority and shows his sense of colour and of timbre to be as imaginative as ever. The Concerto has a marked eighteenth-century feeling with a modest instrumental force (double wood-wind, two each of horns, trumpets and trombones and strings) and a central Andante which omits brass. Considering that Martinů's Concerto appeared only a year before Bartók's first for the piano it is unadventurous; and with keyboard textures which suggest Scarlatti, the solo part is unlikely to attract the virtuoso. (Rudolf Firkušný confirms that the composer, at work on his Second Piano Concerto in 1933, disowned the earlier score on account of its dull solo writing.) However, the Concerto does reveal Martinů's leaning towards a more daring form of instrumental polyphony and in the toccata-like Allegro there is a strong hint of the music of Albert Roussel.

Roussel held an interesting place in Parisian music circles during the Twenties; for after his training at the Schola Cantorum, where he came under the influence of the Franck school and passed through the hands of Vincent d'Indy, he paid homage to the work of Debussy and the Impressionists, made acquaintance with *Les Six* and finally, at the age of fifty-two, took his stand alongside the younger composers, whom he dominated largely by force of musical breeding and sheer discipline. For most Frenchmen his 'modern' compositions were regarded as a sobering force to offset the *avant-garde* and period jazz furniture that cluttered the Parisian salons; but for Martinů his music had a deeper significance. He had become acquainted with it during his days in the Czech Philharmonic when he had been powerfully intoxicated by Roussel's nature symphony *Poème de la forêt* (1904-1906). However, it was to the score of *Le Festin de l'araignée*, with its appealing insect scenario and its delicate and wonderfully transparent instrumentation, that Martinů returned time and time again. He was fascinated by the alchemy of Roussel's pictorial manner and by the ordered logic of his thought; and in *Pour une fête de printemps* (1921) he had marked the way in which Roussel's idiom was developing, with its uncompromising acceptance of simultaneously sounding tonalities and its dissonant underpinning.

Over the years Martinů's admiration for Roussel's music had increased to such an extent that in the winter of 1923 he managed to overcome his natural shyness and introduced himself, asking for instruction in composition. Roussel found Martinů completely different from any of the pupils he had moulded during his years as Professor of Counterpoint at the Schola Cantorum. It was not only that at thirty-three his pupil was well seasoned (after all Roussel himself had been in his late twenties when he had abandoned the navy to work with d'Indy), but lessons with Martinů were severely handicapped since neither spoke the other's language. Nevertheless, in Roussel, Martinů found one of Paris's most hospitable artists who not only took a paternal interest in him and his work, but became a valuable source of strength. Invariably arriving up to an hour late for his Friday morning sessions, he would attempt to play extracts from his scores while Roussel would improvise alterations at the keyboard. It was Roussel who advised Martinů to write more choral music and to think more contrapuntally, and he may even have urged him to explore the music of the early madrigalists. Clearly Roussel's influence on Martinů was considerable and his debt to his teacher is reflected in the tribute which he wrote for *La Revue musicale*, in November 1937.

I came all the way from Czechoslovakia to Paris to benefit from his instruction and tuition. I arrived with my scores, my projects, my plans, and a whole heap of muddled ideas, and it was he, Roussel, who pointed out to me, always with sound reasoning and with precision peculiar to him, the right way to go, the path to follow. He helped show me what to retain, what to reject, and he succeeded in putting my thoughts in order, though I have never understood how he managed to do so. With his modesty, his kindness, and with his subtle and friendly irony he always led me in such a way that I was hardly aware of being led. He allowed me time to reflect and develop by myself . . . Today, when I remember how much I learned from him I am quite astonished. That which was hidden in me, unconscious and unknown, he divined and revealed in a way that was friendly, almost affectionate. All that I came to look for in Paris I found in him. I came for advice, clarity, restraint, taste and clear, precise, sensitive expression – the very qualities of French art which I had always admired and which I sought to understand to the best of my ability. Roussel did, in fact, possess all these qualities and he willingly imparted his knowledge to me, like the great artist that he was.

Evidently there was no normal teacher-pupil relationship between the two, but rather a friendship which grew with time as did Roussel's admiration for Martinů's music. Roussel probably gave Martinů little in the way of dogmatic teaching, but what he did do was to reassure him of his ability to compose and to plant certain thoughts in his mind which helped steer him from descriptive programme pieces to more abstract forms. The first score to reflect Roussel's influence is the String Quartet No. 2. Here Martinů's ideas seem to be crystallising in a more positive way, and though the textures are overloaded in the powerful slow movement and the technique appears somewhat tenuous in the third, the work does show him making a serious attempt to reconcile the disparate components of his former style. The opening calls to mind Stravinsky's *Concertino String Quartet* of 1920 in its use of bi-tonality and its terse and elliptic phrase lengths. The second movement is daring and typical of Martinů in its oscillations around a fixed point, while by contrast the finale is brilliantly good-humoured with a Smetana-like Polka, a solo cadenza for the first violin and a dazzling coda. Flouting Roussel's advice, Martinů followed the Second Quartet with a piece of programme music for large orchestra which like Honegger's *Pacific 231* and *Rugby* is an attempt to create music of an exteriorised kind. Quick to take fire from the new mechanical age, and anticipating Kurt Weill's *Der Lindberghflug* by two years, Martinů seized on Colonel Lindbergh's single-handed transatlantic flight as the theme for his next orchestral composition. Admittedly it is an unusual subject for a symphonic poem, but possibly it appealed because there was something of the lonely aviator about Martinů himself, when, in his early days, he had looked down on the earth as if from the air. However, it was not the sound of an aeroplane in full flight that he hoped to recreate in music; it was more the jostling excitement of the hero's welcome at Le Bourget which captured Martinů's imagination. And it is just this element which places *La Bagarre* in a similar class to *Half-time*. Whereas in that score Martinů portrayed the tension of the spectators at a football match, in *La Bagarre* he transports the same tension to the streets as a mass, in chaos and riot, express their enthusiasm for Lindbergh's achievement. Martinů creates an impressive sonata, violent and complex. Written under the influence of *Le Sacre du printemps*, for all its unmistakable character, the score somehow lacks the force of *Half-time*. None the less, *La Bagarre* remains an important work in Martinů's catalogue; for with it he not only celebrated Lindbergh's transatlantic flight but as a result of it his own name crossed the Atlantic for the first time. Having spotted Serge Koussevitzky at a boulevard café, Martinů is said to have overcome all shyness, introduced himself to the distinguished conductor and presented him with a manuscript copy of *La Bagarre* with the request that Koussevitzky perform it. When, on 18 November 1927, Koussevitzky did in fact première the work with the Boston Symphony Orchestra he established a link between its composer and the New World which was to be of the greatest value in later years. So much for Martinů's temerity. Possibly through his connexion with Koussevitzky and his friendship with Roussel, Martinů was beginning to make a name for himself as a composer in the smaller Parisian music circles. Early in 1926 he was invited by the artist Michel Larionow, a collaborator of Diaghilev, to consider *Karaguez* as a theme for a possible ballet score. At this time Martinů did not feel ready to accept such a commission, which was offered instead to Marcel Mihalovici, a young composer who had come from Bucharest to Paris for a fortnight's holiday and, like Martinů, was to remain for a number of years. From the chance meeting of the two men there grew a friendship which flourished until Martinů's death in 1959. Mihalovici remembers Martinů at this time as a timid, reserved person who used sign-language to express himself when experiencing difficulty in speaking French. Apparently Martinů was unaware of the recognition he was winning in the concerts and recitals sponsored by Walter Straram, whose musical evenings were arranged to show off the works of young and unknown composers. When several of Martinů's scores were heard there for the first time, it soon became evident that besides possessing a talent for composition he had a remarkable ability for turning out new pieces in quick succession. At one of Straram's concerts Martinů and Mihalovici were introduced to two other composers – Conrad Beck who originated from Switzerland and was eleven years younger than Martinů, and Tibor Harsányi, a Hungarian pianist-composer, pupil of Bartók and Kodály and seven years younger than Martinů. Despite their different national backgrounds these four were drawn together and formed a *groupe de quatre*. To describe them as a group was misleading (Roussel had a better name for them when he called them *Les Constructeurs*) for they had few general aims and qualities in common and differed greatly in personal characteristics. Somehow their individualism prevented them from remaining a coherent group for any length of time; however, in the early days they could often be found in each other's company, exchanging manuscripts, discussing technical problems and philosophising into the small hours on the future of music and art. Soon after the group was formed an enterprising publisher, Michel Dillard, of *La Sirène musicale*, began to take an interest in their output and gradually their scores appeared in print under the title of *L'École de Paris* to avoid conflict and confusion with *Les Six*. In addition he organised chamber concerts and recitals where Martinů, the most prolific of the group, was again and again before the public eye; and it was *chez* Dillard that his Sonata in D, for violin and piano, was performed together with the brilliant *Three Czech Dances,* the *Habanera* and a piece for dancing, *Pro tanec*, all for piano solo.

Although Martinů was growing in musical and artistic strength, he was still very poor. He had never valued money, and the little he earned from his performances was quickly spent on books. Martinů's love of reading had in no way diminished since his days in Prague. On the contrary, it had developed, and when he was not composing he would spend hours on the banks of the Seine strolling along the quays, observing the *clochards,* browsing through the *bouquiniste* stalls, sampling everything and anything from Greek philosophy to Dadaist verse. He read avidly and turned his garret in the rue Delambre, where he now lodged, into a cluttered library of periodicals and scores, all of which had passed through innumerable hands before his. He rose early, ate irregularly, cooked occasionally and devoted up to ten hours each day to composition. He rarely sought entertainment and then chose the circus and cinema only because the language of clowns and of slapstick films was universal. He was at home to only a few chosen friends and invariably lived in a world of fantasy. Sooner or later he was bound to want to translate these fantasies into music and towards the end of 1925 he set to work on a one-act ballet-fantasy called *Vzpoura (Revolt)*.

As the title suggests, *Revolt* deals with an explosive situation; but Martinů's rioters are neither revolutionaries nor mercenaries, simply musicians. Sounds rebel. Classical music rises against modern dance tunes. The gramophone mutinies against jazz and ragtime. Chaos develops as musicians become redundant. Critics commit suicide and it is even rumoured that Stravinsky has emigrated to a deserted island to find peace. At this point the libretto, which has a distinct nonsense element, and could well have originated from the pen of Lewis Carroll or Guillaume Apollinaire, reads like the scenario for a René Clair film. From the pandemonium a Moravian girl in national costume emerges singing a folk song. A young composer is moved to take the theme up and develops it into a lovely melody which pacifies the aggrieved musical factions almost as effectively as Tamino's magic bells calm the wild beasts in Mozart's *Die Zauberflöte*.

At this period in his career Martinů was still an experimenter, and each new work represented a stylistic *volte face*. *Revolt* is clearly an invitation for musical cleverness and Martinů was quick to supply this in the five scenes which comprise the ballet-pastiche. Disturbed rhythms and distorted tonalities are treated with the sort of wit and irreverence much in vogue in the Twenties. Displaced accents and shifting key centres are used for comic effect; grumbling ostinatos and bi-tonal passages add to the growing confusion as the Tango competes with the Foxtrot. But for all its brilliance and its attractive invention, Martinů had no prospects for immediate production. Typically, and somewhat stoically, he pushed the score to one side to begin a more serious one-act ballet version of Rudyard Kipling's last 'Just-So' story, *The Butterfly That Stamped*. Martinů's *Motýl, který dupal* includes an overture and twelve dances and is scored for large orchestra with female chorus. The delightful story of King Suleiman's nine hundred and ninety-nine wives who run from his palace when his pet butterfly stamps is one which appealed to the composer because it gave him another chance to explore the Orient. Here Martinů abandons the world of *Istar* for that of the *Thousand and One Nights,* and possibly something of Roussel's opera-ballet *Padmâvatî* coloured his approach to the score. Exotic-sounding flute and cor anglais melismas, typical of oriental music, and evocative rhythms on piano, harp and gong all suggest an Eastern background, but one far removed from that conjured up by Rimsky-Korsakov or Delibes. Although the score was submitted to the National Theatre in Brno, the ballet never reached the stage since Martinů, in a burst of enthusiasm, had forgotten to obtain Kipling's consent before adapting the original. However, an orchestral suite, arranged in 1965, presents 'Suleiman's Palace', 'Oriental Dance', 'Butterfly Waltz', 'Dance of the Flowers' and 'Dance before the King' as a colourful concert selection.

Undaunted by the *Butterfly*'s failure to stamp on a Czech stage,

Martinů began another score for the theatre. At this period he seems to have been as obsessed with ballets as Stravinsky had been between 1910 and 1913; but Martinů's next offering was to be quite different from anything Stravinsky had ever produced. In the mid-Twenties, Paris was the home of a number of experimental dance groups and in February 1927 Martinů was approached by the enterprising Madame Beriza, who ran one such company, with a view to his composing a mechanical ballet for her pioneering theatre. Of course the beauty of things mechanical had been preached by Filippo Marinetti and the Italian Futurists at least ten years before. Milhaud had ploughed the field and scattered the virtues of various mechanical implements – mowers, seed-drillers and binders – in his *Machines agricoles* along with the seedsman's *Catalogue des fleurs*; and in *Pacific 231* Honegger had translated into sound the visual impression of a locomotive speeding at seventy-five miles an hour down the track of the Canadian Pacific Railway. But neither had attempted to write a ballet without dancers – and this was the principal condition of Madame Beriza's commission. Stirred by the challenge, Martinů responded with *Le Raid merveilleux*, a 'mechanical ballet' inspired by the tragic flight of the pilots Nungesser and Colli. Apparently an aeroplane was to have been suspended over the stage while a kaleidoscope of projections, with cloud and seascapes, recreated their abortive attempt to cross the Atlantic. The climax was to have been the plane crashing into the ocean, but instead it was the Theâtre Beriza which crashed for lack of financial support; so, once again, Martinů's score (for two clarinets, trumpet and string quartet) was destined to remain unheard.

A similar fate befell his next ballet *On tourne* (*Shoot*), another experimental work written for the *avant-garde* theatre. Again there are no dancers, but this time the plot unfolds through a combination of puppetry and cartoon film. Aptly Martinů sub-titles his score 'film inédit' and asks for the stage to be divided into two levels. The upper part represents the surface of the sea where a boat carries two puppet sailors and a puppet diver; in the ocean below puppet fish are seen swimming through a web of fantastic seaweed. As a model aeroplane flies across the stage, the puppet diver plunges to the depths and with a torch shines a beam through the seaweed. By means of film projection he reveals the unlikely spectacle of a lobster making love to a fish. For this extraordinary subject, which may have suggested itself to the composer following the Prague performances of Hindemith's Burmese marionette opera *Das Nusch-Nuschi* in April 1923, Martinů demanded an extravagant orchestra to be employed only in the full-length overture. Here, almost certainly, he was cutting his own throat, for the work demanded too much ingenuity and involved too much expense to stage.

With his next ballet, however, Martinů was more realistic. In response to a commission by Božena Nebĕská and to a scenario by Jarmila Kröschlová, he wrote a witty curtain-raiser called *Pokušení svatoušká hrnec* (*Temptation of the Saintly Pot*) and with it scored his first popular success under the revised title *La Revue de cuisine*. Here the dancers play a variety of cooking utensils which swagger their way through a naïve episode of kitchen life. The marriage of Pot and Lid is in danger of being broken up by the suave Twirling Stick. Pot succumbs to his flattery. Dishcloth makes eyes at Lid but is challenged to a duel by Broom. Pot, however, tires of Twirling Stick and longs for Lid's caresses, but Lid cannot be found anywhere. Suddenly an enormous foot appears from the wings and kicks him back on stage. Pot and Lid kiss and make up and, flirting once again, Twirling Stick goes off with Dishcloth. Although Martinů seldom danced himself, he liked the Charleston, the Tango and the Foxtrot, and it was these dances that he used as the basis of this score. Clearly Martinů was going out of his way to be fashionable and popular in this work, and by writing for a chamber group (violin, cello, clarinet, trumpet, bassoon and piano) he was openly making concessions to those who felt his earlier ballets to be too ambitious. *Kitchen Revue* is entertainment pure and simple. There is a Waltonesque lilt to the Tango and a razz-ma-tazz swing in the Charleston, but in spite of these clichés the music contains many brilliant, satirical moments and shows how effective Martinů's ideas could be when he was working with the rhythms of Dixieland jazz and the techniques of free improvisation.

Martinů's jazz period continued with the *Black Bottom* and *Three Sketches in Modern Dance Forms* (both for solo piano) which go through all the motions of the Blues, Tango and Charleston but say nothing new about any of them. There is something artificial in this music; for though the craftsmanship is fluent, the composer comes near to being facile. The same feeling applies to *Le Jazz*, a tuneful if banal orchestral piece which seems to have been prompted by Paul Whiteman or by Jaroslav Ježek, a fellow Czech who had come to Paris where he was making a name for himself in the field of dance music. With a band of clarinets, three saxophones, trumpets, trombones, banjo, piano, drums and a wordless 'boop-a-doop' vocal backing, Martinů attempted to enter the 'pop' world of the day and imitated Ježek's style more in fun and friendly rivalry than seriously. More adventurous was his four-movement *Jazz Suite* for small orchestra, but apart from the syncopated Blues this is not particularly interesting either as jazz or as composition, possibly because Martinů was here little more than an explorer searching for a valid means of expression. The jazz phase was to pass, but not before he had extracted certain rhythmic and melodic elements which were gradually to be evolved into a distinctive style, and not before he had exploited them in no less than three operas.

As early as 1912 Martinů had planned to write an opera based on Przybyszewský's *De Profundis*, but sadly this did not get past the fourth page of sketch. Nevertheless, the idea of composing something for the stage remained with him and seven years later he began to consider Julius Zeyer's *Old Tale* for operatic treatment. For one reason or another this failed to materialise, and when it came to *Lucerna (The Lantern)*, on which he had really set his heart, he was unable to secure author's rights from Alois Jirásek. Jan Havlasa's libretto, entitled *Windows onto the Mist*, somehow failed to convince him, and for a three-act *opéra-grotesque, Who Is the Murderer?*, by J. L. Budín, he was unable to summon any enthusiasm at all. In the early days it seems that Martinů was very uncertain about the operatic subject he was looking for; but he was certain about one thing: he would follow none of the established Czech opera plots – the national, patriotic, folk operas like those of Smetana and Dvořák, or the form of Russian realism which had been adopted by Janáček. The Parisian Martinů was keen to explore the fashionable and the new, and his ballets show just how willing he had been to relish every passing turn of style. In *Revolt, Shoot* and *Le Raid merveilleux* he had consciously been an *avant-garde* composer and with the acceptance of J. L. Budín's text to *Voják a tanečnice (The Soldier and the Dancer)* he now introduced a new genre to Czech opera.

The Czech libretto, taken from Plautus's comedy *Pseudolus*, is deliberately involved and close to farce. Combining revue, operetta, ballet, and musical comedy, Budín's plot merges past and present, sweeps the action from stage to stalls and joins audience and cast in a hilarious topsy-turvy entertainment. The plot revolves around Pseudolus, a cunning and resourceful servant who devises a series of ridiculous situations in which his master Kalidorus outwits Harpax, a Spartan warrior, and wins Fenicie, a dancer in Bambula's household in Athens, as his wife. Librettist and composer use this outline only as a peg on which to hang a whole series of outrageous incidents, and in Act I a carnival develops into a riot when producer, critics, artists and spectators are brought together in a musical mêlée. In the second Act Plautus calls on Cato to disentangle the situation, but, unable to see rhyme or reason anywhere, he settles down to watch a skittish vaudeville as the moon, stars, clouds, street lamps, statues, knives, forks, spoons and

43

plates join in a spirited dance sequence. Later the action moves to a Twenties dance hall where a chorus and Dixieland band exhort the audience to join them in a bustling Black Bottom, the refrain of which is sung through megaphones.

By designing his music as a parody of contemporary idioms and transposing classical antiquity to the twentieth century, Martinů was paying lip-service to a pattern set by Stravinsky in *Oedipus Rex,* by Honegger in *Antigone* and by Henri Christiné whose operetta *Phi-Phi* had run for four thousand performances at the Théâtre des Bouffes-Parisiens. Another opera which might have coloured Martinů's imagination is Prokofiev's *Love of Three Oranges,* where fantasy is mixed with reality, past merges with present and the chorus, masquerading as audience, interrupt the action. However, for all its derivative qualities *The Soldier and the Dancer* is the work of a theatrical craftsman and in the opera house it is as successful today as it must have been at its sensational first performance in Brno on 5 May 1928.

Curiously, Martinů did not wait for the effect of this *opera buffa* on the public before writing another stage work; for two months before (on 24 March 1928) he had completed his second opera *Les Larmes du couteau* (*The Tears of the Knife*), written in only nine days and based on an experimental libretto by Georges Ribemont-Dessaignes. A striking figure in literary Paris during the inter-war years, Ribemont-Dessaignes was a painter, poet, and dramatist as well as being a very individual participant in the Surrealist movement. He was also something of a musician and at one of the Dadaist manifestations in the Salle Gaveau had paraded himself as the composer of a number of bizarre piano pieces, written with the aid of a pocket roulette wheel. Martinů met him at a time when his novels were being translated into Czech and when the Liberated Theatre in Prague was presenting his Dadaist plays *Surinmuet* and *Bourreau de Pérou.* As editor of the review *Bifur* he was in touch with all the literary personalities of the day and his influence was said to be considerable. What attracted Martinů to his writing was not only the brilliance of the language, but also the sadistic cruelty and grotesque irony of his dramatic vision. Written at a time when old ideas of dignity and tradition were swept aside, the libretto of *Les Larmes du couteau* gives satirical treatment to themes such as the ugliness of love, promiscuity and the pathological rivalry of a mother and daughter for the love of a dead body.

The seven scenes which make up this *opéra-macabre* last barely twenty minutes, but in complexity the action seems to take three times as long. The body of a Hanged Man dangles over the stage and as Eleanor tells her mother how she longs to marry such a being, Satan enters proclaiming his love for Eleanor, who shuns him and reiterates her yearning for the Hanged Man. In a parody of the wedding cere- mony Satan marries her to the corpse and Eleanor, celebrating their union, dances an erotic Tango before the suspended figure. Seeing a Negro Cyclist encircling the stage, Satan snubs Eleanor and transforms himself into the form of the cyclist. Anxious to animate her husband's body, still dangling above, Eleanor flirts with the Negro (Satan) while the Mother performs physical jerks at the back of the stage. When Eleanor kisses the Negro, his head splits in two and the face of Satan is revealed. Eleanor stabs herself in fright. The Hanged Man starts to move, and to the strains of a Foxtrot two disjointed legs begin to dance. Next the head is thrown into the air and is juggled with the limbs. The Hanged Man then comes to life, drops to the ground and caresses Eleanor. When she returns his kiss, his skull bursts open and the face of Satan leaps out. Eleanor despairs of loving anybody; but her mother insists that she knows a way of winning Satan's affection. Satan, how- ever, refuses to be courted by a middle-aged woman and disappears, blowing her a kiss.

Curiously here there is no real conflict of character, only grotesque and implausible happenings. Ever since 1916, when Martinů had written *The Shadow*, he had been drawn to the idea of presenting dual personalities on the stage. Then it had been a dancer and her shadow. Now, in the form of the double, Satan-Hanged Man and Satan-Cyclist, he returned to the same theme. But how Martinů imagined portraying these doubles is a mystery. In the score he asks for the metamorphoses to be immediate. Satan, elegantly foppish in top hat, white tie and tails, must turn into the Negro Cyclist within seconds. Quite obviously the concentrated nature of the action and the pace at which incidents develop could not be further removed from the flow of traditional opera or from modern music drama; and a way of effecting the trans- formations could scarcely have been found in the Twenties other than in the silent film. Martinů had previously attempted to use film in his ballet *Shoot,* and long before had developed a passion for Charlie Chaplin shorts. Could his interest in these have coloured his treatment of Ribemont-Dessaignes's libretto? Or did the structure of the text (in dialogue throughout) prompt him to think of it as the scenario for a comic opera-film? Almost certainly poet and composer were aware that film had been used on the ballet stage in 1924 when René Clair pro- duced a Dadist film-interlude in the Picasso-Satie *Relâche,* and Martinů may even have heard about Kurt Weill's introduction of film sequences in *Royal Palace*, given at the Kroll Opera in Berlin in 1927. As it is, Ribemont-Dessaignes's libretto is full of latent film qualities, and indeed many of the unlikely situations seem to come directly from the silent films of the day. Satan's transformations and his changes of costume suggest film cuts; compressed happenings, such as the Mother's physical exercises, the circus-like racing of the Negro Cyclist, the limb-juggling sequence, could all have been made possible with film editing. Moreover, several movements in the action proceed without dialogue: the limb-juggling scene is played against a musical interlude and one of the leading characters, the Hanged Man, is a mime – a character often seen in the films of the Twenties.

Incorporating the sounds of contemporary jazz and elements from the Tango, Foxtrot, and Charleston, but remaining entirely himself, Martinů produces an outrageous extravaganza which is at the same time a model of musical conciseness and instrumental sensitivity. The colour and sound achieved by the fifteen players is remarkable. However, such orchestral subtleties as the score presents did little to convince the Festival authorities at Baden-Baden – to whom *Les Larmes du couteau* was submitted – that the opera was stageable. For the next forty years the score remained unperformed until the National Theatre in Brno bravely premièred it in 1968. Even then the work was not totally convincing, for in many ways it defies stage presentation. Like Berlioz's *Damnation of Faust,* Martinů's opera is years ahead of its time, calling for a visual treatment incorporating all the sophistication of present-day television and cinema media. Possibly by utilising travelling matt film techniques, television colour-separation-overlay devices, and combining these with black theatre, *Les Larmes du couteau* could be turned into an exciting spectacle. As opera, however, it cannot join the ranks of Hindemith's *Neues vom Tage,* Křenek's *Jonny spielt auf* or Weill's *Der Dreigroschenoper*, with which it is more or less contemporary; and as theatre it fails for practical reasons.

Baden-Baden's lack of confidence in *Les Larmes du couteau* did not discourage Martinů or Ribemont-Dessaignes from collaborating on bigger and better things. Evidently poet and musician had come to regard each other as essential to their collaboration. 'If there is anyone capable of persuading me to sign a contract of alliance with a musician it is Martinů', wrote Ribemont-Dessaignes in *Pestrý týden,* a leading Czech paper in 1930. And his next 'contract of alliance' with the composer was an opera called *Les Trois Souhaits (The Three Wishes)*, sub-titled *Les Vicissitudes de la vie (Capriciousness of Life)* which seems to begin where *Les Larmes du couteau* stopped short. This is another experimental work that attempts to marry opera and film techniques, though here the film element is openly used and forms an integral part of the action. Ribemont-Dessaignes's libretto is really a play-within-a-play where situations are presented and developed side by side. The basic theme concerns Arthur and Nina, a middle-aged couple who are given three wishes (wealth, youth and love), the fulfilment of which brings them little happiness and ultimately death. The opera begins in a film studio where the essentially naïve story is being shot amid the paraphernalia of technicians, scene-men, lighting equipment, make-up artists and camera crews. By the end of Act II filming is complete and Act III is devoted to a gala performance of the finished silent film (suitably abbreviated) and attended by the stars of the show. The last scene of the opera is an Epilogue in which the actors introduce their private problems into the plot and extend the story of the film to real life. This, in fact, creates a triple projection and breaks down the barrier between fantasy and reality. The dreamworld of the film studio and plush, luxury cinema, is transformed into the banality of a New York bar, aptly called 'The Three Wishes'. Glamorous actresses emerge as they really are – shallow neurotics with problems. Conflicts between husbands and wives, and wives and lovers are unearthed and buried again. The same conflicts which in the film were only make-believe are transferred to real life and correspondingly developed to similar conclusions as those projected on the cinema screen. Arthur sits alone drinking while his wife, Nina, flirts with her young cousin Serge. Familiar faces from the film come and go, and Lillian, the waitress who, in the film, had played the rôle of the Good Fairy granting the three wishes returns as a stripper. After her dance the bar empties. Nina and Serge, heavily drunk, leave in each other's arms. Arthur remains alone, tired and disappointed. As the lights go out, he dies in the same way as he did in the film. The audience is left to question whether life is like a piece of celluloid action or if the film recreated a life of dreams or a dream-life.

The deliberate, ambiguous ending, the exploration of various levels of reality, and the idea of actors identifying themselves with the characters they portray, were themes Martinů was to exploit years later in *Juliette* and *The Greek Passion*. At this stage in his career he was unable to bring the real force of his musical argument to Ribemont-Dessaignes's slightly sentimental parody. From the beginning the libretto sets out to avoid the traditional concept of operatic text, and from the musical point of view Martinů was determined to avoid the obvious. Instead he chose to make a marriage of opera and oratorio as Stravinsky had done in 1927 with *Oedipus Rex*. Profiting, perhaps, by Stravinsky's device of placing a commenting chorus on the stage throughout the action, Martinů gives us another interpretation of the same idea. But there was another work which helped to inspire him – Křenek's *Jonny spielt auf*.

Almost certainly Křenek's score became Martinů's model for combining jazz with popular and *avant-garde* music, speech-song and ballet which in parts comes close to musical revue. Even the orchestra is forced to combine two cultures with Martinů adding saxophones, jazz flutes, flexatones, banjo, piano and accordion to large symphonic forces. Much of this sparkling music belongs to the idiom of Satie and *Les Six* with catchy dances and sarcastic references to the Blues, the Charleston and the Tango; and when Martinů lets himself go with these parodies then his music comes alive. Overall, however, the score is uneven, and in the more serious moments, generally given to a mysterious quartet of Harlequins instructed to sing falsetto, there is sometimes a lack of conviction. Musical interest at the beginning and end of Acts I and II is maintained by a mosaic of murmuring ostinatos, as studio hands and technicians engage in shouting, talking and even whistling. Apart from the dances and the catchy 'gramophone record' song the most continuous musical period appears in Act III where Martinů provides incidental music to the silent film version of Acts I and II. The Suite, for so-called 'Cinema Band', includes a miniature overture and three pieces depicting the granting of the first two wishes, and four further numbers which acompany Arthur and Nina's expedition to the Golden Island, their shipwreck, Arthur's encounter with the Negress and his death. Throughout these movements the quality of Martinů's invention is less memorable; but in the independent Overture called *Le Départ,* which announces the Epilogue and serves to transport actors and audience from Parisian cinema to New York bar, he produces one of his most urgent and closely argued symphonic movements.

Les Trois Souhaits is an ambitious piece of music-theatre and Martinů's alertness to modern trends had led him to use film in a way which actually anticipated by one year Milhaud's *Christopher Columbus*. But whereas Milhaud's opera (film and all) was first given in Berlin in 1930, Martinů was less fortunate. Negotiations were opened with the Charlottenburg Opera but difficulties, financial and artistic, over the shooting of the fifteen-minute film led to *Les Trois Souhaits* being dropped and as few opera houses in the Thirties were equipped with film projection facilities, managers and promoters steered clear of the score. *Les Trois Souhaits* was considered to be ahead of its time and it was only in 1971, forty-two years after Martinů had put the finishing touches to it, that the Brno Opera Company staged the opera for the first time and with *Les Trois Souhaits* scored one of their greatest post-war successes, possibly because it was produced by a film rather than an opera director.

Refusing to be put off by the lack of interest shown for his latest

venture, Martinů followed *Les Trois Souhaits* with another opera, called
La Semaine de bonté (*Week of Kindness*) in which Ribemont-Dessaignes
continued the association, so firmly cemented in the two earlier scores.
On this occasion, however, the result was less inspired. Based on an idea
of Ilya Ehrenburg's, the plot is a satire on charity and uses wartime
Paris as a backdrop for a tale about two country youths who lose their
naïve views of city life when they come face to face with reality. This
rather unpromising subject failed to hold Martinů's attention; for after
completing the first Act and part of the second he pushed the score to
one side in favour of a light-hearted ballet called *Échec au roi* (*Check
to the King*). Designed as a one-act argument to a scenario by André
Coeuroy, a pupil of Max Reger, and subtitled 'Ballet in Black, White
and Red', *Échec au roi* holds an important place among Martinů's
works since it is one of his last pieces to combine the urbanity of salon
music with jazz discreet enough not to frighten the most traditionally-
minded listener of the Thirties. Like Bliss's *Checkmate* (composed
seven years later) Martinů's ballet is based on a game of chess, but
whereas Bliss's score is dramatic, Martinů's is a three-part burlesque.
Part I comprises a Quadrille for the Rooks, a Solo for the Queens and
a March for the Black and White Pawns. The second part is largely
devoted to a Spanish Pastiche to match the Ruy Lopez opening of a
Chess Game. Play continues in Part III with Checkmate followed by
a Funeral March for the Red pieces and a Triumphal Dance for the
White. The Ballet comes swiftly to a close as the Pawns dance into their
box and an Ace and a Domino roll up the chess-board.

With *Échec au roi* Martinů completed his theatrical apprenticeship.
Between 1925 and 1930 he had produced no less than nine works for
the stage – most of them experimental and exploring the stylish, popular
dance forms of the day. In these scores it is easy to criticise Martinů's
use of the Charleston, Tango and Blues, but these had the same impact
on Europe in the 1920s as the Polka and Waltz had on Victorian
society and the Minuet and Gavotte on the previous age. Being a child
of his time he had not hesitated to adopt a style that paid homage to
jazz and current musical fashions. Yet, despite his acceptance of
fashionable trends, his operas and ballets had brought him little success.
Only three had reached the stage, and while collaboration with Ribemont-Dessaignes had introduced him to an original and imaginative
mind, it had done little more than label him 'Surrealist composer', for
scores like *On tourne*, *Les Larmes du couteau* and *Les Trois Souhaits* were considered unstageable and indeed, at the time of their
composition, they were just that. Clearly it was time to make a break,
time to change course, time for Martinů to settle down.

4 Paris: 1931-7

We had gone to the Cirque Médrano where the famous Fratellini Clowns were presenting their comedy turn. Everyone was laughing including a tall, thin man with blue eyes who sat directly behind me. As I turned around to look at him, he smiled and I wondered how one could possibly respond to such a smile. I became agitated and found it hard to concentrate on the antics of the clowns in the ring below. During the interval the same tall man came up and discreetly slipped a piece of paper into my hand. I opened it with curiosity and read : *Bohuslav Martinů, 11 rue Delambre, Paris 14.*

The words of Charlotte Quennehen, a young French girl who had left Picardy for Paris, where she was making a poor living in a dressmaker's workshop. For Martinů, shy and withdrawn, this introduction could not have been more out of character; yet, for one so reserved, he was capable of the most enterprising actions. Clearly he had lost nothing by presenting himself on Albert Roussel's doorstep and asking for lessons, and he had gained much by making Koussevitzky's acquaintance at a pavement café and pressing him to perform *La Bagarre*. Both men were to play significant rôles in shaping the course of Martinů's career, and his meeting with Charlotte Quennehen in November 1926 was to be similarly fateful. It is difficult to over-estimate the part this remarkable person played in the composer's career; for early on she recognised instinctively that here was an exceptional being, and knowing little of music herself she nevertheless saw in him qualities of a remarkable order, and determined to make it possible for them to emerge. She became his principal means of support and in the evenings worked interminable hours sewing buttons onto dresses to relieve him of the necessity of doing anything except composing. She made a home for him, at first in a smelly, cat-ridden apartment in the rue Mandar, near Les Halles, and later in a rented three-roomed bungalow in the rue de Vanves. She saved him from squalor, and even learnt to prepare the Czech dishes that he liked. She saw to it that his leisure was undisturbed and went out of her way to protect him from every interruption. Together they shared an enthusiasm for the country, for nature and for animals. On Sundays they would go to Versailles, to Fontainebleau or to Charlotte's parents near Compiègne, where they would spend hours in the thick forests gathering mushrooms and flowers smelling of childhood. Once or twice a year Martinů would return to Czechoslovakia and from time to time Charlotte would follow him.

16. *and* 17. Martinů's letter to Mr. Kanka, with details of his examination.

18. *and* 19. Certificate from the Prague Conservatoire, registering Martinů's incompetence in every subject – except his ability to teach.

On one occasion Jan Zrzavý gave her the proceeds from the sale of several of his paintings so that she could take the train to Prague, where Stanislav Novák soon became a true and trusted friend, though he spoke only halting French. In Polička, however, the welcome was less warm. Karolina Martinů, then in her late sixties, had long looked forward to her son settling in Polička with a rich farmer's daughter for a wife; but the arrival of an attractive but penniless French girl who could not speak a word of Czech and knew nothing of Czech ways disturbed her. Though she observed traditional Polička hospitality, she and Charlotte were to remain distant; but when Martinů's intentions became known, his mother openly resented Charlotte Quennehen's presence and for several years refused to give her blessing to their marriage. At the age of seventy-one, however, she relented and sent the traditional Czech feather bed to mark the occasion of her son's wedding. This took place on 21 March 1931, at a Paris Registry Office near the Porte d'Auteuil.

Marriage gave legality and a certain order to the Martinůs' life together, but it contributed little else. While his wife spent the day sewing in the machine shop of a Paris factory, Martinů worked on his scores, either at the piano or at his desk, breaking off only to walk along the banks of the Seine where the *bouquinistes* were his main attraction. Back in his room, another period of work lasted until dinner which his wife learnt to prepare silently in a kitchen where, if she did not freeze in icy draughts, she was roasted by a monstrous stove and choked by its fumes. In the evening he would either go to the Café du Dôme or to a bistro where he would meet friends and make a ten cent cup of coffee or *vin ordinaire* last the evening through. It was a simple existence but he worked hard and with his wife's help he now mastered the French language and learned to appreciate the writings of Cocteau, Labiche and Claudel at first hand. However, reading came second to music, and full of plans he set to work on a number of scores with which he hoped to improve his precarious financial position. Martinů was still desperately poor and with the responsibilities of keeping house and home together he must often have considered whether a return to Czechoslovakia might not bring an improvement in his fortunes. A letter from Jan Kunc inviting him to join the teaching staff of the Brno Conservatoire must have tempted him sorely in November 1930. Certainly security and a regular salary attracted him, but he doubted whether a full-time teaching commitment would give him the freedom he needed to compose. In December 1930 he declined the invitation, promising to return to Czechoslovakia only if and when he had achieved fame abroad. Here was confidence. But Kunc, unwilling to take Martinů's answer as final, recommended him for honorary membership to the Czech Academy of Arts and Sciences in May 1931 and a few months later arranged for him to be invited by the Czech Minister of Culture to accept the Professorship of Composition in Brno. Although it was becoming increasingly difficult for Martinů to make ends meet, in writing to Kunc at the beginning of 1932 he finally refused the offer.

Concerning Brno, I find it hard to make up my mind. Despite the difficult situation here, I feel I really should stay in Paris and would consider leaving to be an act of desertion for which I could not forgive myself, especially if I throw away everything merely for financial gain. I don't believe I could work at my compositions and teach at the same time. There are so many superfluous things involved in teaching that would occupy my mind. I assure you that every quarter-of-an-hour is precious to me. I don't waste a minute, for I have many schemes that must be fulfilled.

The schemes to which he was referring were in the field of chamber music, and Martinů's catalogue for the years 1929–30 shows just how much he felt at home when composing in this medium. It also reveals the immense variety of instrumental combinations which attracted him. In the space of three years he completed twenty-two pieces for chamber ensemble which, if nothing else, amply display his innate gift for judging sounds of various small groups. To Martinů composition was as vital as breathing but often, it seems, he almost suffocated as scores appeared at an incredible rate. Pieces like the *Ariettes* for violin and piano were composed in a matter of hours, others, such as the delightful *Sextet* for wind quintet and piano in four days, while the *Cinq pièces brèves* for piano trio and entertaining *Pastorales* for cello and piano were completed in a week. Such facility has its dangers and it is hardly surprising that the overall quality of these works is slightly more uneven than that in other types of composition. In spite of their descriptive nonchalance, much of the scores sounds like hastily written scrubbing-brush music while some show Martinů relishing technical difficulties at the expense of real invention. However, among the numerous manuscripts which emerged at this time, there are a few which stand out from the rest for showing not only Martinů's technical skill but also the substance of his thematic material and the strength of his musical thought. The String Quartet No. 3 (1929) is one such work. Here Martinů uses the quartet as a vehicle for experimenting with sonority and producing an array of instrumental colours quite new to his vocabulary of timbres. Another remarkable, and in some ways unexpected, piece is the Piano Trio No. 1 (1930), for it exploits three elements which were to form the basis of Martinů's mature style – rhythmic flexibility, gained from his acceptance of overt jazz idioms, an insistence on polyphony, and an avoidance of definite thematic material. By deliberately introducing and combining a number of precise motifs, Martinů produces a harmonic pungency far removed from the unequivocal diatonicism with which each movement opens and closes. The Trio was followed by a Sonata for violin, a cycle of *Études* for cello, and twelve *Esquisses* for piano which are reminiscent of stronger models in Stravinsky's *Ragtime,* but Martinů's most significant efforts were channelled into two Sextets. The first for wind quintet (no horn but a couple of bassoons) and piano is an entertainment piece with two Divertimenti, a brilliant Scherzo for flute and piano and an intriguing Blues, more outrageously jazzy than anything in Poulenc's Sextet of 1930–32 if not quite as instantly memorable. The other Sextet for strings is made of sterner stuff. It has a dramatic fluency and imaginative boldness that was recognised when it was awarded the Elizabeth Sprague Coolidge Prize for Composition in 1932. Here, and in the later arrangement for string orchestra, Martinů speaks with the voice of one totally committed. His imprint is on every bar; and throughout, the structure and balance have the beauty of a logically argued conversation.

Remarkable, too, are a number of *Serenades* for various wind and string combinations and a set of six instrumental miniatures called *Les Rondes.* Each is concise and the brevity is paralleled in the music, but these brittle-sounding dances are important, not so much for their clarity of form as for Martinů's use of Moravian folk song. Here the composer unashamedly looks homeward for his inspiration and selects and tailors Moravian material to his own personal style. Although the value of these pieces is not particularly great, the course they set was one Martinů followed time and again. *Les Rondes* immediately led to other works which betray recollections of home. *Borová*, a set of seven Czech dances for piano, recalls impressions of the delightful Bohemian village a couple of miles north of Polička where Martinů had known much happiness in his youth : and *Staročeská říkalda*, six short choruses for women's voices based on old Czech tales, show his musical horizons being extended by childhood nursery rhymes. However, the first major work to reveal this growing nationalism is the ballet *Špaliček*, begun in January 1931. After his previous period of composition, it is striking that he should suddenly have departed from the kind of music around him in favour of something exclusively Slavonic in feeling and specifically Czech in appeal. *Špaliček* was designed for the Czech theatre and the Czech people, who knew by heart the folk texts and customs that make up the scenario. There could be no question of *Špaliček* being misunderstood (as had been the case with *Les Larmes du couteau*) for it was intended as an echo of home.

Špaliček (*Little Block*) takes its title from the collections of folk songs sold at fairs throughout Bohemia by wandering players in the eighteenth century. Later these songs would be incorporated into an album known as a *špalek*. Martinů's ballet is based on a number of legends and fairy tales taken from various collections and is devised more as an entertainment than a serious contribution to the art form. Besides dances *Špaliček* contains numerous choral items which bring it close to the form of a Czech cantata-ballet. Of course, Karel Bendl's *Czech Wedding* and Janáček's *Rákoš Rákoczy* had presented pictures of Bohemian Moravian and Slovakian life in a series of folk songs and dances, but though Martinů may have been aware of Bendl's score (Janáček's was in manuscript at the time and still is) he is more likely to have been influenced by Roussel's opera-ballet *Padmâvatî* and Stravinsky's *L'Histoire du soldat*. In *Pulcinella* and *Renard* Stravinsky had made the marriage of ballet and song absolute, and in *Les Noces* Martinů saw a model on which to fashion his own piece. Both works draw heavily on folk material, but while Stravinsky's libretto for *Les Noces* is taken from Kireievsky's book of Russian poetry and stems from Russian peasantry, for Martinů's *Špaliček* there was no similar source. He worked on the scenario himself and turning to the childhood memories of home, he selected a number of popular plays and pantomime fairy tales ranging from 'Puss-in-Boots' and 'Cinderella' (in the Czech version by Božena Němcová) to the legend about St. Dorothea and part of Erben's *Spectre's Bride*. The scheme of following one unrelated tale by another was almost certainly modelled on Oskar Nedbal's popular pantomime-ballet *Z pohádky do pohádky* (*From Tale to Tale*) of 1908; and indeed one of Martinů's own tales, that concerning 'The Cobbler and Death' in Act II, calls to mind the hero of another Nedbal ballet, *Pohádka o Honzovi* (*Fairytale about Johnny*), where the simple and good-natured Johnny with the aid of a forest sprite defeats a dragon and liberates a captive princess. However, in his ballets Nedbal makes no attempt to give his scenario local colour and it is precisely this which places Martinů's *Špaliček* in a class of its own. There are references to local Poličkan customs such as 'Bringing out the Death' and 'Opening of the Wells', which reveal a world of homely village culture to which Martinů was to return in his cantata *Kytice* (*Bouquet*), his *Zbojnické písně* (*Brigand Songs*), his vocal duets *Petrklíč* (*The Primrose*) and in the cycle of the four folk cantatas *Otvírání studánek* (*Opening of the Wells*), *Legenda z dýmu bramborové nati* (*Legend of the Smoke of Potato Fires*), *Romance z pampelišek* (*Romance of the Dandelions*) and *Mikeš z hor* (*Mikeš of the Mountains*). Originally *Špaliček* was designed for chamber orchestra, but in

1940 Martinů reworked the score for larger forces and changed the order of some of the pieces. First he extended the tale of 'Puss-in-Boots' and transferred it to Act I; then he decided to omit the *Spectre's Bride* sequence in Act III, and replaced it with Cinderella's wedding dances, formerly in the second act. Although the instrumentation of the 1931 version is much closer to Stravinsky's *Les Noces*, the final score has several remaining links with that ballet, particularly in the extensive use Martinů makes of the piano, which is required to support whole scenes, and in the way the female chorus (accommodated in the pit) is integrated into the musical textures as an intrinsic part of the score.

In *Špaliček* Martinů was championing the cause of Czech ballet and produced in a relatively short time a substantial, vivid and individual work for the stage. The Prologue, attractively brief and sung by a children's choir onstage, leads to four games presented in song and dance: 'Play at the Doll', 'Play at the Prisoners' Base' (a game resembling 'He' in which a water sprite tries to capture anyone who steps into his territory), 'Play at the Little Wolf' and 'Play at the Cock and Hen' (an allegory about a cock who chokes while trying to swallow too large a grain of corn). In each of these scenes the action is danced as the soloists relate the narrative and the chorus comment on the action. Up to this point the score is direct, tuneful and ideally suited to the individual mood of each dance. The remainder of the Act is devoted to the story 'Puss-in-Boots' and from here on the music is more virile, with a more pointed rhythm and a more ambitious score. The chorus is silent and the dances follow without a break. Act II is devoted to the tale of 'The Cobbler and Death' and tells how an old shoemaker, having fallen out with his neighbours, decides to go abroad. He is accompanied by a butterfly who leads him to a black tower where a Princess is imprisoned by a ferocious giant. The Butterfly dances around the Giant until, dazed, he is struck by the Cobbler who liberates the Princess. He is rewarded by the gift of a magic sack in which Death is trapped. For as long as the Cobbler roams the countryside with Death on his back no one dies but, worn and exhausted, the Cobbler makes his way to the gates of Heaven where he releases Death and enters Paradise. Such a tale, with its colourful excursions, offered Martinů great scope for describing atmospheres of sorrow and joy, and it is here that *Špaliček* is most successful. The Act is danced throughout with only three choral and vocal items. From the outset there is a more elaborate involvement of musical means. The score contains many fine strokes of characterisation – the 'Butterfly Dance' with its ornate wood-wind figuration recalling Roussel's *Le Festin de l'araignée*, the 'Market

55

Dance of the Bumble Bee' looking forward to the steely brilliance of the scherzo of Martinů's *Fantaisies symphoniques*, the 'Cobbler's Dance' with its foreboding as he approaches the Black Tower and its strong flavour of *Les Noces* – but none is more telling than the 'Dance of Death' with its dagger violence and its overtones of *Le Sacre du printemps*. Act III opens with the 'Legend of St. Dorothea', a disquieting scene with an atmosphere of frenzied cruelty as the girl is killed by a mob of predatory pagans. Here the music is aflame with feeling and technical brilliance. There are few concessions to artists or audience, but clearly to end the ballet on such a harrowing note was out of the question in a score that was intended to be popular in appeal. As if to redress the balance, Martinů continues with the tale of 'Cinderella' and concludes with a number of Waltzes for her wedding.

That Martinů had great virtues as a composer of ballet music is beyond doubt. *Špaliček* is tuneful, exciting and eminently danceable and the score shows his flair for writing for the stage. There seems to be no end to the fertility of his ideas, but occasionally he is prone to throw styles together in alarmingly quick succession so that we jump from the simplicity of folk theatre to tragedy, from pantomime-revue to classical ballet, with little sense of musical purpose and more than a hint of musical indigestion. However, as entertainment, *Špaliček* won an immediate response at its Prague première in September 1933, and within two months Brno mounted a rival production which was to play successfully in the repertory for the next four years. More important for Martinů was the award of the Bedřich Smetana Prize for Composition which *Špaliček* brought him in 1934. At last he began to feel that he had discovered a means of expressing himself in a language which was valid and his own. After years of searching he had learnt to combine folk lore and folk song in a contemporary idiom and he now abandoned his former universal outlook for an approach more closely allied to the emotions of Czech folk music. The world was changing around him, and though he was being swept along in the hectic atmosphere of the Thirties he felt the need to make himself heard. Admittedly a certain amount of reorientation was necessary, but with *Špaliček* he had discovered a course – a course that pointed homewards and perhaps even more specifically than Prague, towards Polička and the Bohemian-Moravian plateau.

It was only to be expected that Martinů would want to follow *Špaliček* with another work for the Czech stage, but the traditional run-of-the-mill plots were unlikely to provide him with a suitable subject when it came to writing an opera. He needed something simple and direct that could be translated into a modern form of expression, and he found what he was looking for in the half-forgotten religious folk plays of the Middle Ages. Medieval dramas based on Biblical scenes and on freely adapted folk legends had been performed in St. George's Cloister of Prague Castle in the twelfth century, and later the original Latin texts had been translated into the vernacular and accepted as independent dramatic works. Martinů knew of these dramas, but the idea for using them in his own stage works was more likely to have occurred to him when he put the St. Dorothea legend – derived from the *Legenda Aurea*, recorded by Jacobus de Voragaine – to good use in *Špaliček*. With the spectacular revival of d'Annunzio's mystery play *Le Martyr de Saint Sébastien,* accompanied by Debussy's incidental music, in front of Nôtre Dame, and the presentation of Passion Plays in the Courtyard of the Sorbonne in 1931, Martinů was convinced of the practicability of the scheme. Moreover, Arthur Honegger, with whom he was in contact, had achieved considerable success with the incidental music written to René Morax's *psaume dramatique, Le Roi David*, and the *opéra biblique, Judith*, and had made the idea fashionable. Furthermore, he was known to be considering *Jeanne d'Arc au bûcher* as a possible subject for treatment as a musical mystery play.

Originally Martinů had hoped to base his opera on two Czech miracle plays, *The Three Marys* and *The Quack*, but feeling these to be less than ideal, he selected the twelfth century Provençal Mystery about the *Wise and Foolish Virgins*, which was translated into Czech by the poet Vítězslav Nezval, and an early Moravian folk ballad called *The Birth of Our Lord*. Each was to precede two other, more substantial, miracle plays, and with the help of Henri Ghéon, who had devised the *Messe Mysterium* for open-air performance in the Parc des Princes, the fifteenth-century Flemish version of *Mariken de Nimèque* was translated into French (it was later retranslated into Czech by Vilém Závada) and Julius Zeyer's version of *Sister Pasqualina* was cut down to size. *Hry o Marii (The Plays of Mary)* as Martinů came to call his opera, is a cycle of independent mystery plays and from the outset Martinů goes out of his way to emphasise the stage character of each by indicating that he is presenting a play within a play. His score includes detailed notes regarding the presentation and décor of his opera and by avoiding realism, limiting action, specifying mime and formalising gesture he was consciously attempting to produce a type of stylised folk drama new to Czech opera.

The first miracle play, *The Wise and Foolish Virgins*, is treated reflectively throughout. The music is modal-sounding and the drama unfolds in lines of great simplicity and lyrical melancholy. An unaccompanied chorus provides the Prologue and Epilogue, and within this framework nine dancers evoke the atmosphere while seven singers describe the action in music that is melismatic in shape and ephemeral in character. Dramatically the climax of the score occurs with the hymn-like utterance of Christ, the Bridegroom, who is heard but not seen, being represented by a shaft of light. *Mariken de Nimèque* is more ambitious and shows Martinů returning to his idea of the double, previously used in *Les Larmes du couteau*. Here the rôles of Mariken and the Devil are to be sung and danced, and at certain points Mariken the singer hands over to Mariken the dancer, but remains on stage as a spectator until the time comes for her to sing again. Here also Martinů returns to the device of presenting a play within a play, and in order to clarify the course of the action a narrator complements the pit and stage chorus as they comment, warn or express compassion for Mariken, whose fate it is to be seduced by the Devil. Having possessed and destroyed her body, the Devil struggles with a host of angels for Mariken's soul, but as she repents her soul is claimed by the Virgin Mary who grants her forgiveness and leads her to Paradise.

The second part of Martinů's *Plays of Mary* opens with *The Birth of Our Lord,* the shortest of the four miracles and the least dramatic. An orchestral prelude sets the mood while soloists and chorus, with a native folkiness and a directness of expression, describe the nativity scene as a group of children mime the incidents involving Mary and Joseph in the stable. With its simple text and lucid instrumentation Martinů here comes close to creating a form of folk cantata or musical tableau and, incidentally, provides a charming foil to *Sister Pasqualina,* the last and most complex of his miracle plays. Originating in the thirteenth century the legend was known both in France and Spain and more recently formed the basis for Maurice Maeterlinck's *Soeur Béatrice*. Julius Zeyer's version is essentially traditional and concerns Pasqualina, a young novice who runs from her convent to follow the knight with whom she has fallen in love. After much hardship he dies and Pasqualina is accused of his murder. When her innocence is finally proved she returns to the convent to discover that her defection has gone unnoticed since her place has been filled by the Virgin Mary.

Martinů's adaptation is notable for its mixture of Czech folk poetry and lines from the Proper of the Mass and, in fact, *Sister Pasqualina* is the first of his scores to combine secular and liturgical words since the patriotic cantata *Czech Rhapsody* of 1918. It is also the first of his dramatic works to exploit dream elements. From childhood Martinů had been interested in dreams and in later life would ask his wife over breakfast what dreams she had had the night before. For him the dream was a means of escape and in music, as in life, it provided an oppor-

tunity for creating fantasies. Significantly we first meet Sister Pasqualina in a dream. She is being tormented by a group of demons who
dance a symbolic ballet behind screens. Pasqualina calls out for help.
She falls asleep again only to be once more persecuted by the shadowy
apparitions. At this point it becomes clear that Martinů is arranging
his first scene in units of chorus and ballet alternating with extended
meditations for Pasqualina, each of which is followed by poignant,
unaccompanied supplications for the repose of her soul sung by a
chorus of nuns. Unable to sustain her vows Pasqualina leaves the
convent, but the details of her elopement, her love for the Knight, his
death at the Devil's hands and the events leading to her arrest are not
exploited dramatically. To have portrayed these incidents on stage
would not only have created problems for the composer but would
have extended the score to unreasonable lengths. Instead Martinů
writes a descriptive intermezzo in the form of a Moravian folk ballad in
which the chorus outlines the course of the action in music of granite
hardness and sustained determination. In Scene 2, however, the action
continues with Pasqualina's trial and march to the stake where, in an
aria, she looks back over her life with regret. She accepts her fate, but
in Scene 3, with the divine intervention of the Virgin Mary – a rôle
which is mimed throughout – the flames are commanded to subside.
Pasqualina is saved and led to the convent where, with a restatement
of the dream music from Scene 1, she awakes. Martinů now poses a
question. Has all this been a dream or should the action begin again?
It was an issue he was to raise at the close of his opera *Juliette*, but here
he makes a positive ending. Pasqualina falls dead and the Sisters celebrate a Requiem over her body.

In *The Plays of Mary* Martinů was creating a special dramatic form.
Recitatives are minimal, and arias, if they do not assume a folk-song
character, are notable for their mysticism. The chorus, while remaining
outside the action, comments and reflects on the stage pictures which
sometimes resemble *tableaux vivants*; but in the way the miracle plays
proceed in song, dance, mime and narration *The Plays of Mary* reveal
a logic and economy of dramatic design quite new to Czech opera.
At its Brno première in February 1935, it was felt that here Martinů
had produced his finest work to date and later the same year *The Plays
of Mary* brought him the Czechoslovak State Prize for Composition.
Gradually his reputation was growing. Within twelve months Prague
had mounted its own production of the opera and now, regarded as one
of the leaders of the popular Czech theatre movement, Martinů's
latest scores were awaited with interest. Clearly there was a responsive
and ready-made audience for the folk-inspired stage entertainments he

59

was devising, and he immediately set to work on another opera, not for the theatre this time, but for radio, a medium through which he hoped to reach a much wider public.

Important pioneer work had been done in broadcast music in Czechoslovakia by Stanislav Goldbach as early as December 1928, when his specially-written radio cantata *Der Rundfunkhörer* (*The Radio Listener*) had been transmitted. By 1935 Czech Radio was developing strongly, but although there were occasional relays of operas from the larger theatres in Prague and Brno (the first to be broadcast from the National Theatre in Prague was Smetana's *The Two Widows*, given on 12 February 1925), there was no agreement for regular operatic transmissions. Theatre managements feared that relays would adversely affect box office attendance and consequently there grew up a tradition of mounting operas and operettas in the studios of Czech Radio. One of the earliest pieces to be presented in this way was Dvořák's *Pigheaded Peasant* (6 September 1931) and in the same year Rudolf Kubins was commmissioned to write a one-act opera which he called *Letní noc* (*Summer Night*). The next move was made by the German Service of Czech Radio when they invited Horst Platon to produce a score for radio, and it may well have been his *Die schweigende Glocke* (*The Silent Bell*) which provided the stimulus and model for Martinů's *Hlas lesa* (*Voice of the Forest*) written between April and May 1935 to a libretto by Vítežslav Nezval.

The meeting of Martinů and Nezval was a happy event, for composer and poet had much in common and were drawn to each other in Paris by a desire to create something positive out of the destructive tendencies of the Surrealistic circles in which they had both moved. In *The Voice of the Forest* they produced a whimsical chamber piece that has all the homespun naïvety of a folk tale. Myselenka, a hunter, is overcome by brigands as he travels through the forest at night. His calls for help are heard by his peasant-bride Nevěsta who disguises herself in brigand clothes and joins the outlaws to save her lover. When the brigands decide to elect one of their group to kill Myselenka, it is the disguised Nevěsta who is chosen, and who leads him out of the forest where she reveals her identity and takes him to safety. Although Martinů calls his new score a radio opera, its importance lies not so much in establishing new techniques but in its acceptance of Czech folk lore as subject matter for broadcast music. Certainly the plot is slight but in its direct presentation Martinů was going all out to ensure that the action would be comprehensible to a listening audience. To avoid any possible confusion a narrator sets the scenes and links the action. The choruses are vigorous and short and the arias have a happy grace; but so that the words should be clearly heard the musical lines are simply arranged, the only sophistication being the use of the Aeolian mode, which gives the score a folk song quality. The instrumental accompaniment is deliberately transparent, but apart from an occasional echo device – itself a characteristic of Bohemian folk idiom – there is little attempt to give the opera local colour or, more important, sound perspective. This was something Martinů was to explore in his next opera; for following the favourable reception of *The Voice of the Forest* (Radio Prague, 6 October 1935), he was stimulated to compose a second work for broadcasting, and by the end of the year had completed *Veselohra na mostě* (*Comedy on the Bridge*) to a classic Czech play by Václav Klicpera.

Although Klicpera's play was nearly a hundred and fifty years old when Martinů decided to set it to music, it remains modern and topical even today. The opera tells of the difficulties encountered when neighbours wishing to visit each other find that their respective homes happen to be located in territory held by hostile camps. While their own authorities allow them exit permits, these documents do not entitle them to enter enemy zones or to return to their own. They are thus caught on a bridge linking the two areas. Into this comic situation, which bears many similarities to the tragic reality of today, come Josephine, a Fisherman, a Brewer and his wife and the Schoolteacher. All are trapped on the bridge: all fear for their lives except the Schoolteacher who is concerned only with the solution to a riddle. Hostilities break out and those on the bridge begin to confess their past indiscretions as nerves become frayed and tempers lost. Sometimes the confessions are embarrassing but the situation is saved when an armistice allows the villagers to return to their homes. In its witty solution of problems concerning unity of action, time and place, and in its restriction of character movement to one tiny area, Klicpera had, unknowingly, provided the substance of an ideal radio opera. Acoustically, too, the play gave Martinů the opportunity of making use of distance and space between the characters situated at either end of the bridge, while the military nature of the plot provided every excuse for writing a score built on fanfare rhythms and reveille calls. The short Prelude grows out of these ideas and presents two themes, the first in D major, the second in B flat minor, and the ensuing clash of harmonies nicely establishes the conflict which exists between the two hostile forces. The score, for chamber orchestra with piano and battery (used to represent gunfire and shell explosion) is much more integrated than that of *The Voice of the Forest*. The six scenes are linked, not by the use of motifs, but by a continuous web of sound which breaks off only for the spoken recitatives of the guards at either end of the bridge. Musical characterisation is barely suggested, and although the music assumes different qualities for the entry of each villager, this scheme is not developed after the initial phrases. Only the Schoolteacher emerges as a fully rounded person, and then the theme which represents him seems to have been taken from one associated with Kecal in Smetana's *The Bartered Bride*. None the less, *Comedy on the Bridge* is unmistakably Czech in subject and spirit, and the music's spontaneous, refreshing good humour was quickly appreciated by those who heard the first broadcast on 18 March 1937. Fourteen years later the opera was translated into English and presented by the NBC Television Network in the United States. As a result Martinů, then living in America, was awarded a prize for the best chamber opera of 1951. In an excess of enthusiasm the New York critics also recommended that Klicpera be recognised for his text. Unfortunately he was unable to accept his prize in person, having died ninety-two years before.

The *buffo* element which plays an important part in *Comedy on the Bridge* returns in Martinů's next opera *Divadlo za bránou* (*Theatre Beyond the Gate*) written between June 1935 and April 1936. The intriguing title does not refer to one specific theatre, but was intended to epitomise entertainment in its broadest form as played by a travelling company on a trestle stage at a fair, in a market place or on a village green. Here the composer was returning to his scheme of presenting a play within a play, and in the form of an opera burlesque he attempts to draw together elements from the *Commedia dell'Arte* with figures from popular Czech theatre. The result was a three-act divertimento in which neither subject nor story seems important and where the libretto (if it can be called that) is a patchwork of different scenes and situations. Colombine is in love with Harlequin but the jealous Pierrot refuses to allow the course of true love to run smoothly so he shoots his rival. This does not, however, prevent the story from continuing since the deceased Harlequin rises from the dead and takes Colombine as his wife. Act I is a ballet-pantomime and in Acts II and III the plot is repeated as *opera buffa* with Harlequin and Pierrot being joined by masked characters from Czech folk lore and figures created by the famous French mime Jean-Gaspard Debureau, who had been born in Bohemia and so had a special attraction. Tongue in cheek they bounce their way through scenes from Molière's *Le Médicin volant*, or a parody of it, and sketches from the Parisian *Boulevard du crime*. The overall impression is of improvised mimicry, an intriguing marriage between French farce and end-of-term revue, typically Czech in its exuberant dance music and totally captivating in its humour.

When Martinů set out to create his cantata-ballet *Špaliček* in 1931, he can little have imagined that it would lead to so stylised a form of popular entertainment as *Theatre Beyond the Gate* five years later. That score holds a unique place in his catalogue and clearly it could not be repeated or surpassed. Wisely, therefore, Martinů shifted his attention from riotous work for the stage to choral music, and in the cantata *Kytice* (*Bouquet*) he continued the idea of setting folk dramas to music, but in a more serious and disciplined style. As the title suggests, *Kytice* is a collection of folk texts drawn from the Bohemian-Moravian Highlands, and there the composer comes very close to home. Though the orchestral and vocal forces are large (four soloists, children's and mixed choirs and an orchestra including two pianos and harmonium) Martinů succeeds in balancing his values and matching the simplicity of the folk poems with a clarity of sound that is obviously a product of the Bohemian countryside. Five- and three-bar phrase lengths lend the orchestral Prelude a native folkiness, and irregular rhythms and firmly contoured melodies distinguish the ballad 'The Girl who Poisoned her Brother', a setting of the morbid fourteenth-century folk tale *Juliana, a Maiden Pure*. 'Selanka', an orchestral idyll, leads to the pastoral-sounding 'Kravařky', for which it is difficult to find an English equivalent (perhaps 'Cowgirls' is sufficiently close to the Czech). Of all Martinů's choral pieces this is the most imaginative. It is designed for soprano and alto soloists and a women's chorus whose singing describes a picture of cowherds grazing in the fields. The music, marked *volně* ('to be sung freely'), takes its origin from a special form of yodelling called *halekačky* which Martinů heard in his youth in the Vysočina. Of course Smetana had made use of this device in his chorus *Píseň na moři* (*Song of the Sea*) as early as 1877, but in Martinů's hands it was put to particularly telling effect in the second Act of *Theatre Beyond the Gate* of the previous year. Here the *halekačky* consists of a number of exultant ejaculations to the sound 'ej' or 'hoja', and begins with a rising interval that gives prominence to the principal note of the melody. This form of vocalism is still performed in parts of Moravia, where country folk take pride in it. Obviously it is difficult to convey the magical effects as these cries travel from one peasant to another across hilly slopes and silent dales until they are lost in a series of fading echoes. None the less, Martinů precisely captures the feeling of these calls at the very beginning of his movement as soprano and alto soloists hail each other across a valley of wordless perfect fourths. This is one of the most original pieces in the cantata and throughout the chorus provides a modal support which is subtly heightened and pointed by skilful handling of the modest instrumental forces. Here,

63

surely, Martinů is evoking memories of the Vysočina and using folk idiom as part of his patrimony. The peace of this rustic scene is dispelled by an orchestral Intrada, a boisterous dance with irregular, polka-like rhythms, in which, with the exception of the two pianos, the instrumentation calls to mind the small itinerant bands that Dr. Burney referred to in his Journal of 1772. Its raucous-sounding, bucolic good humour makes an ideal foil to 'A Sweetheart is Better than a Mother', a thoughtful meditation for solo tenor and chorus. The cantata continues with a short carol for children's voices which reveals a debt to *The Cunning Little Vixen*. The movement in parallel thirds and sixths and three-bar phrase lengths not only evokes memories of Janáček's opera but gives Martinů's music an authentic folk-song spirit. *Kytice* concludes with 'Man and Death', a full-length cantata in its own right, in which the four soloists declaim the action and the chorus reflect on it in music of power and vision.

With *Kytice* Martinů came close to the soil of the Vysočina, for when he worked in his native Czech he was describing home; and he was clearly at home in the simplest circumstances, in the intimacy of the folk-poem, in the directness of the folk song. Here the folk element is all pervasive, but vocally the furthest Martinů was prepared to go from the simple line of a folk melody was to a parallel line of thirds and sixths, and this consideration may account for the fact that in *Kytice* the contrapuntal style is hardly ever to be found where it might be expected – in the choral writing. Martinů, it seems, for all his interest in polyphony, thought of it as a sophisticated technique used in choral music more traditionally, though not exclusively, for public worship. In *Kytice* his aim was not to interpret the mind of tradition, but to communicate with his compatriots in his own tongue.

Although Martinů had drawn freely upon Czech folk idiom for pieces written since 1931 he had achieved more success with his operas and ballets than with his orchestral and chamber works. Possibly he had found it easier to express nationalistic feeling in legends and plays than within the framework of the concerto or instrumental suite; and, realising this, Martinů had turned to another source of inspiration for his orchestral works. Along with other composers he had taken to looking back to the compositional forms of the eighteenth century; but, surprisingly, it was not the music of Handel or Bach which roused his interest – though some years before he had considered writing a group of *Prague Concertos* modelled on Bach's Brandenburgs – but the scores of Corelli, whose *Concerti Grossi* and *Sonata da Camera* Martinů had come to admire for their clarity of design and musical vitality. Yet while these were to be the direct source of his inspiration he did not regard them, as Stravinsky sometimes did, as vehicles for pastiche or neo-classical parody. It was not a question of savaging the past, for in Martinů's hands eighteenth-century forms were to be adapted in a special way, and during the early and middle Thirties he began to fill the concerto grosso framework with bi-tonal harmonies, linear textures and a type of germinal development that he was making peculiarly his own.

The first of his works to show a leaning towards Baroque forms is the Cello Concerto No. 1, written in 1930, rescored in 1939 and revised in 1955. With a basic antithesis between solo cello and orchestral ripieno, the introduction of ritornelli and the episodic construction of movements, the Cello Concerto pays handsome lip service to concerto grosso principles. But in this score Martinů seems to be saying, thus far and no further; for the opening movement is written without key signature, the ritornello theme has a marked pentatonic character and the astringent combinations of chromatically altered chords show evidence of the influence of Albert Roussel. In the meditative second movement the argument is based on a method of organic growth from an initial note pattern and bound by a number of pedal points, grumbling ostinatos and plagal cadences. If the Cello Concerto No. 1 shows Martinů composing to the letter of concerto grosso form, then the Concerto for String Quartet and Orchestra confirms his acceptance of Baroque spirit. Here a solo quartet is pitted against a large symphony orchestra but the language is noticeably more forceful than hitherto. Pedals, ostinatos and polytonal clashes again underline Roussel's influence while the continuous development of terse musical ideas into closely knit textures emphasises the composer's germinal approach to composition. Only the divertimento-like rondo, with its polka rhythms and engaging antiphonal interplay between solo quartet and orchestra, allows a moment of respite to the harsh dissonance of the preceeding movements.

To the same period belongs the *Serenade* for chamber orchestra, designed in homage to Roussel. The dedication to Martinů's teacher is symbolic for the score shows him filling old bottles with new wine. In its neo-classical form the *Serenade* is most obviously linked to the music of Roussel and here Martinů merely underlines the classical characteristics of the music by his use of asymmetric rhythms and primary diatonic harmonies simultaneously combined and chromatically altered. The *Partita* (Suite No. 1) for strings and *Sinfonia Concertante* (both completed in 1932) show varying degrees of Roussel's influence; but emerging from these busy scores are glimpses of something as yet undefined, but not far removed from the complexity of harmony which developed in the orchestral works of 1938 and 1939. The *Partita* is a concise four-movement essay with a rhythmic flexibility that brings it close to dance music – a quality that was quickly appreciated by the Corty Dance Ensemble, who adapted it as a contemporary ballet in the Netherlands in 1934. In the *Sinfonia Concertante* Martinů treats his two orchestras in true concerto grosso style, devising harsh sonorities as the two groups engage in antiphonal opposition. In this respect Martinů was anticipating his own *Double Concerto* (1938), and in his use of developing textures from an initial motif the *Sinfonia Concertante* also looks forward to the later work, though at this stage the motif appears in only one movement.

Two Concertinos for Piano Trio and String Orchestra (Nos. 1 and 2) are sister works, close in time and spirit to the Concerto for String Quartet and Orchestra; but it remains a puzzle why Martinů should have composed two scores each of four movements and each for the same combination within the space of five months. Clearly both are complete works and it seems unlikely that one would have been a preparation for the second. There is no evidence, apart from the manuscript, that the earlier Concertino ever existed. It is not mentioned in any correspondence and is not found in any list. Possibly Martinů, having written the first work, carelessly mislaid the score, and in order to fulfil an obligation to the Trio Hongrois rapidly composed the second, working on similar lines as far as memory would permit. An examination of the two pieces shows that this is not a case of serving the same meat with different gravy; for the musical substance of the first Concertino is quite different from that of the second. Formally, both works are concerned with the expansion of unity and each score displays material derived from a ritornello theme and controlled by a rhythmic drive which is neither relaxed nor contradicted.

In these Baroque pieces Martinů's style was developing into something more positive, and with his *Inventions*, composed for the 1934 International Music Festival in Venice, he approached orchestral music with a freshness and individuality that had sometimes been lacking in the earlier scores. For the first time since 1928 when he had composed *La Rhapsodie,* Martinů was working with a large orchestra, and in his *Inventions,* which have nothing in common with Bach's keyboard works except the title, he intensified his system of germinal composition, though here the motifs are briefer and more percussive than before and are developed from one movement to another. Like Sibelius, Martinů does not announce his material and then deal with it. Instead he allows the motif to emerge from the general textures, and it is only through a process of weaving and building that the importance of the basic unit is realised. In the *Inventions* he laid the foundation of the

20. Stage set from the 1922 Prague National Theatre production of Martinů's ballet, *Istar*.

21. Stage set from the 1924 Brno National Theatre production of Martinů's ballet, *Who Is the Most Powerful in the World?*

22 Martinů in Paris.

23. The Group de Quatre : Conrad Beck, Marcel Mihalovici, Bohuslav Martinů, Tibor Harsányi.

six Symphonies. But to regard the *Inventions* as symphonic would be misleading. They may be cellular, but more often than not Martinů seems to be concerned with building a mosaic of sound. This is not to deny the lyrical and folk-inspired central andante with its two contrasting, ill-tempered outbursts for piano which look forward to the ruthless threat of the *Double Concerto*; but generally, Martinů seems to be concentrating on changing tone colours, and in their emotionally charged, kaleidoscopic climate the *Inventions* look forward to one of Martinů's finest scores, the opera *Juliette,* which was now beginning to take shape in his mind.

5 *Paris: 1937-40*

The play is a desperate struggle to find something stable on which man can lean, something concrete like memory or consciousness which does not disappear as soon as it is grasped or transform into tragic situations as soon as it is seized . . . Through a whole network of unforeseen situations and illogical conclusions runs the thread of human memory, but if this thread is cut we enter a world where man's deepest desire is to renew his memory, pick up the thread of the past, even somebody elses, and make it his own . . . but if man is unable to maintain his own stability and keep his common sense he must remain in this timeless world of no memory.

This is how Martinů described *Juliette ou le clé des songes*, a very personal play by the French writer, Georges Neveux. Written in 1927, Neveux's *Juliette* was first presented at the Théâtre de l'Avenue in Paris three years later with much publicity. Its intangible elements of longing and searching and its ephemeral plot that is hardly a plot at all provoked mixed reactions from its first audiences, but were just the sort of thing to attract Martinů, who became totally absorbed in its dream fantasies. *Juliette* comprises a number of absurd, irrational situations. Michel, a travelling bookseller, arrives in a small harbour town to discover that the inhabitants have lost their memories. They can imagine and believe everything, but have no recollection of the past. Michel stays in this community, where he gets involved in the strange things that are going on, but all the time he is searching for Juliette, the young girl with whom he has fallen in love on a previous visit. He hears her singing and sees her everywhere, but she eludes him, for she, too, belongs to this nebulous world where there is no past and no future. Like the other inhabitants she knows only the present and to know more leads to a world of dreams. Neither Juliette nor Michel are capable of breaking the barrier which separates them. They exist on different planes. Michel realises that one of them is living in an unreal dimension. Is it he or is it Juliette? The local Commissar proposes that the winner of a game of cards will show who is dreaming and who is not. For Michel this is nonsense. There can be only one way to Juliette. He must cross the barrier that separates light from dark, that bridges consciousness and dreams, that divides sanity from madness, where these mindless creatures seem to exist. Juliette calls him. Shall he betray his love and return to civilisation or plunge into this bizarre world? Juliette calls again. Slowly Michel feels himself drawn into the unknown and in a haze of distorted shapes all that has gone before returns to haunt him in a dream. There is no ending. The dream begins again.

Juliette is a profoundly disturbing and highly original opera. It is a work of darkness and shadow in which Michel wanders through streets in a feverish state calling to people who answer but who do not understand. With their loss of memory they have also lost their ability of connecting things and events. For them there are no relationships, only incomprehensible phenomena, and they regard Michel as if he did not exist. Michel feels, desires, loves and struggles to penetrate the strange armour of indifference surrounding him. He fights to find something tangible to hold onto, but memory and the vestige of reason that remain are insufficient for him to maintain his sanity. Finally he succumbs to the world of dreams.

Martinů's music for *Juliette* is full of human warmth and seems to be expressing the strength of human longing. The idiom is sensuous and highly charged and by adopting a form of musically defined speech the composer seems to be returning to the world of Debussy's *Pelléas et Mélisande*. In *Juliette* there is little distinction between song and recitative. The vocal lines are unemphatic and follow the rhythms of everyday speech in the form of spoken *melos*. The action is presented in terms of musical dialogues, and curiously there is only one real song in the opera – a song for Juliette – which haunts the entire score. However, the work does show an overall unity sometimes lacking in the earlier operas. While there is not the feeling of classical form which pervades Berg's *Wozzeck* and Britten's *Turn of the Screw,* there is a sense of homogeneity which results in part from the structure of Neveux's play. The three acts are designed in an arch, with the climax occurring in Act II after the attempted shooting of Juliette. The other Acts are fragmentary but are linked by two motifs which dominate the symphonic textures. The first, heard in the opening bars of the opera, evokes the fantastic world of Juliette, and the second motif, a 'Moravian cadence', represents Juliette herself. By association this suggests Juliette's longing for love, and although Martinů had used a similar chord progression in *Špaliček,* it was not his own invention, and can be traced back to Janáček's *Taras Bulba* (Coda, Part III – bars 168-9). By adoption, however, it has become a distinct mark of Martinů's harmonic style.

Juliette reveals the composer's ability to portray character and mood in a way that had not always been evident in the earlier operas. The musical characterisation is firmer and Juliette's music itself is distinguished by a melodic movement in parallel thirds and sixths, consecutive six-four chords and chords of the added sixth. The townsfolk, too, are effectively well drawn. The Commissar's lines move in leaps; the garrulous Fish- and Bird-Sellers are suggested by rapid semiquaver units accompanied by strident sevenths on the xylophone; the Grandfather of Youth is portrayed in monotonous, almost static lines. When we examine the other inhabitants – the Fortune-Teller who forecasts the past, and the Vendor of Memories who reminds people of journeys they have never made – it becomes clear that Martinů is concerned with painting musical pictures of pathological states of mind. This is not to suggest that *Juliette* is a psychological or philosophical opera. Far from it. But in Act III we come across a number of very remarkable dramatic situations where Martinů's expression is compelling to the point of being gruesome. With the Convict who comes to dream of freedom, the Little Boy who believes he is Buffalo Bill, the Beggar who longs to see the sea and the Engine Driver who gazes at photographs in an album whose pages are blank, Martinů was creating a handful of thumb-nail sketches which are the musical analogue of the Homunculi, the amorphous, distorted figures in Goya's *Caprichos*. These fragments, in the same class as those Berg created in *Wozzeck* and *Lulu*, make the music of *Juliette* the precise analogue of the dramatic situation. Moments of relief are rare, and even though Martinů includes a light-hearted episode when Michel is elected Mayor because he can remember that as a child he played with a toy duck, we are soon caught up with the fate of Michel – a character whom the composer regarded with an auto-biographical affection. Like his hero, Martinů was a dreamer, a fantastic idealist, looking and longing for beauty and peace. For Martinů *Juliette* was a child of love. The score remained his favourite and it was a motif from it that he remembered in 1953 when completing his *Fantaisies symphoniques* (Symphony No. 6). It was also the composition on which he was working in the days immediately before his death in 1959. Furthermore, the 'Moravian cadence' mentioned earlier haunts each of the six Symphonies and nearly every work up to 1959. *Juliette* was the work of a man whose own torments find expression in its music, and if Michel was intended as a self-portrait of the composer one must question who provided the model for Juliette. It could, of course, have been Martinů's devoted wife Charlotte, but a more likely source of inspiration was his twenty-one-year-old pupil Vítězslava Kaprálová, who had come to Paris for further study after graduating from the Conservatoires in Brno and Prague, where she had studied composition under Vítězslav Novák.

Vítězslava Kaprálová, daughter of the Czech composer Václav Kaprál, was born in Brno in 1915 and lived with her father at Tři Studně

(Three Wells) in the Vysočina. In his younger days Martinů had known the family well and had watched the little girl twenty-five years his junior grow into an attractive pianist. Following in her father's footsteps, Vítězslava had devoted herself to music and had revealed a talent for conducting. In Prague Zdeněk Chalabala and Václav Talich, at that time preparing for the première of *Juliette,* were her teachers, and on Talich's recommendation she came to Paris in 1936 to continue composition with Martinů, and conducting with Charles Munch at the École Normale de Musique. By all accounts Kaprálová was a remarkably gifted musician and a striking woman as well. For Martinů her arrival in Paris was like a breath of Czech air. She was beautiful and full of life, and her delicate figure fluttered across his path at a time when he was settled in a well-ordered routine. They spoke the same language, were bound to the same geographical spot on the map and shared a passionate interest in music. She became his devoted follower, and lessons took the form of discussions which suggest a subtle relationship between master and pupil. Martinů was a man of ready emotional response, and he was naturally attracted towards her. He was fond of Kaprálová and genuinely believed in her ability as a conductor. In the autumn of 1936 he entrusted to her the première of his Harpsichord Concerto (written in September 1935) and was excited when her *Military Sinfonietta* was selected for the 1938 International Festival of Contemporary Music in London. When he was not fully occupied with composition himself he wrote for her a number of short songs to Moravian folk poems, and there is no doubt that her personality invested these trivia with the charm that had stirred him deeply – the charm he was never to forget. Twenty years later, in 1957, he was to recall her memory in a poignant piano piece called *Vzpomínky,* but the work in which he remembered her most closely was the String Quartet No. 5, written in May 1938. Although the printed score bears no dedication, the original autograph sketch, preserved in the Moravian Museum in Brno, shows an inscription to Vítězslava herself. Remarkably, the twelve-page manuscript is adorned by a number of whimsical cartoons in the composer's hand which suggest that Martinů, like Janáček in his *Intimate Letters,* was thinking of the quartet as the ideal vehicle for expressing his most private communications. Martinů's intimate marginalia record a series of events, personal thoughts and incidents resulting from a difference of opinion or quarrel he had had with Kaprálová and from her sudden departure to Monte Carlo. The Quartet therefore reflects a sense of loss which finds expression in the music itself. Tempting though it is, it would be wrong to attach a definite programme to each of the four movements on the strength of these sketches alone. Clearly Kaprálová had stimulated Martinů's creative powers to their highest pitch and in this deeply felt quartet he responded with a work that is the sum and quintessence of his artistic growth as a composer of chamber music. Without doubt it is one of Martinů's most significant contributions to the form. Here he comes closer than ever before to the world of Bartók's string quartets, and Martinů's Fifth immediately invites comparison with Bartók's Third. Its contents are tragic, uncompromising and harsh to the point of aggressiveness. It is a work demanding much of listener and performer alike. The mood of the first movement is sombre: the string textures are fragmentary, the part-writing percussive. Moments of tenderness are rare, but at one point the second violin intones a baleful variation of the opening notes of Dvořák's *Requiem,* here enharmonically altered and transposed. The spirit of the episodic Adagio is melancholic and may well have been prompted by a sudden moment of anger, for at this point the manuscript is prefaced by a musical quotation from one of Kaprálová's songs, a setting of Nezval's poem *Sbohem a šáteček* (*The Farewell Handkerchief*), written in 1937 and revised the following year. Obviously the song had some significance for the tormented composer, who writes a meditation upon it which is full of a sense of isolation. The third movement is a furious Scherzo and its relentless rhythmic drive, boisterous syncopations and turbulent percussive chords are almost certainly the result of temperamental pique. The finale begins with an impassioned Lento, but when the tempo changes to Adagio the music assumes a tragic character. The expression grows bitter in dissonance and the effect is overwhelming. A virile motif in octaves on all four instruments is unleashed. This undergoes a process of organic growth until the Coda is reached where powerful and widely spaced chords punch home the impression of strength and originality.

The Fifth Quartet is a disquieting score: it is also the most intellectual in Martinů's catalogue of chamber works. Though prompted by personal experience, its force and resilience are phenomenal and it strikes notes of emotional violence which Martinů had tentatively sounded in his *Concerto Grosso* several months before. One wonders if Bach or Corelli would not have written something of the nature of the *Concerto Grosso* had they lived during this century. The score is laid out for wind, brass, strings and two pianos and Martinů's scheme of antithesis usually involves setting the pianos against the string and wind bands. Although this method is not strictly followed, he restricts the percussive dissonances to the pianos whilst the remainder of the orchestra is engaged in melodic invention (here the *Concerto Grosso* looks forward to the Concerto for Two Pianos of 1943) with chord progressions that are logically contrived and move, as in the music of Hindemith, towards a definite cadence formed by a concord in an established key. The outer movements show how well Martinů can subject an initial note pattern to his system of continuous evolution, while the central Adagio demonstrates his ability to develop a simple melodic idea through increasingly contrapuntal tissues to a climax of dissonant intensity. The *Concerto Grosso* is music of high calibre and in the following *Tre Ricercari* and Concertino for piano and orchestra Martinů was no less inspired.

The *Ricercari,* commissioned by the Venice Music Festival in 1938, have little in common with the strict fugal devices of Frescobaldi, and though Martinů's three pieces abound in elaborate free-contrapuntal weaving, it is conceivable that the composer was using the title in the sense of a fantasia. Here the general style and idiom is noticeably more melodic than that of the *Concerto Grosso*, but again Martinů treats the introduction and development of an original pattern as the cut of his musical argument. The *Ricercari* stand halfway between chamber and symphonic music and link Martinů the composer coloured by years of residence in France with Martinů the future American citizen. On the one hand the instrumentation looks back to the *Brandenburg Concertos*, and on the other its technique of composition looks forward to the six symphonies. From this score alone it is possible to determine the direction of Martinů's later orchestral compositions.

The June of 1938 saw Martinů working over the score of his Concertino for piano and orchestra, a work which, like the lovely Czech-sounding Piano Concerto No. 2 written three years before and the Harpsichord Concerto of 1935 with its modish partiality for eighteenth-century figuration, treats the solo instrument in concertante fashion. But whereas the earlier concertos show Martinů writing keyboard textures which move in contrapuntal sequences with an undeniable feeling for the Baroque, the Concertino shows the composer treating the piano in a more percussive way. Lush phrases and melodic passage work are replaced by a sharp, brittle style that is determined in its *martellato* writing and harsh in its use of minor seconds. Throughout the three movements the mood is serious and, despite its cheerful front, even the finale fails to hide the composer's distraught feelings – feelings which show his reaction to the serious political situation in Europe.

Martinů spent the summer in Czechoslovakia where even he could not fail to notice how Dr. Edvard Beneš, who had succeeded T. G. Masaryk as President in December 1935, was preparing the country against the growing threat of Hitler. A plan of national rearmament was being pushed ahead at a tremendous pace and those in Czechoslovakia who had been life-long pacificists began to feel that their existence was again at stake and laid aside their anti-militarist sentiments. For once the Czech Army was becoming popular. Smart young officers thronged the Prague streets and people talked enthusiastically of an Air Force and of the 'maginot' lines of fortifications being constructed along the most vulnerable positions of the Czech frontier. Dr. Beneš had begun a drive to treat those Sudeten Germans ready to show loyalty to the Czech Republic with greater generosity than in the past. He travelled into German-speaking districts attempting to win friendship and faith, but many wondered if the time was not already too late for such actions, and others questioned the wisdom of the President's conciliatory policy, which he was vigorously sponsoring throughout 1938.

In Polička, Martinů tried to comfort his seventy-eight-year-old mother, who was recovering from a stroke, but even here he could not dispel the misgivings and doubts which Hitler's annexation of Austria had sown in his mind. But for the Anschluss his *Concerto Grosso* would have been printed in Vienna and premièred in Paris. As it was, the score was blocked in the Austrian capital, where the situation was becoming increasingly grave. Everywhere he sensed growing insecurity, and little realised when leaving home for Paris that he was never again to cross the Czech border and never again to see his family or native land.

Nothing about the journey through Germany indicated that we were so close to the tragedy which was to hit our country within a few months and later the whole world. Here and there we saw an aeroplane or a soldier guarding the track which led to the frontier. None the less, world tragedy was being prepared along these frontiers. Plans to destroy Europe were in progress and each day brought stronger confirmation of the unbelievable cataclysm that was about to explode over our heads.

Back in Paris, composition became Martinů's only possible reaction to events around him. The future of Czechoslovakia under the increasing threat of Nazi invasion caused him anxiety and the future of those in Polička was foremost in his mind. In this oppressive atmosphere he found it hard to concentrate and moved to the peaceful countryside outside Compiègne where, in August, he began an orchestral work commissioned by Paul Sacher for the Basle Chamber Orchestra. Five years earlier, in 1933, Sacher had begun to take an interest in Martinů's music when he included the *Partita* in one of his Lucerne concerts and, in 1936, he again championed the Martinů cause by premièring the Concertino for Piano Trio and Orchestra (No. 2) in Switzerland.

Now, in 1938, he invited Martinů to write something especially for the Basle Chamber Orchestra, but sensing the composer to be ill at ease he suggested that Martinů and his wife became guests at the Sacher home. Gratefully the Martinůs accepted, and in a Swiss mountain retreat near Pratteln, a region full of summer sunlight and bird song, the composer continued the *Double Concerto* which he had started the month before.

It is lovely here. We are in the garden and I am working on the terrace. We have a chalet to ourselves and seem to be alone in the mountains, but as I look down to Germany on our right I can see the defence lines they are setting up against the helpless frontiers with France. We listen every day to the news bulletins on the radio trying to find encouragement, but it never comes.

It was only to be expected that fear should touch Martinů's work at this time and much of the *Double Concerto* for two string orchestras, piano and timpani, was written as a violent protest against the atrocities of war that were being committed in Europe.

When I look at my *Double Concerto* I have the impression that the atmosphere of tragic events which we remember so well is engraved on the pages of the score and that in it I even presented something of the future incidents and danger which threatened my homeland . . . But events followed their course and I continued to work in a state of anxiety, waiting to hear what tragic and desperate things were happening every minute of the day. In this uncertainty, which weighed heavily on the conscience of the world, I came to the end of my score.

The *Double Concerto* is a work of strong emotions, dramatic violence and intense sadness. But what Martinů omitted to mention in his programme note to the first performance (9 February 1940) was that he completed the score on the very day of the Munich Crisis. The work was conceived in tragic circumstances and the emotions it expresses are not those of despair, but rather of revolt, courage and unshakeable faith in the future.

In the *Double Concerto* Martinů again turned to the form of the concerto grosso, yet he found a new source of nourishment in a well he had almost drunk dry. Here he brings his highly personal form of neo-classical expression to a peak, with the two string orchestras used antiphonally and as complimentary bodies, and the piano and timpani as extras. The closely-knit textures, which are woven in determined and unrelenting rhythms, find their origin in Bach, but the spirit in which Martinů writes is far removed from the *Brandenburg*

75

Concertos. The rigours of the composer's utterance are matched by an economy of material and an intense concentration of expression which make the score a landmark in twentieth-century composition. This is music without themes, and here Martinů is obsessed with germinal development. The sonata-like opening is uni-cellular. The two orchestras challenge each other in feverish outbursts. There is no respite. In the middle section rests become fewer, note values shorter. Textures thicken. The part-writing becomes more contrapuntal and the recapitulation is reached, but implied rather than restated.

The Largo offers no relaxation. The intensity of the first movement continues with massive chords – pillars of sound which rise with ascending confidence. These chords play a significant part in the movement and symbolise the firmness of a structure enclosing the torments of a troubled world. The music is intense. As tempos change note values diminish and the two orchestras develop in canon. A new level of violence is reached as the piano sweeps upwards in harsh glissandos. The disorder fades. The solo piano quietly reflects on the desolation while sinister ostinatos lead to the final section where the string writing is in eight real parts. The climax is sounded and the movement, harrowing in its pathos, ends with a reprise of the pillar-like chords.

In the Finale Martinů enters a nightmare world of torment. This is not programme music but absolute music calling to mind Bartók's *Music for Strings, Percussion and Celeste* and Vaughan Williams's Symphony No. 4. Here Martinů is anticipating the horrors of World War II, and the fragmentary nature of the material and irregular patterns convey a sense of terror and pain. Phrases from the slow movement, sometimes in augmentation, are tossed from one orchestra to another and there is even a restatement of the eight-part contrapuntal section from the slow movement and a return of the opening chords. Significantly the work closes on an unresolved discord – a mark of style not found elsewhere in the composer's work. And his decision to end on a discord almost certainly suggests his misgivings for the future.

The *Double Concerto* is an intensely disturbing work. It stands not only as a superb piece of writing, but as a confession symbolising the composer's desire for freedom and peace. It in Martinů crystallised in sound a tragic moment in history. It is not an easy work to understand or listen to and needs great concentration, but once its idiom has been accepted it emerges as Martinů's most profound achievement. This is not just because of its originality, but because it poses questions that are at once vital and important and because it attempts to solve them convincingly and logically. The *Double Concerto* is an inevitable work which remains a remarkable example of the triumph of the human spirit, not in spite of suffering, but through it.

Returning to Paris from the peace and safety of the Swiss mountains, Martinů was overwhelmed by the impending tragedy of his own country. The resignation of President Beneš on 5 October 1938 and the arrival of German forces on Czech soil on 18 October filled the composer with horror. 'I can't find words to describe the despair I have experienced since leaving Switzerland. We live in a vacuum since all our plans are upset; Paris is organising the Resistance, but we still hope for better days.' The avalanche of war was in motion and Martinů found it increasingly hard to settle down. He spent hours deliberating in which direction he should move. He toyed with the idea of going to North America, but at heart felt morally obliged to try to return to Prague where he could be in contact with his family. He corresponded with the Prague Conservatoire, hoping to be considered for the Professorship in the Master Class of Composition, a vacancy that had been created by the retirement of Joseph Foerster, but unexpectedly his application was refused and even his appeal for an ordinary teaching post at the Brno Conservatoire fell on unsympathetic ears. Neither Václav Talich nor Stanislav Novák could help, and everywhere, it seemed, Martinů's efforts were in vain. In the spring of 1939 he desperately submitted his score of *Juliette* to Prague with the request that he be awarded the Bedřich Smetana Prize for Composition. But this was hardly the time for prive-giving and its receipt was not even acknowledged.

It was as if everything had stopped at the touch of a hand. Ideas found no support and vanished as if a void had opened and swallowed humanity up. The futility of any kind of activity hammered on my mind. Everything I had been doing, I had done, written or thought seemed pointless, as if someone had rubbed a chalk mark off a blackboard and left only a smudge. There now seemed nothing worth composing.

As the atmosphere of war began to sweep across Europe, Martinů tried hard to compose, but his heart was not in a set of five pieces for piano trio called *Bergerettes*, nor in the *Promenades* for flute, violin and harpsichord. He made little headway with the *Suite Concertante* for the violinist Samuel Dushkin and corresponded far more about it than he actually composed. However, in a set of amorous Bohemian folk poems by František Sušil, to which he gave the title *Madrigals*, he captured the spirit of music of an earlier age. He still talked of going to America, but at this time considered it more as a safety measure to ease his troubled conscience. With the Nazi invasion of Czecho-

slovakia on 15 March 1939, however, he realised that the road home
was finally closed and that the United States might be his only means
of escape. For the time being Martinů resolved to stay in the city, but
without money he was glad to take up the provisional post of Cultural
Attaché at the Czech Legation. Martinů was no diplomat, but at least
this gave him a roof over his head and time to compose. However, the
only piece for which he could muster any interest was the Sonata
for Cello and Piano No. 1, completed in May. In its unusually dramatic
character this score speaks a similar language to that of the *Double
Concerto,* and almost certainly voices the perturbation of spirit caused
in the composer by the sad news brought from home by Kaprálová,
now a refugee.

In September 1939 war was declared, and although many Frenchmen believed it would mean little more than mobilisation, the Czechs
living in Paris regarded it more seriously. With General Svoboda
campaigning in Russia to form an army and Dr. Beneš in North
America and then London organising a force of Czech paratroops,
patriots in Paris enlisted into the Army, and one of the first to volunteer
was Martinů. Being in his fiftieth year, he was not called up, but he
responded by composing a Military March for the other volunteers and
the *Polní mše* (*Field Mass*) which he designed as a powerful anti-war
protest.

The *Field Mass* is not a setting of the liturgy, but a collection of
texts by Jiří Mucha and passages from Bohemian folk poetry interspersed
with lines from the Psalms and phrases from the Common of the Mass.
Designed for performance out of doors, the *Mass* was intended to unite
soldiers at the front with compatriots at home. Preference is given,
therefore, to brass and wind instruments and strings are omitted altogether. An impressive percussion section, bells and hand bells of the
type used at the altar during Mass (the so-called sistrum) and the
crotola, an instrument tuned to two notes a perfect fifth apart, piano,
harmonium, solo baritone and male chorus complete the forces. Though
the score is continuous it falls into several episodes, the first of which
includes a setting of the Lord's Prayer. The harmonium introduces the
soloist, a soldier on duty at the front reflecting on the remoteness of his
homeland and imploring God to save him. Dramatic trumpet calls
sound an alarm and the chorus responds with an impressive unison
setting of Psalms 44 and 42. A deeply felt apostrophe to the fatherland
follows in which Martinů, with charmingly observant music, recalls the
sweet, holy place of his childhood and muses on the mourning boom of
the funeral bell that used to sound from the Polička Church. A piano
cadenza introduces the final section which establishes the mood for a

setting of the Kyrie, the first petition of which is chanted to a transposed plainsong phrase that can be found note-for-note in an eleventh-century version of the Sanctus. Throughout, Martinů uses the transposed Dorian and Phrygian modes and continues in the same vein for Christe Eleison, where the tenor part is taken from a plainsong sequence for Whitsunday, *Veni Sancte Spiritus.* Here the choral writing suggests a knowledge of composite organum and points to Martinů's research into early music. The soloist, representing the sentry on duty in the field, calls to God for solace in his troubled hour. The chorus chant 'Dominus vobiscum', and intone the Agnus Dei with a slow and assured simplicity. While drums beat a retreat the unaccompanied chorus sing a chorale-like setting of verses from Psalms 57, 56, and 54 and, as if in reconciliation, the *Field Mass* ends with a touching 'Amen'.

The *Field Mass* is Martinů's nearest approach to sacred music and anticipates in a very remarkable way Britten's *War Requiem* and Bernstein's *Mass.* Just as Britten alternates the liturgy with the highly personal poetry of Wilfred Owen, and Bernstein juxtaposes the individual voice of Stephen Schwarz with the ordinary aspirations of mankind as expressed in the Common of the Roman Mass, so through the words of Jiří Mucha, Martinů alternates the fears and resentment of the threatened Czechs with fragments of liturgy. Although the *Field Mass* is a smaller, more unpretentious work than either Britten's or Bernstein's, it is an impressive score showing Martinů writing with great sincerity.

In the first days of the war, musical life continued in Paris much as it had before. The Triton, renamed *Societé de la Musique Contemporaire,* still functioned but in a state of unease. The political situation in the city was serious and 1940 brought more anxiety. Early in February Martinů travelled to Switzerland to hear the *Double Concerto* played for the first time – an event charged with emotion and one which was to be among the most memorable in his career. Returning to Paris several weeks later, he learned that performances of his music in Czechoslovakia had been banned and that all sums from his international royalties had been blocked. To be black-listed by the Nazis, as he had been, was one thing, but to be barred from his own country, as man and musician, reduced him to despair. Between April and May the Martinůs lived in conditions which were becoming increasingly frightening, and although many could foresee the fall of Paris the composer remained for the première of his First Cello Sonata given at the Triton on 19 May. For Martinů, this was a kind of leave-taking. He had planned to stay for the première of the *Concerto Grosso* and the first performance of the *Double Concerto,* promised for 14 June under

Sacher's baton. But on 10 June, Rudolf Firkušný, one of Martinů's staunchest friends, sensing that the fall of Paris was imminent, advised the composer to leave the city. The German invasion of France meant that Martinů and his wife were directly threatened, and with no money and only one suitcase they left in the same way as tens of thousands of refugees all over Europe. By a stroke of luck they caught a train which put a safe distance between them and Paris.

From Limoges, Martinů sent word to Sacher in Switzerland.

Here is our news. We suffer hard times and for days have looked for shelter, no matter what, no matter where. For the present we are primitively fixed up in Rancon, a village not far from where Charles Munch is living. We have no news of our friends who, like us, left Paris at the last moment . . . We remember you with pleasure, but recent events are stronger than remembrances. We don't know where we are going or what the future holds. We have left everything in Paris and we look to the future with uncertainty.

To escape the threat of advancing German forces, only a dozen miles away, Martinů and his wife set out on foot to cross the French frontier and find the home of Colette Frantz, a violinist friend; but after hours of travelling they arrived at Cauterets in the Pyrenees only to find their host's house deserted. Exhausted and bitterly disappointed they made their way to Aix-en-Provence, where reluctantly Martinů was forced to face the facts. Having been black-listed for his support of the Czech National Council in Paris, he could no longer expect to stay in France. He was obliged to begin formalities to leave for the United States. Time and again he applied for a permit but each time his application was refused. Relying entirely on the help of friends in the Composers' League and the generosity of the I.S.C.M., he eventually secured a North American entry visa; but as he was Czech, no exit permit was forthcoming from the Vichy authorities. Delays were long, departure dates postponed. The procedure for applying for a visa was tedious and long-winded. Martinů's spirits were low. He was homesick for Paris and little that his dutiful wife did could bolster his morale. Then he received news of the death of Vítězslava Kaprálová. Martinů was wretched. He wanted to communicate with her family in the Vysočina, but was unable to send even his condolences since postal services with Eastern Europe had been cut. However, he could still write to Switzerland where the faithful Paul Sacher awaited his latest news. 'My spiritual state is such that I would rather let everything go . . . I keep thinking of Prague and our countrymen and how they must be feeling. Perhaps it would be better if we did not have to think at all . . . Here in France everything is slowly disintegrating. One can't help feeling sad. Nevertheless I have the will to work and thank God there is still the possibility of doing so here!' Each day Martinů had to spend four or five hours travelling in an electric train between Aix and Marseilles and the only way he knew of passing the time was to sketch ideas for new compositions. During August and September he produced one of his finest piano pieces, the *Fantaisie and Toccata*, a dramatic and deeply-felt study for Rudolf Firkušný. And when in October Martinů learnt that he had been granted a French exit permit he set to work on the lively *Sinfonietta Giocosa* for piano and orchestra which aptly reflects his high spirits at the prospect of leaving France. By November the four-movement *Sinfonietta* was ready in score and five weeks later the *Sonata da Camera* for cello and small orchestra, a commission from Henri Honegger, was nearing completion. The only check to Martinů's flow of ideas at this time seems to have been the painful chilblains on his hands, but financially he was checked in every direction. Paul Sacher was a constant source of help, and while an anonymous group of Swiss admirers appealed through the paper *Dissonances* for funds on Martinů's behalf, Ernest Ansermet in Geneva organised a collection to aid the homeless composer. The response was encouraging, and while this helped to provide what food and clothing were available, it did nothing to speed formalities involved in granting a Spanish transit visa. The fateful year 1940 was coming to an end. What hope, the Martinůs wondered, did 1941 hold for them? It certainly began brightly when, in the first week of January, their papers were finally put in order. On 12 January, Martinů and his wife travelled to Lisbon where, having missed the *Excambion* by a matter of days, they were forced to wait for yet another two months until Paul Sacher was able to reserve berths on the *Exeter*. Finally, on 25 March 1941, the Martinůs set sail for New York.

For more than nine months Bohuslav Martinů had been homeless. He had endured and survived privation and appalling winter conditions. He was now emaciated and weak and during this period had slept in more than forty different beds and on countless railway platforms. He had experienced insecurity and bitter distress, but escape from Europe was a necessity accepted without joy. Something had come to an end, and it is little wonder that the fifty-one-year-old composer wept to leave France, his adopted home for more than seventeen years.

6 *America: 1941-8*

Believe me, New York's endless avenues and streets are not exactly the best source of inspiration . . . They fall in on you, hold you fast so escape is impossible. No, I can't say my recollections of New York are of the happiest.

These were Martinů's first impressions of New York, written in April 1941, forty-nine years after Dvořák had arrived in the same city. Dvořák's sojourn in the United States was undertaken in circumstances and for reasons far different from those of Martinů; nevertheless the reactions of the two men to their new environment were not dissimilar. Both looked back with nostalgic regret to the countryside of Bohemia and Moravia, to Prague and other ancient cities of Europe, to a culture ripe, established, certain and mature. Both men felt ill at ease amidst the industrial wealth and efficiency of the young continent. Dvořák, sensing a kinship with the exiled negroes, discovered their idiom and conveyed their sadness in music which bears an affinity to their religious songs. For Martinů, however, there was no such outlet.

The *Exeter* reached New Jersey on 31 March 1941. Yet again in his life Martinů was cut off from the surroundings he had grown accustomed to: again he was among strangers whose language he did not know, whose environment he did not understand. Now it was a question of starting again, for everything he had done previously seemed to have lost its meaning. He had to establish himself once more, not only to make a place in the American musical scene, but to secure a means of existence. He was penniless, self-effacing, armed with only four manuscripts and no other evidence of his gifts. He was but one of many musicians seeking refuge in the United States. It was not going to be easy.

Martinů was ill and exhausted after his harrowing experiences in Europe. He had changed radically. His thin, haggard face and soft eyes showed what suffering he had gone through since leaving Paris, and though he was met by friends, Firkušný and Dushkin among them, there were considerably more problems in settling down than he had expected. The question uppermost in his mind was what was he to do in New York. Martinů's reputation rested entirely upon scores he had written in pre-war Europe, but only a few of these were known in America. Even the composer himself was unable to trace valuable manuscripts somewhere in occupied territory. Certainly the fear that

24. *Half-time* : caricature of himself by Martinů.

25. Caricature of Martinů by Sekora.

26. Scene from Martinů's ballet *Špaliček*. Production of the National Theatre, Prague, 1932.

27. Scene from Martinů's radio opera *Comedy on the Bridge*.

he had lost everything made him especially low-spirited. However, New York gave him little time for brooding as he became caught up in the bustling pace of its daily life. A reception given by the Mayor helped refugee musicians to meet each other, but Martinů had never enjoyed socialising and now found it hard to jump onto the social ladder. More and more he felt the need for retreat. He was not at home in the American scene and could never get below the hard, polished surface of the city. He was at bottom a Czech who had, at various stages, grown to love the leisured, artistic life of Prague and Paris. He found hotel life in Fifty-Seventh Street stifling. He missed the boulevard cafés, and his quay-side walks along the Seine, and no matter how often he strolled around Central Park his thoughts were always elsewhere. Though the New World was at peace, there was little peace in Martinů. The war in Europe was at its height and in Czechoslovakia the nation was fighting for survival. The awareness of his affinity to the struggling Czech people inevitably affected his attitude to life. He became more introverted and suffered acute bouts of depression. Composition was next to impossible and he had to summon every effort to complete by the end of April a forty-five-bar *Mazurka* for inclusion in a piano album intended to pay homage to Paderewski. 'Life is very difficult here . . . I had the firm intention of writing but did not expect such a big change or such a reaction. I began to compose in June (1941) but the results are not good. I must confess this new life leaves me little time to myself, but I hope by the summer that I shall have been able to put some of my ideas in order.' After three months Martinů could stand New York no longer. During the summer he and his wife found lodgings in Pleasantville, then in Edgartown, Massachusetts, and finally in Jamaica where a fellow Czech, Frank Rybka, a cellist and pupil of Janáček, made them especially welcome. Here Martinů got down to the task of learning English, though his monthly allowance of three hundred dollars from the Czech Consulate in New York was hardly sufficient for private lessons. Instead he developed the habit of going to the cinema each day to see the same film over and over again in order to study its dialogue phonetically. Unorthodox the system may have been, but it was certainly effective. Martinů stayed in Jamaica for nearly a year during which time he learned, as far as he ever could, to adjust himself to the American way of life. At last he began to regain his former interest in and facility for composition. But whereas in France he had devoted himself to operas and pieces for small ensemble, in Jamaica he began to think of large-scale works. The period of experimental composition was behind him. Now the balance of intellectual maturity and seriousness was leading him to think about symphonies

G

and concertos into which he was about to pour his life's experiences as an artist.

As if to flex his creative muscles, he reworked the chirpy *Sinfonietta Giocosa* and revised the *Suite Concertante*, begun in Paris, interrupted by the Czech crisis, resumed after Munich, broken off by the outbreak of war and taken up again in America. Between October and December 1938 the piece had started life as a portly Scherzo for violin and piano, but now it acquired several off-shoots including an orchestral accompaniment (revised in 1945), which does little to disguise its zig-zag growth or the variety of its idioms. Somehow the pendulum swings unconvincingly from tart modernism to suave Impressionism as the music moves through a breezy Toccata, an elegiac Aria, a whimsical Scherzo and an episodic Rondo.

The *Suite Concertante* was little more than a preliminary for a larger, more significant concerto begun in July 1941, in response to a commission from Paul Sacher and the Basle Chamber Orchestra. In the *Concerto da Camera,* as the piece was to be called, Martinů returned to the principles of the Baroque concerto and found his old form. The *Concerto da Camera* is close in spirit to the dramatic *Double Concerto* of 1938 and is almost as deeply felt. The score breaks no new ground, but shows a continuation of the pre-war style with harsh harmonic clashes, pedals and ostinatos, polyphonic weaving and a growth of textures from continuously developing motifs. The solo writing is spontaneous and finely judged, and though concertante in nature it provides opportunities for brilliant passage work in the outer movements, especially the finale which is notable for its cadenza with piano accompaniment.

Martinů's next work, the Concerto for Two Pianos, must rank as one of his major accomplishments. Perhaps he recognised this himself, for it remained a favourite of his. Musically it grows from scores like *Kytice,* the *Tre Ricercari* and the *Concerto Grosso,* which employ two pianos as the backbone of the orchestra; and here the two instruments are not used in skeletal fashion but assume solo significance. Pianistically the Concerto presents great difficulties and its technical demands for the soloists are close to those in Bartók's Sonata for pianos and percussion. Possibly for this reason, it has been championed by few duos. This is sad, since the musical invention is of a high order, and the balance between the two pianos and the orchestra finely judged, especially in the opening Toccata. The Rondo finale is something of a marvel, with exuberant interplay between the solo pianos, brilliant scoring and inexhaustible rhythmic vitality.

The Concerto for Two Pianos was followed by a full-length Violin

Concerto, written for Mischa Elman in 1943, in which the composer treats the solo part in a retrospective nineteenth-century fashion with an accompanying symphony orchestra, instead of the more usual ripieno ensemble. With the exception of piano and harp the instrumentation is identical to that of the First and Second Symphonies, with which the Concerto is roughly contemporary. In a way it is possible to regard Martinů's previous essays for the violin as a series of experiments for this major offering. Like Brahms, he was approaching middle age when he composed the work. But unlike Brahms, Martinů has not completely solved the problem of writing a romantic concerto, for the three movements, lyrical though they are, seem to have been conceived for orchestra with violin added. The solo writing appears less important than the accompaniment, and in the outer movements the soloist sometimes sounds like a persistent insect whose buzz the orchestra often manages to chase away. When this happens there is an exciting display of sonority and timbre, and it is upon this that the first movement depends for its effect. The form of each movement is classical, but the content, based on Martinů's system of germinal development, makes it modern. The arresting opening is rhapsodic, with many contrasts and several references to the four-note motif from Dvořák's *Requiem*; the pastoral Intermezzo is a well-rounded meditation in which the composer uses folk idiom as if it had been coursing through his veins from birth, which it had, and the finale is a Rondo with polka-like episodes in which folk dance lingers. The Violin Concerto is a lovely work, and while the Cello Concerto No. 2 continues in the same style, it does not contain material of such substance. The germinal process of composition that forms the basis of the outer movements of the Violin Concerto is less apparent in the Cello Concerto. The serious-sounding Allegro is well thought out, but the following movements seldom rise above mediocrity. The fantasia-like Andante suffers from long-windedness and the Rondo from note-spinning. As a whole the Second Cello Concerto is not an excursion to any particular place, but rather a trip through countryside which remains basically dull. Along the way there are points of interest – traces of folk idiom, deft touches of instrumentation – but the unpromising finale with its lengthy cadenza and mechanical coda is like an unexpected return to the starting point of the outing.

With each new concerto Martinů was making a name for himself, not only in New York, where Samuel Dushkin played the *Sinfonia Concertante,* but in Philadelphia where Eugene Ormandy premièred the Concerto for Two Pianos, and in Boston where Koussevitzky introduced the Violin Concerto. There were other Martinů premières in

Boston too, and in November 1941, after friends had retrieved the score from war-scarred Vienna, the *Concerto Grosso* was heard for the first time under Koussevitzky's baton. In January 1942 it was given a repeat performance in New York's Carnegie Hall, where nearly fifty years before Dvořák had heard his *New World* Symphony for the first time. In Koussevitzky, Martinů had obviously found a true champion and friend, and through him the composer was invited to take up a teaching post at the Berkshire Music Centre in Lennox, where, despite his patchy English, he spent six weeks of the summer instructing and making music. It was during this stay that the finely-written Piano Quartet was first performed, and here, too, that Martinů put the finishing touches to his First Symphony, begun in May in Jamaica.

It is curious that Martinů, one of the most prolific composers of the century, should have waited until his fifty-first year before attempting a symphony. In a way his case is again similar to that of Brahms, who was forty-three when the C minor Symphony appeared. But there the parallel ends; for Brahms was so severe a self-critic that he may well have destroyed works, perhaps including an early symphony, barely distinguishable from those known today. Martinů showed no such sensitiveness, but apart from two early attempts he waited for his more than mature years before tackling the difficulties of symphonic structure.

The incomplete sketch of a symphony dating from 1912 can be discounted, and a work which Martinů himself called *La Symphonie* refers not to the structure of the piece but rather to its texture. After the première, given by Koussevitzky in Boston in 1928, Martinů changed the title to *Allegro symphonique*, but for the first performance in Czechoslovakia in 1930 he renamed it *La Rhapsodie*. Fourteen years separate this from the Symphony No. 1, which Koussevitzky commissioned to be written in memory of his wife. (Natalie Koussevitzky's death was also to prompt Stravinsky's *Ode* and Bartók's *Concerto for Orchestra*.) In Martinů's case the conditions of the commission specified only the composition of a large orchestral work, so it was almost certain he turned to the symphony of his own volition. Admittedly, during the early days of the war, Charles Munch had urged him to think in terms of composing a symphony or set of Slavonic Dances for symphony orchestra; but the time had not been right then. In 1942 Martinů felt better able to respond and between 21 May and the end of August, in the amazingly short space of fifteen weeks, he completed his First Symphony. As if some barrier had suddenly been removed Martinů turned avidly to the composition of symphonies and, like Brahms, he followed his First with a Second twelve months later.

In June 1944 the Symphony No. 3 appeared, and by June 1945 the Fourth was ready for performance. Only eleven months were to pass before the Symphony No. 5 was in score; but with this Martinů's series of annual symphonies were brought to a close. Five years elapsed before he sketched his *Fantaisies symphoniques* (the so-called Symphony No. 6) in 1951. Over the course of eleven years the six Symphonies show Martinů developing his ideas in a significant way. In each of the series he created a very personal type of work which goes some way to substantiate Ernest Ansermet's view that of his generation Martinů was one of the great writers of symphonic music.

The symphonies can be divided into two groups according to the number of their movements. The First, Second and Fourth are four-movement compositions while the rest fall into a three-movement pattern but without any trace of classical order. Nevertheless it is interesting to follow the structural changes the composer made from symphony to symphony and to see how his concept of sonata form developed from near orthodoxy in the First Symphony, to a movement with a reduced central section in Symphony No. 3, transformed itself into a two-part structure in the Fourth Symphony, and became a number of variations in the *Fantaisies symphoniques*. Furthermore, the three-movement form of the Third, Fifth and Sixth Symphonies suggest that Martinů's series could well have been extended to include the three-part symphonic poems *The Frescoes of Piero della Francesca* (1955) and *The Parables* (1957-8) which are so closely bound in concept and in musical expression to the idiom of the Symphonies that they might well have been styled Symphonies Nos. 7 and 8. As it is, these works break down the traditional barrier dividing symphony from symphonic poem.

While Martinů's six Symphonies are individual, each has a distinctive quality which stems from *Juliette*. Six years separate the First Symphony from the opera, and though many of the composer's most important scores date from the period in between, not one is the logical successor of *Juliette*. The Symphonies are linked to the opera as much by their common musical expression as by the use of a correspondingly large orchestra. However, the forces called for are not quite as extravagant as those required for *Juliette* : the accordion, celeste and xylophone, for example, appear in none of the Symphonies, but the piano used as a continuo and sometimes combined with harp (in all but one of the six), is strikingly individual and looks back to the stage work.

But if the symphonies have a common ancestor in *Juliette* they are not written in the same mood. In spite of its dedication the First is a romantic rather than solemn affair. The Second is pastoral in feeling and very Czech-sounding. Symphony No. 3 is tragic. No. 4 is lyrical and the Fifth, while difficult to classify, is sanguine in the bright optimism of its outer movements. For the Sixth Symphony there is no need to look any further than Martinů's own descriptive epithet. He called it 'fantastic'. There is no denying the individuality of the Symphonies. Each is *sui generis,* not least in form and construction, and Martinů's freedom from academic training in his youth no doubt accounts for the looseness of some of his formal schemes. Of course his wide reading of scores had made him as fully conversant with classical concepts as with serial techniques – a system of composition he accepted and watched develop, without venturing into himself – and in the *Inventions, Partita, Tre Ricercari* and *Concerto Grosso* the Baroque could be seen in more than just the titles. Equally, when it came to writing a symphony, Martinů could not ignore the past, and his originality as a symphonist can be seen to stem from his use of modified ritornello principles which result in episodically-constructed movements. By sometimes developing his episodes from the same material as his initial ritornello Martinů was returning to his own system of continuous growth and thus creating a free musical structure from a few thematic and rhythmic fragments. Needless to say, this technique was not Martinů's invention. Among others, Sibelius and Roussel had put it to considerable purpose in their own symphonic works. In Martinů's hands, however, it was to be manipulated, often in masterly fashion, so as to produce an organic unity by means of melodic and rhythmic variation, inversion, augmentation and diminution and by continuous repetition. Of these the last is the most important, but it is not only note patterns that are repeated. Often whole passages reappear with minor modifications in scoring or transposed into different keys, and sometimes, it seems, Martinů seized on repetition merely as a means of patching a movement together. Clearly he was no slave to orthodoxy and was apt to rely, if anything, rather too much on the spontaneity of the moment. Caprice often dictated the pattern of keys he used and in the symphonies each movement is allowed to follow its own course of progressive tonality – a scheme Mahler and Nielsen had adopted earlier in the century. Thus the opening movement of the Second Symphony moves from D minor through B flat to G minor and closes in B flat. Of Martinů's twenty-one symphonic movements no less than fourteen show him ending in keys different from those in which he began.

The First Symphony begins where the dream world of *Juliette* stopped, but the modal-sounding note-pattern on which the first movement is based could not be further from it. Martinů's initial note-theme for the Symphony is derived from a cadential phrase to be found in the twelfth-century Bohemian chorale *Svatý Václav* (St. Wenceslas). This fragment of plainsong had appeared in Martinů's cantata *Česká rapsódie* as early as 1918, and returns in the *Memorial to Lidice* and *Fantaisies symphoniques* with such force that it seems to have had some special significance for the composer. Indeed, the chorale is one of the most fervently national of all Bohemian hymn tunes, and the words accompanying the final petition 'Holy Wenceslas, don't let us perish!' have been used by the Czechs as a protest against oppression from the Hussite Wars to the Nazi invasion in 1938. Among others, Josef Suk had used the chorale as the basis for his *Meditations* for string orchestra; and in a more personal way, Martinů's brother, František, had painted a representation of St. Wenceslas on the exterior of his house in Polička in 1940, with the words 'Don't let us perish' marked symbolically between the window and the front door. Clearly the chorale held a special meaning for the Martinů family. The chorale finds no place in the Scherzo, which is conventional in form but unconventional in the energy it generates. There is nothing in the earlier scores that is comparable to the drive and urgency of this motoric music, which may well have been suggested by Martinů's experience of living in New York City. Respite is found in the Trio where strings are silent and wind and brass engage in folk idiom. In the elegiac third movement Martinů abandons his system of germinal development, possibly for the reason that it is less satisfactory in passages where slow tempi have little forward motion of their own and because his principal melodic motif, the 'Moravian cadence' from the opera *Juliette*, refuses to be transformed organically. For his finale, the composer makes no ambitious attempt to build an elaborate edifice leading to fugue or passacaglia, and again he put to one side his technique of germinal development. Instead he writes a Rondo in which folk song lingers, and in one of the episodes he even introduces a haunting phrase that seems to echo the opening bars of Skřivánek's G major aria in the first act of Smetaha's *The Secret*.

The appearance of his First Symphony is a landmark in any composer's career. Martinů's is an interesting solution, not least for the way it exploits germinal techniques of composition. The Second Symphony follows similar lines but is designed in chamber-music style. There are no rhetorical gestures here, and the belief in restraint and clarity referred to in the composer's note to the First Symphony is evident in the scoring of the Second where climaxes are modestly indicated with the dynamic marking never going beyond *sfz* or *ff* and no excess of emphasis. Martinů's original sketch for the opening movement shows an Allegro in the form of a spruce little march, but the final version reveals no trace of this. Instead the movement grows from a simple note-pattern and from a number of arpeggio figures, not unlike an Alberti bass, which demonstrate Martinů making use of an old technique in modern guise. The pastoral Andante is allied to Moravian folk song with a melody that hovers modally around the tonic and mediant (major alternating minor), while the third movement departs from the accepted form of Scherzo and Trio. Here Martinů returns to the material of his original sketch and writes a continuous march with a sustained central section. Rhythmic interest replaces melodic content as ostinatos and pedal devices draw the various textures together. In the last few bars trumpets stridently declaim the passage of the *Marseillaise* to the words 'Aux armes, Citoyens! Formez vos bataillons!' Though there is no reason to suppose that the movement was conceived programatically, the date of completion, not long after the extermination of the Czech village of Lidice, leaves little doubt that this gesture was intended as a clarion call to the Czech refugees in Cleveland who commissioned the Symphony. By contrast, the finale is one of the most jubilant rondos Martinů ever penned, and nowhere reflects the agony and horror he felt on reading about the carnage which the Nazis had perpetrated in the Lidice blood-bath in June 1943. The Hitler Youth had wiped the tiny village in North-west Bohemia off the map as a reprisal for the assassination of Heidrich in Prague. No Czech could remain unmoved by this calculated act of cruelty and, spurred on by the Free Czech Government in London, Martinů in Darien, Connecticut, commemorated this outrage in a short symphonic meditation called *Památník Lidicím* (*Memorial to Lidice*). Far from crushing Martinů's Czech spirit, the horror of Lidice became a banner for revolt and in this music the composer proclaims his faith in ultimate victory. The work has no specific programme, but the distillation of tragedy is there, as the music pushes forward like a gigantic funeral cortège. It is not surprising, therefore, that Antony Tudor found Martinů's score an ideal vehicle for his ballet on the theme called *Echoing of Trumpets,* given in London in 1973.

In *Memorial to Lidice* Martinů is concerned with dramatising in sound a moment of shock in history. The mood is one of grief and despair, and throughout the pace is slow and deliberate. In bar 2 clarinets and bassoons balefully intone the cadence figure from the St. Wenceslas Chorale (previously heard in the First Symphony) as a resolute petition for salvation. The tragic atmosphere prevails until the full orchestra announces an ascending phrase in parallel thirds and sixths directly related to those passages in the *Field Mass* which symbolise the Czech homeland. The music becomes more animated, the expression more determined. A climax is reached on a powerful E flat chord. The music plunges into F minor and horns quote the

opening notes of Beethoven's Fifth Symphony; one is reminded
that this was the motif used by the B.B.C. to represent freedom from
tyranny and oppression during the war. The *Memorial* ends with a
return of the opening material. *Lidice* occupies an important place in
Martinů's output. It is a score at once noble and solemn. Even if it does
not quite approach the significance of the *Double Concerto* it makes
its effect in a different way : by revealing glimpses of optimism.

By contrast, the Third Symphony replaces *Lidice*'s gloom with a
tense dramatic argument which reflects Martinů's sense of desolation
during the early months of 1944. The Third Symphony is tragic in the
Aristotelian sense. Here Martinů seems to be communing with himself
on the fate of Czechoslovakia, and he bases his first movement on a
three-note motif which is not far removed from two works bearing the
epithet 'pathétique' – Beethoven's Piano Sonata, Opus 13 and Tchaikovsky's Sixth Symphony. The central slow movement is unlike anything
in the preceding symphonies. The elegy of the First and nostalgic
meditation of the Second have no connection in either mood or work-
manship with the complex, contrapuntal fantasia of the Third. Only in
the *Fantaisies symphoniques* of 1951-3 does Martinů again indulge
in polyphonic writing of a similar nature. Though the melodic lines
recall the *Concerti Grossi* of Corelli and Vivaldi, the motif on which
Martinů muses stems from a different age and tradition and is similar
to the 'fate' motif in Tchaikovsky's Fifth Symphony. The finale takes up
the motif from the previous movement, developing and transposing it
until it assumes a four-note shape similar to the subject Bach used in the
second Kyrie of the *B Minor Mass*, the phrase Mozart turned to
account in the Miserere of the *Missa Brevis* (K. 49), the theme Dvořák
used as a leading-motif in his *Requiem*, and the motif Suk introduced in
the second movement of the *Asrael* Symphony. The very fact that this
theme should have been used in the works of Bach, Mozart and Dvořák,
and by Suk as a 'fate' motto, makes its appearance in Martinů's Symphony more than a coincidence – at a time when hostilities in Europe
were about to cease. Though the composer was later to admit that he
was unfamiliar with Dvořák's *Requiem*, it seems inconceivable he was
ignorant of the *Asrael* Symphony and even more surprising if he did
not recognise the connection between his four-note motif and that of
Bach's Kyrie. Nevertheless he intended this motif to have some extra
meaning, for after a restatement of the opening material the violent
form of expression is replaced by a Coda in which a beautiful, chorale-
like melody is given to a solo string quartet and accompanied by a
delicate web of violin and harp figuration. As this fades, cor anglais
and horn intone a transposed and distant-sounding allusion to Dvořák's

'Requiem' motif. Martinů has left no explanation for this curiously muted conclusion; but it may be that he was working on the final section of this score when the allied armies were about to land in Normandy. Martinů could hardly have remained unmoved by the liberation of France, so the explanation for the final section of the Symphony, completed on D-Day itself, may be found in these external events. Whatever the source of inspiration, the Third is an intensely moving and memorable Symphony, in which the music is tinged with tragic feeling, except in the closing pages where it seems the composer is making his own supplication for peace.

Ten months after completing the Third Symphony, the Fourth was sketched; but though the two works are close in time they are poles apart in other ways. In fact, the new Symphony looks back to the four-movement pattern of No. 1 and the pastoral moods of No. 2. The Fourth Symphony might well have been sub-titled 'lyrical', for it is full of warm melody and the most felicitous instrumental touches. The tragic qualities of the Third Symphony are nowhere to be found here; instead the score is romantic in mood, almost lush, and breathes the air of a peaceful countryside somewhere in Massachusetts where most of it was composed. The opening is like bird music, music of impalpable texture, transparent and beautifully judged. Here Martinů's specific technique of developing a long and varied discourse abounding in interesting incident from the slenderest of material is fully displayed, and while this is clearly symphonic writing of high order, one is conscious that the composer has almost completely dispensed with accepted symphonic form. (There is no formal development section as such, the movement being binary in design with a continuous growth from two slender ideas announced in the first bars.) In the second movement Martinů was anticipating by three months his own boisterous orchestral Scherzo called *Thunderbolt P-47,* written 'in praise of speed' and the American fighter pilots who flew the P-47s across Europe during the war. In the Symphony the Scherzo second movement brings a happy fusion of the traditional and the new: the outer parts bustle with strenuous bi-tonal clashes while the Trio is fragile and folk-like. Once again Martinů looks toward his native land by using a melody strongly reminiscent of *Bolavá hlava* – a folk song which was later to colour the finale of Symphony No. 5 and the opening movement of the *Sinfonietta La Jolla.* For his romantic third movement Martinů glanced back to his concerto grosso days by setting two violins and a cello as a concertino element against a ripieno of strings, horn and piano. In contrast to eighteenth-century practice, however, there are bi-tonal clashes, and the principle of organic growth from note patterns; but on this occasion the motifs seem too slight to carry the inflated shape of the movement, which is overloaded by Martinů's ornate figuration. The composer is much more successful with his good-humoured finale, which teems with attractive and immediate ideas presented in bold orchestral colouring. As a whole the Fourth Symphony must rank among Martinů's most successful orchestral works. It is also the one which, on account of its strongly diatonic tendencies and exceptional lyricism, comes closest to Dvořák.

The Fifth Symphony, originally intended for the Red Cross but finally dedicated to the Czech Philharmonic Orchestra, is the last of the series Martinů began in 1942, and with it he came to the end of a number of experiments. Possibly he finished here simply because he felt he could go no further on the same lines. As one might expect, many features from the earlier Symphonies return, but generally the music is happier, more shapely, with recognisable architecture, and briefer. Once before, in Symphony No. 3, Martinů had produced a three-movement composition and here he returns to the plan of making the central Larghetto serve as slow movement and Scherzo. The opening movement falls into five sections – Adagio alternating with Allegro – but is not a rondo. The structure is built on pace, not material, and the contrasting of five slow and quick episodes finds a precedent at least in Beethoven's Piano Sonata, Opus 13, in his String Quartet, Opus 130 and in the first movement of César Franck's D minor Symphony. However, the essential difference is that Martinů knits his five sections together much more organically by his technique of continuous musical growth, which is based on a three-note motif presented in the opening thirty bars or so. Despite the composer's organic thinking, the Czech character of the music shines through, and is brought forcibly to mind in bar 86 where the melodic contour seems to have been influenced by Skřivánek's First-Act aria in Smetana's *The Secret*. The Larghetto middle movement is episodic with a semiquaver ritornello figure alternating with more relaxed sections in longer note values. Here the music displays a neo-classical, almost Stravinsky-like, character, and shows Martinů's complete freedom in his use of the bar line. In the Finale the composer returns to the idea of juxtaposing slow and quick sections, with germinal material drawn from the same three-note pattern he had used for metamorphosis in the opening movement of the Third Symphony. In the Fifth this is built into an ever-changing mosaic of sound, which helps to make it the most convincing finale of the Symphonies. The feeling and character of this Symphony strike a new note, and though Martinů does not cover quite as wide a field of styles as he does in the Fourth, in the Fifth he accomplished what he had been striving to write over a number of years. For the composer this was the end of the search, and there was little point in continuing along similar lines. The time had come to make a break.

In February 1945, Slovakia was liberated. Two months later Bratislava was free and by May German forces were driven from Prague. In August postal services were re-established with Europe and Martinů spent days writing to Polička and Prague. His first thought was to return home, but though he had made contact with Czechoslovakia the news he began to receive was not always good. In Polička both his brother and sister were safe, but his mother had died the year before. From Prague came word that Stanislav Novák, shattered by the loss of his wife and children in the Auschwitz gas chamber, had died of a broken heart months before the Armistice. For Martinů a return to Czechoslovakia with neither mother nor devoted friend to welcome him seemed hard. He decided to take a holiday to Cape Cod where he hoped to put his ideas in order. In between he relaxed by writing the lyrical *Czech Rhapsody* for violin and piano (dedicated to Kreisler), a Sonata for flute and piano, the finale of which is said to have been inspired by the song of a whippoorwill, and a cycle of sixteen *Polkas* and *Études* for solo piano. Despite his new surroundings Martinů was ill at ease. He longed to be left on his own and wondered in which direction he should turn. While admitting that he owed America a great deal he was naturally drawn towards Prague, but uppermost in his mind was what the future held for him in Czechoslovakia after so long an absence. He returned to New York in September to find a letter offering him the Professorship in the Master Class of Composition at the Prague Conservatoire. This was beyond Martinů's wildest dreams, and he immediately cabled his acceptance; but by some quirk of fate he was to hear nothing officially from Prague until November 1946.

For months he waited in a state of uncertainty – uncertainty which slowly turned to despair. Feeling better able to work from a European base, Martinů decided to return to Paris, but a week before his departure Koussevitzky suggested he should lecture at the Berkshire Summer Music School at Tanglewood again. Though Martinů did not wish to be separated from his wife, the offer was tempting, not least for its financial remuneration, and it was agreed that the composer should join Charlotte in Paris when his teaching commitment was over. With the score and parts of his Fifth Symphony already corrected, Martinů hoped to devote his afternoons and evenings at Tanglewood to an orchestral composition commissioned by Paul Sacher, who was planning to mark the occasion of the Twentieth Anniversary of the founding of the Basle Chamber Orchestra with a festival of new works. Stravinsky had agreed to write a Concerto for String Orchestra, Honegger was preparing his Fouth Symphony and Martinů had promised a three-movement work in the style of a concerto grosso. He had begun to sketch the *Toccata e Due Canzoni,* as the piece was to be called, in March 1946, but had made little headway with the second *Canzona* in New York. In Tanglewood he hoped to forge ahead, but at the start of the course he had an accident which not only prevented him from teaching, but made composition impossible. Returning late at night on 25 July, the composer stumbled in the darkness of his room and fell from a second-floor balcony to the ground-floor below. Unconscious, he was discovered by a cook who rushed him to hospital where he laid in a coma for two days. On examination Martinů was found to have serious head and ear injuries resulting from a cracked skull. He was confined to bed for five weeks and only at the end of August was able to convalesce in Vermont. Here he slowly learned to walk again, for following the fall he had lost his sense of balance; but most disturbing were the buzzing noises in his head which were to plague him for many months, with partial deafness in the right ear. How often at this time must he have compared his condition with that of Smetana? For weeks he suffered continual headaches. He was nervous, experienced difficulty in holding a pen and found all movement an effort. His doctors advised him not to undertake any journey, so a return to Europe was clearly out of the question. Depressed, Martinů tried to forget himself in composition, but now he was unable to concentrate for more than a couple of hours each day, and in this condition he slowly reworked the *Toccata* and completed both *Canzoni* by the middle of October. Despite its skilfully-written appearance, the score somehow falls short of the standard set by the composer's most significant works. The *Toccata e Due Canzoni* belongs to Martinů's maturity and shows him developing complex musical structures in concerto grosso style most convincingly, but neither of the *Canzoni* present much musical contrast and what seems to be lacking is a sustained breadth of imagination and ready invention. Originally Martinů had planned to follow the *Toccata* with two light and gay dances, but in the event the music assumed other characteristics. The first *Canzona* emerged as a doleful lament while the second is a deeply-felt fantasia in which the expression is tragic. Somehow the total effect makes less impact than it should, and *Canzona* No. 2 in particular lacks cohesion. Where, for example, the earlier pages are vehement, dissonant and percussive, the coda is full of gloom and the optimism with which Martinů's last movements generally close is entirely absent. The *Toccata e Due Canzoni* is disappointing. Though the state of the composer's mind is not known during the time of its composition, the marked difference between the earlier pages of the score and those at the end suggest that his accident had taken a greater toll of his critical faculties than might at first have been suspected. Certainly his return to writing for chamber orchestra is not wholly convincing as demonstrated here.

In the three years following his illness there was a decline, both in the quality and quantity of Martinů's compositions. The lovely String Quartet No. 6, written between October and December 1946, is an example of music conceived without full strength. If the Fifth Quartet is the most intellectual of his output, then the Sixth marks a certain retreat from the rigours and austerity of the previous quartets. This is not to suggest that it is a less personal work. It is unmistakably Martinů, but its utterance had been tempered, the textures simplified and the mood muted. The opening movement is modal, and the episodic Andante is concerned with the presentation and variation of two contrasted ideas, but suffers from long-windedness, while the last movement serves for scherzo and finale. It opens with a boisterous dance which may well have a folk song origin. Between bars 30 and 70 Martinů suggests a Trio with corresponding lightness of texture, but his return to the Scherzo is cut short by a vigorous polka which develops into an exciting rondo.

In November 1946, Charlotte Martinů returned to New York to find her husband much changed. Following the death of her mother she had been detained in France for months longer than she intended, and though Rudolf Firkušný had sent regular reports on the composer's condition she had been held up even longer on account of a French dock strike. Five months had passed since the accident and she now discovered a different Martinů from the one she had left in May. He had aged considerably and was noticeably more withdrawn. He was irritable, short with his friends and troubled by the slightest noise or disturbance. Most of all he was concerned by the mounting hospital bills which had to be met. With little money in the bank and only occasional royalties coming in there seemed no alternative but for Charlotte Martinů to take up her needle again, and before long she was installed in a New York garment factory where she was obliged to stay for the next five years in order to make ends meet. Meanwhile, Martinů had instructed his solicitor to claim compensation for the injuries he had sustained in Tanglewood, but after months of litigation he was awarded a sum that barely covered half the medical costs. Life at this time was gloomy; but on 14 November, after a silence of fourteen months, Martinů at last received word from Prague confirming his appointment, not at the Conservatoire as he had previously been led to expect, but at the Academy of Music and Dramatic Art. Despite this unexpected promotion, no positive move was made, for Martinů's doctors forbade any journey to Europe; and even by May 1947, he was still unfit to travel for the First Prague Spring Festival, at which Rafael Kubelík planned to give the world première of the Fifth Symphony and Paul Sacher the first Czech performance of the *Double Concerto*. Since Martinů was obliged to stay in New York, his wife flew to Prague to represent him. There she began the unenviable task of looking for suitable living accommodation, for the composer had every intention of taking up the Academy teaching post the following year. Through friends, Charlotte Martinů discovered that Count Collerado Mansfield was prepared to turn his castle at Zbiroh, on the outskirts of the city, into an artists' colony and was willing to put it at the disposal of needy Czech painters and musicians. Martinů, whose works were warmly received at the Festival, unquestionably qualified for consideration, and it was agreed that a flat would be ready during the summer of 1948. The prospects of living on Czech soil again spurred him to take a greater interest in composition, for the year (1946-7) had been unproductive. Only three scores, all of them chamber pieces, had appeared. A set of wispy and well-meaning *Madrigals* for violin and viola, and a graceful Quartet for oboe, viola, piano and cello, modestly pay tribute to Mozart, while the Seventh String Quartet, sub-titled 'Concerto da Camera', records Martinů's enthusiasm for the music of Haydn. The Seventh Quartet is the first of a number of works culminating in the Haydnesque *Sinfonia Concertante* (1949) and the Piano Trio in D minor (1950) that belongs to Martinů's 'classical period'. Unlike any of the earlier String Quartets, the Seventh displays a simplicity of form, harmonic expression and transparency of texture. It is a happy, unassuming work which nicely demonstrates Martinů's germinal technique in the outer movements and displays a sustained breadth of invention in the lyrical, Dvořákian Andante. The light-weight finale confirms that the composer's style was in a process of simplification – a state which pervades the Third Piano Concerto on which Martinů was also engaged at this time.

As early as 1945 Rudolf Firkušný had asked the composer to write a concerto especially for him, but with various scores on hand Martinů had not been able to oblige. Now in the autumn of 1947 he felt the urge to write something Czech with which to celebrate his return home – and why not a concerto that would be optimistic, in bright major keys and with an appealing lilt throughout? Unfortunately the ideas for the concerto did not come to Martinů with his usual speed and facility and in the event he produced a determined work,

intense and predominantly in minor keys. In writing this Piano Concerto Martinů was consciously looking back to *Juliette,* hoping to recreate the lush romantic phrases from the opera which had made it
a favourite among his children. To this extent the instrumentation of
the two compositions is similar, and quotations of the 'Moravian cadence'
from the opera certainly suggest the earlier score; but the marked
Brahms-like quality of some of the piano writing contradicts the dreamworld of *Juliette* altogether. For the music of Brahms Martinů, it seems,
had little sympathy, yet curiously it pervades the Second and Third
Piano Concertos and is strongly felt in the finale of the Third Cello
Sonata as well. The opening movement of the Concerto, dramatic
and full of purpose, is followed by a meditative lament and by a polka
which tries to be happy but does not convince; and the return of the
powerful first movement opening in the finale must be regarded as
more than a gesture on the composer's part to create formal unity. A
cloud seems to hang over the music – a cloud which may have
gathered following the sudden death of Jan Masaryk on 10 March
1948. Years before, Jan Masaryk had befriended Martinů when he was
struggling for recognition in Prague. Later, despite the composer's move
to Paris, the two friends had remained in touch, and when, as Foreign
Minister in President Beneš's Government, Masaryk had travelled to
New York in the spring of 1945 for the inauguration of the United
Nations, he spent some time with Martinů before returning to Prague
in July. It was the last time the two men were to meet. In March of
1948 Martinů was so deeply grieved by Masaryk's death that the new
Concerto now assumed a special significance, with the opening notes of
Dvořák's *Requiem* deliberately woven into the textures of the second
movement. With the setting up of a new regime in Czechoslovakia on
25 February 1948, it became clear that Martinů could not easily return
to a Prague which was no longer free. Feeling unable to accept Communist policies, he decided with reluctance to stay in North America.

28. Martinů and his wife Charlotte in 1931.

29. Charlotte Martinů, the painter Jan Zrzavý, Martinů, and the poet Vítězslav Nezval in 1934.

30. *The Plays of Mary*; scene from the Brno production of *Sister Pasqualina*, 1935.

31. *The Plays of Mary*; scene from the Brno production of *Mariken de Nimèque*, 1935.

7 America: 1948-53

By the summer of 1948 Martinů was fit enough to holiday in Europe, but the Europe he discovered had changed since the dark days of 1940. In these eight years, he too, had changed. He was nearing sixty, but appeared much older. As a newly-registered American citizen he had come to France to consult specialists about his hearing, but the return to the land of culture and tradition did little to initiate a new period of creative composition. Earlier in the year he had completed two piano pieces, *Les Bouquinistes du Quai Malaquais*, a souvenir of his pre-war walks in Paris, and *The Fifth Day of the Fifth Moon*, a tribute to the Chinese wife of the composer Alexandre Tcherepnin. In addition he had produced a set of seven *Czech Madrigals*, and for the Martha Graham Dance Company a ballet called *The Strangler*, which is based on the theme of Oedipus and the Sphinx. With an occasional reference to the composer himself, in such lines as 'child of the tower and light', the libretto by Eric Hawkins and Robert Fitzgerald is on a low level, while the music is memorable only for Martinů's receptive use of Mexican percussion including deer hooves, rattles, logs and metal discs.

After three months' holiday Martinů returned to the States. It was September, and the time when he should have been teaching in Czechoslovakia, but instead of Prague he found himself at Princeton, where he became Visiting Professor of Composition for the next three years. Since his appointment was on a part-time basis he was glad to lecture at the Mannes Academy in New York for one day a week and to teach privately. Obviously his time for actual composition was limited, and in 1949 he produced only five new scores. The *Barcarolle* and *Bagatelles*, both for solo piano, are trivial and the *Mazurka Nocturne* for oboe, two violins and cello is a *pièce d'occasion* written at the request of UNESCO to celebrate the death of Chopin. With *Three Czech Dances* for two pianos, however, Martinů produced a work of greater significance. Somehow he had always seemed more relaxed when writing for two concert grands, and usually responded to the variety of sound these instruments could produce. Here each of the dances becomes a vehicle for experimental colour, not percussive, but chattering, dry sonorities, often in brittle seconds and ninths similar to those which distinguish the outer movements of the Concerto for Two Pianos. In the *Dances* folk idiom and melodic movement in parallel thirds and sixths

H

give the music a typical Czech feeling, while the brilliant and often demanding piano writing place the set above Martinů's average at this time.

The work to which Martinů devoted most of his attention in 1949 was the *Sinfonia Concertante* for solo violin, oboe, bassoon, cello and orchestra. From his own programme it seems that the composer had been haunted by the memory of a pre-war performance of Haydn's *Sinfonia Concertante* and only in Princeton was he able to examine the score which was to inspire his own *Sinfonia*. Martinů's note leads us to expect a certain degree of plagiarism but, apart from identical solo instrumentation, similar key schemes and tempo indications, there is little in his score which could be directly attributed to Haydn's influence, except that both works look back to a pre-classical era. In their own language both composers were attempting to revive the traditions of the Baroque Concerto. Both artists were concerned with the problems of contrasting a group of solo instruments against a larger orchestral force and both saw the Sinfonia as an ideal testing ground. Martinů's score belongs to the period when his style was in a process of simplification and here harmony, line and texture are matched by a clarity of form and lucidity of instrumentation. The solo writing is well focused but since the solo instruments vary greatly in technical possibilities Martinů elects to use them either in pairs or as a four-part ensemble.

The concerto grosso principles of the *Sinfonia Concertante* are continued in the Concerto for Two Violins, written in 1950 for the Beal twins. The Concerto is really an extension of the form set by the *Duo Concertante* of 1937, though here the expression is more lyrical, the underlying harmony less astringent. A similar process of simplification is to be found in the *Sinfonietta La Jolla,* ordered by the Musical Arts Society of La Jolla, the Californian town near San Diego. A condition of the commission was that the music should be tuneful and easy on the ear, and in writing his piece Martinů decided on the form of a three-movement divertimento for small orchestra with obbligato piano. The *Sinfonietta* breaks no new ground. In fact it looks back to the Fifth Symphony with an obvious quotation of the folk-song theme which had been put to good use in his finale there. The second movement gives Martinů the chance of writing a pastoral fantasia on Czech folk tunes, while the last, an attractive rondo, might well have been styled 'homage to Haydn'.

The spirit of Haydn's music also pervades the Piano Trio No. 2, written to celebrate the opening of the Haydn Library in Cambridge, Massachusetts in May 1950. Here Martinů emphasises a healthy respect for tradition by giving his Trio the key signature of D minor; but this

is only superficial, for each movement follows a definite system of progressive tonality, the outer ones resolving in B flat. In other respects
the work is more conventional. The first movement is in sonata form
with a recapitulation section implied rather than restated. The Andante
displays to good effect Martinů's technique of developing musical para-
graphs from minute note patterns, while the rondo finale, more rhythmic
than melodic, contains the most memorable pages of the score, possibly
because it is the movement least indebted to Haydn.

With various commissions on his desk, and frequent performances
of his Symphonies and Concertos being given on the radio and in the
concert hall, Martinů was becoming recognised as a forceful figure on
the American musical scene. Gone were the days when he was regarded
merely as a nostalgic purveyor of Czech folk music. But despite his
growing reputation he was no nearer to accepting the American way
of life than he had been nine years before. He still felt ill at ease. He
complained of being swallowed up by the all-American routine. For
him New York was one vast, monstrous sky-scraper. He deplored the
mechanical world around him. He reacted violently to the humdrum
dullness of city life. He had little opportunity for contemplation or
for coming to terms with himself, and there were no quiet retreats
where he could seek inspiration. Books were still his best friends and
only in the second-hand bookshops of Twelfth Street could he find
relief in the art and literature of the old world and the old life. For
Martinů, who had loved cities like Prague and Paris, the feeling for
American towns turned to hate : 'I am sick for home and yearn for our
hills! My work is that of a Czech tied to the homeland by a cord
nothing can cut. I detest America! How I long to escape!' For Martinů
there was no escape and no act of creation could exorcise his state of
estrangement. Nevertheless, in composition he found some peace of
mind, and now work after work began to appear at an incredible rate.
Fluent though most of these pieces are, they are often little more
than undistinguished examples of a composer's facility in putting pen
to paper. The Piano Trio No. 3, for example, is sub-titled 'grand', but
this applies more to its scale than to its content; the *Intermezzo*, a
cheerful piece of orchestral music, is neither experimental nor re-
actionary and remains pleasantly unremarkable; the *Serenade,* for two
clarinets, violin, viola and cello, flirts agreeably but says nothing new;
and if a set of *Pastorales* for five recorders, clarinet, two violins and cello
has won a certain acclaim, it is not for its elfin shyness or stylised charm
but because it is dedicated to the Trapp family, later of *Sound of Music*
fame.

Martinů was now sixty-one, and though he felt the need to relinquish his post at Princeton, there was no retirement for him. His mind was teeming with new ideas, his mail full of requests for new works. And following the successful revival of his opera *Comedy on the Bridge* in New York on 28 May 1951, he even received an invitation to write a musical for Broadway. But the dramatic work on which he eventually decided was far from suitable for Broadway and was, in fact, not even intended for the stage. In June, Martinů accepted a commission to write a television opera, the subject being taken from one of Tolstoy's *Tales for the People* called *What Men Live By*.

Martinů designed his new chamber opera for seven characters with a small choir and orchestra, and by selecting a morality he was deliberately returning to the type of subject which had formed the basis of his *Plays of Mary* seventeen years before. Not surprisingly the two operas have much in common. Again, action is suggested rather than played and realism is relegated to stylised gesture. A narrator (out of vision this time) introduces the characters and comments upon their reactions. The dream element, which had played an important part in *Sister Pasqualina,* returns in this score, though here it is Martin Avdeitsch, an old cobbler, who experiences a vision and is told to prepare for the coming of the Lord. Recalling how Christ moved among ordinary people, talking to them and giving them food, Martin decides to play host first to Stepanitch, an old soldier, then a mother and her child, and finally to a beggar woman. In the final pages the three characters return to Martin in a dream and sing from St. Matthew's Gospel :

> I was hungry and you gave me meat,
> I was thirsty and you gave me drink,
> I was a stranger and you took me in.
> In so much as you have done it unto one of
> the least of my brethren, you have done it also to me.

The opera ends with Martin's revelation that the Saviour had visited him.

The process of simplification which has been noted in connection with the *Sinfonia Concertante* and Second Piano Trio continues in *What Men Live By*. Here Martinů's expression is direct and matched by an instrumental accompaniment that is always transparent. The five scenes are not continuous but Martinů adopts a system of motifs to unify them and to represent the cobbler and his visitors. However, they are not used to give the music a symphonic force. On the contrary the score has a distinct chordal structure in which polyphony is pruned to a minimum. With its oratorio-like qualities, *What Men Live By* does not make a very serious contribution to the development of television opera. Apart from the obvious superimposition devices used for Martin's visions the score cannot claim to have furthered the cause of opera on television as the works of Menotti may have done. If Martinů was treading his way cautiously through the complexities of television in *What Men Live By*, in his next opera, also written for television, he was only marginally more adventurous. For years the composer had been on the look-out for a subject for a comedy, but Klicpera's *Comedy on the Bridge* had been little more than an amusing flirtation and had not provided what he really wanted. Admittedly André Wurmser's text to *Alexandre bis* (1937) had had potential. Alexandre, deciding to test the fidelity of his wife, Armanda, shaves off his beard so as to resemble his cousin and then returns unrecognised to seduce his own wife. Until now Armanda has faithfully rejected the amorous proposals of Oscar, an admirer; but with the arrival of Alexandre II (her husband) she begins to weaken and ignores the warning of Alexandre's portrait which springs to life admonishing her to be true only to the real Alexandre. Oscar returns with renewed ardour. The portrait declares the old maxim 'There's never two, that there isn't a third' and Armanda and Oscar elope leaving the shaven Alexandre with his wife's ironic laughter ringing in his ears. For all its similarities to Milhaud's *Le Pauvre Matelot* (written ten years before) Martinů's score never really catches the spirit of the libretto. The music is fluent enough (there's even a quotation or two from a jaunty music hall song of the Twenties), and the vocal lines are eminently singable, but somehow the invention is mechanical; and the persistent use of the piano as a chattering continuo becomes tiresome after a while. Conscious of his shortcomings in this direction, Martinů decided to try his hand at opera buffa once again, and in 1952 turned to Gogol's *The Matchmaker*, adapting the libretto himself and reducing the three-act original to two. But again the result is not convincing and the music is sometimes limp. Martinů's aceptance of arias, recitatives and formal ensembles marks a moving away from the pattern set by *Juliette,* and in details of characterisation *The Marriage*, as the opera came to be called, shows little development over his earlier scores. Fyokla, the matchmaker, Ivan, the government official, Anuchkin and Zhevakin, the retired officers, are all presented in humorous fashion, but remain cardboard stiff. Nevertheless, Martinů parodies their conventions of courtship in a sequence of waltzes which luxuriate in a wealth of happy ideas. The opera also contains a number of witty touches, including an obvious quotation from Mendelssohn's *Wedding March,* but generally, the humour stems from the satire not the music – and only for Podholyosin who, in good *Bartered Bride* tradition, develops a stutter as he approaches Agafya does the score spring to life and reflect the brilliance of the original.

The Marriage was written in the space of seven weeks and the score reveals traces of the composer's haste. This was inevitable, for apart from studio production dates, Martinů had other deadlines to meet, other commissions to complete. The *Rhapsody Concerto* for viola and orchestra was sketched and scored in the space of a month; the lovely Cello Sonata No. 3 was written in just over three weeks; two sets of Choruses for women's voices were turned out in a matter of days, and a three-movement Concerto for Piano, Violin and Orchestra which the composer had promised Benno and Sylvia Rabinof was ready for performance within three months. But the work which took up most of Martinů's time was a new Symphony written for Charles Munch to celebrate the seventy-fifth anniversary of the Boston Symphony Orchestra. Along with Britten, Milhaud, Petrassi, Copland, Villa-Lobos and Martinů's own pupil from Tanglewood days, Leonard Bernstein, the composer agreed to write something for the Orchestra and in so doing returned to work on a large symphonic canvas for the first time in six years. After producing one symphony annually between 1942 and 1946 Martinů had written no more. The break could possibly be attributed to external circumstances, to his serious accident and to subsequent ill health; but it is also likely that he felt there was no point in producing symphonies on the lines he had so far used. He approached the symphony therefore with a different outlook and originally intended not to link it with his symphonic series by calling it 'Symphony'. It was only respect for the memory of Berlioz which caused him to abandon his first title – *New Fantastic Symphony* – and rename it *Fantaisies symphoniques*, which goes some way to explain the character of the work. In spite of his wish to make a break with the past, the break is by no means complete. The score falls into three movements, as did Symphonies Nos. 3 and 5, though in fairness to the composer it is more to the point to call these movements fantasies. Each of these fantasies is filled with Martinů's marks of style and none is more prominently displayed than his technique of musical development from germinal themes. But where in the earlier symphonies he had used several germs to support the weight of each movement, here he carries virtuosity to a new level by fashioning this astonishingly varied work on a three-note motif and sustaining each of the fantasies on the same slender material. The originality of the score and its newness in Martinů's development can be seen in the extremes to which the composer can push tendencies already long displayed. After years of strenuous activity, he had mastered a highly original style which, by the time he came to the *Fantaisies symphoniques,* could be used exactly as he wished. He could speak as he chose, following his whims, changing his mood, reflecting the caprices of his thoughts in a spontaneous, natural way.

In the first movement Martinů imposes an external framework by the use of an impressive Lento section which acts as a prelude and postlude to a set of ingenious variations. As muted strings and flutes engage in a riot of insect-like figuration, two muted trumpets intone a three-note motif which forms the theme on which the *Fantaisies* are built. Here is a sonority that begins where Bartók's *Concerto for Orchestra* stopped. From this busy texture emerges a solo cello, which adds one note to the motif and translates it into a transposed version of the opening of Dvořák's *Requiem,* a motif Martinů had already used in the finale of the Third Symphony and elsewhere. Until the return of the opening Lento material, Martinů builds a series of continuous, yet widely differing and fragmentary variations on this theme, treating it in augmentation, diminution, as a bass, rhythmically altered, transformed into two grotesque marches and orchestrated with the greatest variety and skill. The central movement is a Scherzo in spirit and depends more on rhythm than melody for its momentum; but wherever the interest of texture or rhythm gives way to melody, the *Requiem* motif from the first movement is prominent. Here, however, Martinů allows himself one extra fantasy. With a feeling of nostalgia for his native land he quotes a phrase from his *Field Mass,* which with its patriotic associations seems to underline the composer's longing for home. A similar quotation is heard in the last movement where the original three-note motif, now inverted, is extended to resemble the cadence figure from the St. Wenceslas Chorale which Martinů had used to good advantage in the First and Third Symphonies, where he recorded his reaction to the horrors of World War II and his sympathy for the victims in occupied Europe. From a slow and deeply nostalgic opening, Martinů proceeds through a series of rapidly changing episodes and widely differing variations in what is possibly the most complex movement in his whole output. While it is possible to draw a parallel between the form of the finale and the opening movement, in the last movement the changes of mood are more rapid, the mode of composition more contrapuntal, the whole more fantastic. Also in the finale Martinů allows himself an additional fantasy – a quotation from his opera, *Juliette,* which is itself a fantasy.

The references to Dvořák's *Requiem,* the St. Wenceslas Chorale, the *Field Mass* and *Juliette* suggest that for Martinů the *Fantaisies symphoniques* had a strong personal significance, and in a letter to Miloš

Šafránek he said that the work had a very private meaning and that only he, Martinů, knew it. Unlike the String Quartet No. 5, the music has no known extra-musical stimulus, but is decidedly Czech and may have sprung from the composer's intense longing to return to Europe. Whatever the force behind the *Fantaisies symphoniques*, the score remains a deeply felt and highly charged record of Martinů's development as a symphonist. It is an outstanding work, and its originality was recognised when the New York Critics' Circle awarded the composer their Diploma for the best orchestral work performed in America during 1955. Since then the *Fantaisies symphoniques* has become part of the standard orchestral repertoire on both sides of the Atlantic and has even been adapted by Kenneth Macmillan for the third part of his ballet *Anastasia*. With the *Fantaisies symphoniques* Martinů closed a chapter in his life. The score was not only the high-water mark of his American sojourn but also the last work he wrote in America for nearly two and a half years. In fact it was in Paris that Martinů put the finishing touches to the score and there that he decided to strike out the parts for three pianos which had featured prominently in the original first movement.

On 5 May 1953 Martinů sailed for Europe. North America had been kind to him, had been his home for twelve years – at least seven longer than he had intended. Circumstances, political, financial and medical, had prolonged his stay and the memories he was taking with him were mixed. In the United States he had found safety, won recognition as a teacher, fame as a composer; but in return he had been obliged to surrender his Czech nationality for American citizenship. For Martinů this had been the hardest thing to accept. His roots had been firmly and deeply set in Czechoslovakia and in France, and these were the two countries where his affections lay. What else could he feel as he approached the shores of Europe again except that he was nearing home?

8 A Spiritual Homecoming

O Praga! quando te aspiciam?

Thus Hector Berlioz, who in his sixth letter to Humbert Ferrand, and in circumstances far different from those of the Czech composer, anticipated by nearly a hundred years the question Martinů must often have asked himself during his exile in the United States. Now, in May 1953, he was returning to Europe, but uppermost in his mind was the same thought: *O Prague! When shall I see you again?*

It was not Prague that welcomed Martinů but at least it was Paris, his adopted home, and she greeted him with all the freshness of a breath of spring. It was good to be back, good to be staying in the Avenue Mozart, not far from where he had lived in the dark days of 1940. At sixty-four, Martinů was looking forward to enjoying the fruits of life. After thirteen years it was reassuring to see old friends, to know he had not been forgotten. However, he badly needed rest, and after fulfilling an obligation in Brussels (he had been nominated to the jury for the Queen Elizabeth of the Belgians Competition) he travelled to his wife's home at Vieux-Moulin in the depths of the French forests, where he rediscovered the peace and peasant solitude he had so long sought in North America. After a couple of months the Martinůs moved to the Côte d'Azur, and in a small villa on Mont Boron, in the Cimiez district above Nice, they enjoyed the natural, simple atmosphere they had known there in the autumn of 1937. For Martinů, Nice had always held a special attraction, and in the warm Mediterranean climate he hoped composition would not be the problem it had sometimes been in North America. Now his moments were filled by sketching musical ideas, which were not simply discarded but stored at the back of his mind for a new opera.

Hoping to find a text for a large-scale dramatic work commissioned by the John Simon Guggenheim Memorial Foundation, Martinů spent most of his evenings reading, and after several months convinced himself he had found the ideal subject in Georges Neveux's *Plaint contre l'inconnu*. Secretly he believed he could turn this into a second *Juliette*. But for all his enthusiasm, Martinů had failed to recognise that generally the happiest length for an operatic source is the short story of the type of Merimée's *Carmen*, the Abbé Prévost's *Manon Lescaut* or more recently James's *Turn of the Screw*. So expansive is the nature of music that ordinary novel length creates serious problems of compression and in Neveux's complex argument about five unhappy individuals who plan to commit suicide, but first file an accusation against God, there could be no question of a systematic or clearly consecutive treatment. Nevertheless Martinů persevered and after three months had the first Act – all seventy-three pages – complete. Here the opera stopped. Suddenly the composer grasped that the text contained too many words. He was describing everything but revealing nothing and the result was a form of musical journalism, apt to each stage of the drama maybe, but unable to enhance or to concentrate in musical form a character or particular situation. Three months behind schedule, Martinů began to search for a new play and before long he stumbled on Goldoni's *La Locandiera.* Though this was not the drama he had set his heart on, there was nothing in the Guggenheim commission which precluded a comedy; and while *Mirandolina,* as he eventually called the opera, is a conventional theatre-piece, it would be wrong to regard it as a 'second best' subject, in spite of the fact that he had selected it with his back against a wall. Ever since 1937 when he had rejected Anouilh's *Bal de voleurs* as a possible operatic plot, Martinů had been on the lookout for another comedy and in *La Locandiera* he found what he had been searching for. The three acts are concerned with the schemes of an attractive Florentine hostess to win the admiration of one of her guests, the Knight of Ripafrata, a confirmed woman-hater. After several attempts Mirandolina secures his love, but promptly rejects it along with that of other suitors in order to marry Fabrizio, a waiter, whose fidelity she wanted to test.

It was appropriate that Martinů's first opera to Italian words should have been written on the Riviera, for the score is full of light and warmth quite missing in *The Marriage.* For the composer, *Mirandolina* was the end of a three-thousand dollar search, and the attractive waltzes, lilting intermezzos, and colourful Saltarello admirably capture the spirit of Goldoni's comedy, though, as always with Martinů, the music is Czech-sounding rather than Italian. Sketched and scored in just over six months, the music nowhere suggests the sense of haste which marred *The Marriage.* Here the invention is of a higher order, and if too many casual ideas gain admission and prolong the comedy, Martinů compensates with nicely scaled arias, lyrical duets and lively ensembles, treated with a healthy respect for tradition. In the Knight of Ripafrata and Mirandolina he found a pair of decorative tragic and comic masks, and by regarding them as singers in a singers' opera he had no need to excuse himself for writing vocal display. In Act I (Scene 6), the hoyden-ish Mirandolina is given a brilliant coloratura aria which seems to make her the Florentine cousin of Rossini's Susanna, and the lyricism of her utterances sounds no less genuine for their obvious debt to *The Barber of Seville*. In fact the characterisation is so sympathetic that when the subject of fidelity moves her in musical lines almost identical to the 'Moravian cadence' of another Martinů heroine – Juliette – there is no apparent loss of identity. In *Mirandolina* Martinů produced his most successful comedy. It holds a place in his output similar to that of *The Betrothal in a Monastery* in Prokofiev's, except that in the Martinů the humour is less hollow, the situations not so contrived.

After working on a major score Martinů's habit was to relax, but instead of gardening, reading or taking an excursion he preferred to spend his time writing pieces which were not intended as compositions, but which were compositions nevertheless. These trifles were often intended for his own pleasure or for that of his friends and over the years he had produced many charming miniatures such as the song cycles *Nový Špaliček* (*New Špaliček*) and *Písničky na jednu stránku* (*Songs on One Page*) which had proved to be gems of real worth. With *Mirandolina* behind him Martinů now began a number of vocal and choral items, the first intended as a tribute to his birthplace, the Polička Tower. In *Hymnus k svatému Jakubu* (*Hymn to St. James*) to words by Jaroslav Daněk, priest at St. James in the 1950s, Martinů wrote a patriotic song of thanksgiving for three solo voices, mixed choir and organ. Here he opened his heart to the Vysočina he had not seen since 1938. The music is unpretentious, but it served to stimulate the composer's nostalgic remembrances of home, and in *Petrklíč* (*The Primrose*), intended for friends in Brno, he produced a sequence of duets for soprano and alto voices accompanied by violin and piano which sing unashamedly of the Czech culture and tradition in which he had been bred. This cycle celebrates in a scattered, fragmentary way the loyalty and love which, in a more systematic and monumental form, Smetana expressed in *Má vlast* (*My Country*). What Martinů writes here is genuinely folk-inspired. All five pieces are marked with a freshness and simplicity and in 'Poledne' ('Noonday'), with its polka rhythms and apparently artless three-bar phrase groups, it is hard to imagine another composer who has been more successful in employing art to conceal art. Notwithstanding the uninhibited gaiety of this song, it is the beautiful 'Žaloba' ('Plaint') which makes the most appeal. Here the marriage of voice and accompaniment is of the happiest: simple yet well-devised, with a support that heightens Martinů's modally flavoured melodies. In *Petrklíč* he reached a pinnacle of vocal writing which, if he did not surpass, he at least equalled in *The Mount of Three Lights*.

The idea of writing a cantata was not new, and during the war Martinů seriously considered a liturgical text on the basis of Cavalieri's *Sacra Rappresentazione di Anima e di Corpo*. For one reason or another the project had never materialised and it was only in November 1954 that the composer could bring himself to write this very personal essay on episodes in the life of Christ. After an organ prelude has set the tranquillity for the Passion of Our Lord, the Narrator recites a prayer. Tenors and basses relate the Christmas story and the organ directs our attention from the Nativity to Christ's agony. We are now in the Garden of Gethsemene and the choir meditate on the words: 'O, my Father, take away this cup from me; not as I will, but as thou wilt!' The Narrator prepares for the betrayal and over a twenty-bar ostinato the choir shout 'Crucify Him!'. Tenors and basses demand 'Art thou the Christ?'. There is a climactic moment of suspense. The soloist replies 'I am' and the cantata closes with a chorale-like setting of the words: 'O Son of God who created Heaven, Earth and Man in the splendour of his own image.' Martinů's Passion is simple but written with a conviction no less sincere. There is no pious comment as in Bach's arias and chorales, nor does the composer try to suggest the greatness of the theme by the use of impressive harmony or decorated melody. Yet Martinů's directness conceals a profound art. The symmetrical form, organ interludes, the dramatic climax and hymn-like conclusion are impressive in a way that more ambitious writing cannot be.

Though Martinů was by adoption a child of the West he relied upon few Western traditions in his choral music. When it came to writing for a choir he invariably fell back on a number of simple Czech verses welded together with a folk melody, accompanied by a number of supporting chords or their embellishments. Poignant these may be, but they are too closely allied to Bohemian-Moravian folk idiom to have much effect in oratorio. For this reason Martinů turned to the fourth-century Assyrian-Babylonian poem, *The Epic of Gilgamesh*, when he was invited to compose a large-scale work for Paul Sacher's choir in Basle. As early as 1949 Martinů had read about the twelve cuneiform tablets containing *The Epic,* but five years were to pass before he could turn these to account in an oratorio. Originally he had been keen to set those sections of the poem which deal with the Flood, but these were omitted in favour of a three-part picture of Gilgamesh, the legendary King of Ourouk. In Part I, which corresponds to Tablets I and II, we are introduced to Gilgamesh, a solitary figure with neither friend nor relative. His people implore the Goddess Aruru to find a companion for him and in response to their wailings she moulds from clay a warrior called Enkidu. Enkidu is a primitive who lives among the works of nature with only animals as friends, completely ignorant of any other mode of being. Gilgamesh learns of this strange person, and desiring to befriend him, sends a dancer from the Temple of Istar to seduce him and lure him from his simple environment. The King's plan is successful. Enkidu loses his innocence and the animals desert him. Friendless, he follows the girl to the city where his life changes. Now he must work to live, and disillusioned he attacks Gilgamesh. The two warriors fight, but since they are so well matched neither will submit to the other and finally they become friends.

Part II incorporates extracts from Tablets VII, VIII and X and begins with the death of Enkidu. The question of death presents itself to Gilgamesh, who cries bitterly but fails to comprehend that his friend has gone for ever. He fears death himself and begs the Gods to restore Enkidu to him. There is no reply and Gilgamesh begins to search for immortality.

The final Part, 'Invocation', is a setting of Tablet XII and tells how Gilgamesh fails to learn the secret of immortality. Again he makes passionate supplication to the Gods to allow him to see his friend. In response to his plea the earth opens up and the spirit of Enkidu emerges. Gilgamesh asks what he has seen in the other world but there is no reply. With the King's searching enquiries the oratorio ends.

Gilgamesh is unquestionably one of Martinů's most powerful works, but unlike Bartók's *Cantata Profana*, it has a certain lack of cohesion. It could hardly be otherwise; for the episodic nature of the text (in Roy Campbell's English translation) militates against unity. Nevertheless, the oratorio is in the composer's most mature style, and the vocal score gives little idea of the imaginative instrumentation, where deliberately created sonorities match the passionate and sorrowful stretches of beautiful writing. Though the forces called for are modest (oboes, bassoons, horns and tuba are omitted) the orchestra is as much a protagonist in the action as the soloists, speaker and chorus. Much use is made of percussion, and piano and harp playing in combination are put to good effect in the barbaric chorus which depicts the combat between Gilgamesh and Enkidu and ends Part I.

In the choral writing *The Epic of Gilgamesh* shows Martinů at his most enterprising, and throughout he displays a variety of techniques absent in previous works. The chorus engage in delightful counterpoint or massive pillar-like chords. At times they are divided antiphonally, used in bold imitation or employed as part of the orchestra in a series of wordless melismas. But for all its expertise the most memorable sections are those where Gilgamesh implores Enkidu to appear from the dead. Here Martinů's use of the female chorus to produce unearthly wailing, not unlike the howling of the wind, is highly effective. As the chorus implore the God Ea to raise Enkidu from the earth, the voices graphically soar upward in wordless glissandos. The invocation becomes urgent. Chorus and soloists make a barbaric appeal to the heathen deities. An eighteen-fold repetition of a two-bar ostinato leads to the climax – a desperate shriek which flashes across the score like forked lightning. The earth opens and the spirit of Enkidu issues forth to answer Gilgamesh's questions with an enigmatic 'I saw'.

The Epic of Gilgamesh is a work of imagination which bears an interesting resemblance to Honegger's *Le Roi David* in alternating the voice of the speaker with normal oratorio forces, to Holst's setting of the *Rig Veda* in the similarity of its subject and to Walton's *Belshazzar's Feast* in the effect and use of chorus and orchestra.

For *Otvírání studánek* (*The Opening of the Wells*), Martinů's next choral work, there was no obvious model on which he could hang his homespun material, so he turned naturally and instinctively to the childhood dialect of home – Moravian folk idiom. This fitted like a glove the verses Martinů had received in July 1955, on the Czech springtime custom of opening the wells; and the Poličkan poet, Miloslav Bureš, can hardly have realised how these would affect the ageing composer, out of touch with his homeland. Martinů is said to have wept bitterly on reading the poem, which not only aroused memories of youth but made him deeply homesick. From these simple recollections there arose indirectly not one but four chamber cantatas which became the composer's credo, a profound affirmation of all that he held dear in life. Though not intended by Martinů to form a cycle, these pieces have nevertheless been connected as a tetralogy for the obvious reason that they seem to spell out the message of the seasons. *The Opening of the Wells* breathes the air of spring, *Romance z pampelišek* (*Romance of the Dandelions*) suggests summer's greeting, *Legenda z dýmu bramborové nati* (*Legend of the Smoke of Potato Fires*) announces the arrival of autumn and *Mikeš z hor* (*Mikeš From the Mountains*) is a Czech winter tale. When Martinů began composition he had no intention of designing a work on the plan of Vivaldi's or Haydn's *Seasons*: all he realised was that in company with Bureš he was celebrating an indelible memory and unfading love of his native land. Bureš's simple vernacular with its rustic figures of speech and naïve imagery were exactly what was needed to unloose Martinů's deeply felt music. Czech poet and Czech composer shared an identity of feeling. Their affections were fastened on the same geographical spot and their memories nourished similar sentiments. Bureš's *Opening of the Wells* touched a nerve in Martinů who was moved to produce his most nostalgic recollections of home.

The place of this work in Martinů's catalogue can profitably be compared with that of *Juliette;* for it was in the course of writing the opera that the composer found his symphonic style. From *The Opening of the Wells* stem many of the features which distinguish the works of the last years. There is nothing contrived or self-conscious about this adaptation of local folk custom, and the composer matches the directness of the text with a simplicity of line, harmony and instrumental accompaniment which is quite remarkable. The formal scheme is clearly defined with choral passages, recitatives, spoken verse and orchestral sentences integrated into a continuous whole.

The Opening of the Wells is a Maytime custom celebrated in the country between Litomyšl (Smetana's birthplace) and Polička. Today it is as compelling and colourful as it must have been when Martinů observed it in his youth, and when, in Act II of *Špaliček*, he described the children who greet the spring by processing into the Moravian highlands to clear the brooks silted with winter mud. Martinů welcomes us to the Vysočina with a recitation and short instrumental prelude which seems to evoke impressions of the little fiddle and toy drum he used to beat around the gallery of the Polička Tower sixty years before. As the chorus takes up the narrative, one wonders if Martinů is not singing with the children as they pass the Rampart Gate on their way to the hills. Here the music has a childlike simplicity, and moves in the lines of parallel thirds and sixths so typical of Moravian folk music. Martinů's hovering around the third degree of the scale, his natural acceptance of the Mixolydian mode, and his barless phrases with repeated cadential figures stamp his music as unmistakably Czech. The speaker describes how the Queen (solo soprano), elected from the children, is followed by a group of boys who make their way to the forest pools where, armed with rakes and hoes, they release the water. As spring 'like a happy bird begins to sing' the children dance and Martinů captures their enthusiasm in a lively round over a *dudy* (bagpipe) drone. The Queen, addressing the well, casts a spell against witches; and the children exorcise the powers of evil by singing a phrase in honour of the clean pool to make it healthy and strong. A baritone soloist representing the forest spring pensively describes its newfound freedom as it nourishes streams and rivulets. At the words 'I, like you, was born of all this. I take the well-known path and see my home again through hopeful eyes. What does it matter that my days are over and gone, for from one to another we hand down the heavy key and open the doors of home,' the composer himself seems to be speaking; and symbolically the piano intones yet again the theme Martinů had used to represent his homeland in the *Field Mass* in 1939. As the cantata fades with echoes of Moravian folk music, there ends one of the most moving and beautiful panegyrics ever penned for Czechoslovakia. No wonder Martinů was able to write shortly after completing it: 'How lucky I am to be a composer, for through my scores I can speak to the whole world. Thus, I can return home, making a spiritual journey in which distance cannot diminish the sound, music or memories of home.' For Martinů *The Opening of the Wells* was a homecoming, and though the Czech wells of refreshment were miles away, they nourished him to produce *The Romance of the Dandelions,* possibly the most original of all his choral works and certainly the one most intimate in mood. This is the only part of the cycle to be written for unaccompanied mixed choir, yet it is conceived on similar lines to *The Opening of the Wells,* with the equivalent instrumental interludes incorporated into wordless choruses.

It is unlikely that Bureš's poem refers to any genuine folk custom in the Vysočina, for a peasant community dependent upon agriculture for its livelihood is unlikely to have invented a legend in praise of the weed which stifles its crop. The *Romance* is more imaginative than folk-inspired, and in its literary form comes close to a Moravian ballad, verging on a type of written love-song. It tells of a peasant girl who waits seven years for her lover to return from the wars. When he at last comes to her village she does not recognise him and questions whether he has met her betrothed on the field. Smiling, the soldier reveals his identity and embraces his love.

In his setting of Bureš's tender verses, Martinů distils his music into relatively simple lines but allows the textures to be more intricate, with the chorus singing in chords analogous to those in the piano accompaniment of the previous cantata. Again folk idiom lingers, and the *halekačky* (mountain call) returns. The most remarkable features of the score, however, are those where Martinů displays his sensitiveness for musical pictorialism. The way he relishes Bureš's reference to the fluttering of the grey dove, the rustling of leaves and murmuring breezes is delightful, but most striking is the passage describing the soldier's return. As tenors relate the narrative the remainder of the choir tap their fingers on the backs of their chairs to suggest the beat of his approaching drum. Such moments show Martinů's feeling for timbre to be as keen as it had always been and give his music a disarming strength.

Just as impressive is the third cantata, *The Legend of the Smoke from Potato Fires.* By using an accompaniment comprising piano, accordion, recorder, clarinet and horn, Martinů was here consciously

32. Martinů with his brother, sister and mother in 1937.

33. Martinů with Vítězslava Kaprálová and her father in 1938.

34. Martinů's manuscript for the fifth string quartet, dedicated to Vítězslava Kaprálová.

returning to the Czech-sounding chamber group reminiscent of the bands of itinerant musicians that used to frequent Bohemia and Moravia in the eighteenth and nineteenth centuries – an apt touch for a legend which is more generally Czech than coming specifically from the Vysočina. The Legend, which is said to have originated as potato haulms were being burnt in the autumn, describes how Mary, Mother of Christ, steps down from the stained-glass window behind the altar of a small church, adorns herself in a peasant robe and leaves the village to toil on the land. Noticing her absence, the congregation eventually finds her working in the fields. In Martinů's setting a final chorus underlines the moral : 'Mary had no need of churches dark and gloomy or for wax candles when all around her are bright sunflowers and the images of her son in the lads that vigorously mow the hay'.

The mood of this harvest-time cantata is suitably reflective. Melodic lines are serious and the subtle instrumentation evokes a church atmosphere with the accordion used to suggest a distant organ. Throughout, the choral writing is hymn-like with melodies that seem to grow from chorales; and for the episodes where Mary stops before a shrine, Martinů actually takes up an old Czech Pilgrim's Hymn. For the remainder his musical expression is simple and direct with a wealth of two-part counterpoint favouring the Mixolydian mode.

Mikeš from the Mountains, the last of the cycle of cantatas, more closely resembles the first than the middle two, and with an identical accompaniment to that used in *The Opening of the Wells,* the integration of vocal and instrumental passages is achieved with the success that is conspicuous in the first. Only in one respect is there a distinction : here the introductory and concluding sections are sung, not spoken. But whereas *The Opening of the Wells* celebrates an authentic folk custom in such a way that it is the precise musical analogue of the event, *Mikeš from the Mountains* merely perpetuates a legend which is said to have originated around Kadov or Fryšova pod Žákovóu Horóu (Fryšova under Žákov Mountain). The legend describes the exploits of Mikeš, the wily shepherd boy who gets the better of the elements by settling his herd on Fryšova Mountain in such a way that Jack Frost mistakes their white coats for snow and moves to another area, leaving the Vysočina to enjoy a mild winter. Bureš's charming version of the allegory is set to music in masterly fashion. With *dudy* drones, modally-flavoured tunes, the *halekačky* and polka interludes, the Czech authenticity of this score is stamped through and through. But perhaps it is the music's mellowness and feeling of intense nostalgia, conceived out of love for the homeland, which gives this cantata a special place in the composer's catalogue.

With these four chamber cantatas Martinů created a personal and highly successful vehicle for treating the folk customs and legends of the Moravian Highlands. In each of these pieces he speaks as an unselfconscious Czech who had absorbed the idiom of folk art into his very being in such a way that few have been able to equal. In the *Zbojnické písně* (Brigand Songs) he did not seek to find a new idiom but returned to the same source from which he had taken his earlier works. Here he produced a collection of pieces which must be regarded as the pinnacle of his part-song writing. In the *Brigand Songs* Martinů turned to a number of outlaw poems gathered from various regions by Methoděj Florian, who had lived in the Moravian Highlands all his life. The outlaw songs first arose from the experiences of people who had known oppression in an area of the Carpathian Mountains. Gradually the *zbojník* (the brigand from the hills) came to be regarded by the peasants as the protector of the poor – a Czech Robin Hood – who fought against their feudal master's tyranny. Brigand legends spread quickly through the nation and for the serfs the brigand became a hero. They sang of his courage, of his daring, strength and honour, his hatred of traitors, of his militant vigilance and in some cases they even accorded him supernatural powers. Such ideas form the nucleus of an infinite variety of songs and poems. Mostly of a morbid nature, these offer reflective comment on the death of a brigand or pessimistically describe the fate which awaits him at the gallows. Such a poem is 'Stavajú, stavajú šibeničky dvoje' ('They are building gallows'), the third of the ten songs Martinů set for unaccompanied male voices in January 1957.

> They are building gallows, they are building two.
> Johnny, you must decide which of them shall bear you.
> I shall hang on whichever one they select.
> From the crown on my head shall grow a tulip quite erect.
> 'Tulip fine, on which day shall I pluck thee?'
> 'Wait 'till next Sunday, for green shall I then be!'

Not all the songs anticipate death. The fourth, 'Jede Janóšek' ('Johnny rides'), relates how an outlaw defends himself when attacked 'swinging his sword aloft twelve heads roll before the smiter', and 'Pijú chlapci' is a vigorous drinking song. Moments of brigand triumph or exuberance are rare and Martinů seizes on them as a contrast to the predominantly gloomy sentiments of such poems as 'U téj bíléj hory' ('By the White Mountain'). In this cycle Martinů does not merely describe the texts in musical terms: he is inspired by them. His characteristic hovering around the third degree of the scale, sometimes major, sometimes minor, is a recurring feature and he takes pride in incorporating it into the various melismas and mountain calls. There is little contra-puntal writing here, but a variety of texture is achieved by recitatives, solo passages and instrumentally-designed wordless accompaniments of striking originality. While Martinů's debt to the part-song style of Janáček is enormous, it is with Szymanowski's *Songs of Kurpie* (Opus 58) that his *Zbojnické písně* can best be compared. Both composers were writing about brigands, but whereas Szymanowski's made direct contact with the *gorales* (the highlanders of the Tatras) in Zakopane and assumed with great success their improvisatory idiom he was, never-the less, an observer, as Martinů in writing of the *zbojník* in his *Brigand Songs* was not. Martinů's brigands were his contemporaries. He had heard about them and their exploits from childhood and when speaking of them was renewing the bond which bound him to home.

Martinů wrote the four chamber cantatas and the *Brigand Songs* over a period of years in various parts of France, Switzerland and Italy, and these were sent to his native country like greetings from afar. From time to time, however, he was moved to write more than a greeting and for Rafael Kubelík, who like himself had chosen to live abroad, he had long wanted to create something special. Martinů had pro-duced nothing of an orchestral nature since leaving North America, but as a result of an excursion to Perugia in the spring of 1955 there arose the idea of *The Frescoes*, a set of three symphonic movements for large orchestra. Travelling down the Tiber Valley, Martinů discovered the little town of Borgo San Sepolcro, where *The Resurrec-tion* by Piero della Francesca (1420-1490) had been brought to light. Moved by the beauty of this work, Martinů went on to Arezzo, where he spent days in the Church of San Francesco examining Piero's famous frescoes which make up the *Legend of the Holy Cross,* an elaborate history with its roots in the Crusades. Here, in the full excitement of the encounter, Martinů found the substance of all that he wanted to put into music, the peace and colours of nature, the simplicity of form, the philosophy of acceptance and resignation. Piero's frescoes were to inspire Martinů much as Wilhelm von Kaulbach's mural had prompted Liszt to write *Hunnenschlacht* and Mathis Grünewald's ambitious altar-piece at Isenheim had led Hindemith to produce his *Mathis der Maler* Symphony in 1934 and opera in 1938; but though *The Frescoes* find their origin in extra-musical forces, Martinů chose not to depict each of the ten panels as a symphonic poem. Rather it was the solemn, frozen silence of the whole series that he tried to suggest, by approxi-mating in musical terms the emotional state which is aroused in the onlooker by Piero's work. For his first movement Martinů took as his subject a group of views in which the Queen of Sheba, on her way to Solomon's Palace, is seen on the bridge over the Siloe, after having received the revelation that the wood of the bridge had been cut from the tree destined for Christ's Cross. The source of the second fresco is 'The Dream of Constantine', in which an angel shows Constantine the sign of the Cross in the sky. The last movement takes no particular fresco as its subject but is a general view calling attention to two battle scenes: the first depicts Constantine, Cross in hand, defeating the army of Maxentius, Emperor of Rome; while the second concerns the rout of the forces of Chosroes, the Persian King, who had forcibly taken the Cross from Jerusalem. While this might be considered program-matic, the only descriptive moment in the whole score admitted by the composer occurs in the second movement where a solo viola imitates the military call of a distant trumpet.

For some time Martinů had consciously been simplifying his style, removing many of the harsh, astringent qualities in his harmony and softening the scoring. Like Bartók, Bloch and Schoenberg in their final years he, too, was anxious to make his works as accessible to the musical public as possible and in *The Frescoes* he produced a distinctive three-part fantasy without any loss of musical personality. From his corres-pondence we know that Martinů was keen to match the opaque coloured atmosphere of Piero's frescoes with an opaque instrumentation, a fact which possibly explains why he here returned to the sensuous sounds of the Impressionistic period. The subdued, veiled scoring is highly imaginative and enhanced with wood-wind filigree and delicate string writing, with as many as six solo diversions for first violins and two for each of the other string sections in the first movement. Form-ally, *The Frescoes* break no new ground and there is no attempt to link the movements thematically. If the pieces do not equal the *Fantaisies symphoniques* in virtuosity or technique of composition, it is not because they fail to mirror the meaning of Piero's originals as well as they might. Piero della Francesca was renowned for his sense of perspective and for the impassivity he brought to his work. In a very personal way Martinů's *Frescoes* convey something of this quality as well as a feeling of the artist's use of light and shade.

The Frescoes was followed by an Oboe Concerto which confirms that the composer's style was in a process of simplification. The score is a rich quarry of melody, and echoes of folk song ring through in the Andante. Even so, Martinů's concern is not with content but with balance. Although the Concerto is wisely laid out for chamber orchestra, excluding oboes, the instrumentation is generally too heavy. By using the piano as a continuo and writing passages which move from soloist to keyboard in quick succession, Martinů was adding problems of ensemble to those of balance. It is not that the piano writing is unattractive, simply that the composer does not always regard the oboe in a purely melodic way. It is rarely allowed to sing, and in the second movement the lovely folk-song melody is given to the oboe only after a long and exacting recitative-cadenza when the soloist cannot enjoy it. By this time the Concerto has developed into an endurance test of breath control. Marking down the dynamics in the orchestral parts certainly lightens the texture, but this cannot remove the predominantly thick accompaniment. The Concerto was intended for a fellow Czech in the Melbourne Symphony Orchestra and it was Jiří Tancibudek, the first soloist, who begged the composer to release the oboe from its surrounding muddy textures. Though Martinů contemplated reworking the Concerto he never lived to do so.

In the two-and-a-half years Martinů had spent on a sabbatical in Europe, the United States had not forgotten him. His compositions were being regularly performed and in 1955 alone the *Fantaisies symphoniques* was given twenty-eight times. Also in 1955, the *Fantaisies* was pronounced by the New York Music Critics Circle to be the best orchestral work of the year, and in the summer the National Institute of Arts and Letters elected him to life membership. Obviously the time was coming when the adopted mother country would want to see her adopted son, and in October Martinů went back to North America to take up a teaching post at the Curtis Institute in Philadelphia.

For most of his life Martinů had enjoyed the freedom of composing when and as he wished, and though he was to teach only one day a week he found the timetable long and conditions limiting. The Curtis Institute offered few opportunities for individual tuition, and among his classes there was no one whose ability Martinů considered outstanding. Most of all he resented the time spent travelling between New York and Philadelphia, and even the Great Northern Hotel in Fifty-Seventh Street, where he lived, brought him little escape from the noise and bustle of New York's streets. He lacked the quiet retreats he needed for composition, and once again the old habit of strolling around at night returned. 'You have to go on walking block by block. You are driven tormentingly on by the external sameness of your surroundings. You go quicker and quicker until you stop thinking that the corrosion and cheapness of the ordinary world is terrible and inhuman.'

His dislike for New York once again turned to hatred, and his aversion was reflected in his work. The rhapsodic Viola Sonata rattles emptily along and the Sonatinas, for trumpet and piano and clarinet and piano, were a labour in vain. Martinů was not composing well, but the suffering of an artist is ironically often the seed of passion and beauty. Reasserting his deepest convictions, and feeling them to be at variance with the values of the superficial world into which he was again thrown, Martinů began work on a Piano Concerto (his fourth) that was dictated not by any whim but by his desire to exorcise the spirit of mechanisation around him. He regarded the new concerto as a work apart. By subtitling it *Incantation* and providing a note for it, he was indeed departing from his normal practice.

Webster's Dictionary defines the word *Incantation* as 'magic charm' and this corresponds exactly with my own idea. The creative artist is always on the lookout for the significance of life, humanity and truth. He resents oppression and opposing forces which dominate his existence and weigh heavily upon him. He would like to find a common denominator to all the contradictions around him, but somehow a system full of uncertainty rules our destiny. Automation and uniformity calls the artist to protest. But a composer has only one method of protesting and that is with music. While he gathers his emotions, hunts for a melody which can be translated into substance, form contradicts him. And when he puts his finding on paper he begins something entirely different because music must speak for itself.

Incantation is a powerful, compelling two-movement Concerto in which Martinů has something trenchant to say and says it convincingly. There is nothing tawdry about this music and in the originality of its material and scoring the work poses vital problems and argues the solutions in a positive fashion. Convinced by the urgency of his argument, Martinů concentrates his attention on particles of raw material with little attempt to recommend them by ornament. There are no unrelated elements in the conception. All is inevitable and indispensable : all thought is dissolved in the image. For this reason the instrumentation is as important an element in the thought as are the motifs. The two are inseparable and the score presents a musical mosaic where each instrument is spotlighted, even if only for a few notes. Here Martinů calls for many detailed effects : the harp and strings produce 'thunder' in a series of rapid glissandos; violins and cellos play in high and low registers in flageolet tones; *col legno* and *au talon* are frequent indications for the string players, and flutter tonguing and *cuivré* are commonplace directions for the flutes and horns. The harp has a vital rôle in supplying frequent harmonies and rapid ostinatos, and the player is sometimes asked to work '*près de la table* with the nails'. The full score is as precisely marked as any of Debussy's, but Martinů is not just experimenting with timbres, still less indulging in stunts, any more than Debussy was at his best. The keyboard part is among the most highly developed of its kind in the composer's catalogue and by devising it especially for Rudolf Firkušný he was placing the work's formidable difficulties in the preserve of the gifted minority. Here Martinů joins Bartók and Stravinsky in regarding the piano as a percussion instrument, with writing that is often harsh and savage. In the course of the two movements he draws on every type of piano technique, save only the cantabile. He produces unusual sustaining pedal effects, staccato and legato devices in the outer registers of the keyboard and in the second movement acknowledges the 'Hawthorne' movement of Charles Ives's *Concord* Sonata by instructing the soloist to depress chord clusters silently with the left hand while the right engages in *martellato* passagework which causes the depressed chords to vibrate and add subtle colours to the music. Unlike Ives, however, Martinů does not call for a strip of board fourteen and three-quarter inches long, nor does he ask the soloist to assault the keyboard with the palm of his hand or the clenched fist.

Incantation is a complex musical structure, and its logic and continuity depend not on traditional form but on the growth of tension. The first movement is cast in a loosely fashioned ternary structure and moulded from a motif, dominated by the interval of a second. This is developed into a succession of dense textures. The same meagre material serves for the expression of a number of different, highly intricate ideas and as each is presented it seems that Martinů is saying something individual. Each moment of inspiration is independent, but the textures are bound by pedals, sometimes simultaneously sounded, which take the place of harmonic progressions. There is little relaxation in the second movement, a series of variations which come from the same source as the *Fantaisies symphoniques*. Here each variation exploits a different sonority ranging from the percussive to the lyrical, from the dolefully modal to the persistently fantastic. And as always, it is the first-movement motif, with the omnipresent interval of a second, which dominates the music and gives it a monothematic feeling. However one considers Martinů's contribution to mid-twentieth-century music, *Incantation* is a score which cannot be ignored.

Depressed by the New York environment and disappointed by his teaching post in Philadelphia, Martinů resigned and applied for a situation in Rome where a vacancy existed in the American Academy of Music. His application was successful and in May 1956 he left the United States. There were no tears, only feelings of regret for the years he had been obliged to spend there. In conversations and letters to friends his thoughts were constantly in Europe. Clearly it was time to return once and for all.

Travelling first to Paris where Charles Munch and the Boston Symphony gave the first French performance of the *Fantaisies symphoniques,* and then on to Switzerland, the Martinůs arrived in Rome in August. At the airport they were welcomed by a group of the composer's new pupils, who were surprised to see what little luggage they carried. Travelling light was the Martinůs' speciality. However, thanks to the understanding Director of Studies, Laurence Roberts, they soon had all they needed and were installed in a comfortable flat overlooking the Porta Pancrozio. With an easy timetable which left him free to discover the Eternal City and to socialise, Martinů soon felt at ease. Here he renewed his acquaintance with Petrassi, Menotti, Berio and Jacques Ibert and resumed the old pattern of life he had enjoyed in pre-war Paris – working in the mornings and walking during the afternoon. From time to time he would break his routine to visit a museum or to read; and while browsing in the library of the American Academy he discovered William Bradford's *New England Memorial,* a collection of speeches and quotations by the first Governor of New England State, which prompted him to take up another work for large orchestra.

The Rock, as Martinů finally called his score, has no connection with Lermontov's melancholic poem which inspired Rakhmaninov's early orchestral fantasia. Standing halfway between *The Frescoes* and *The Parable,* Martinů's piece is a symphonic prelude which takes its title from the rock off Cape Cod (Manomet) near Plymouth, New England, where the Pilgrim Fathers are said to have set foot in 1619. The composer had stayed near Cape Cod himself in 1942 and a year later had considered writing a memorial in music for the isolated souls who had landed there three hundred and twenty-three years before. However, in 1956 it was a commission from George Szell, who was looking for a new work with which to celebrate the fortieth anniversary of the Cleveland Orchestra, that led Martinů to reconsider *The Rock* as the basis for a symphonic movement. Secretly he hoped it would be a typically American or New England score and the manuscript is aptly prefaced by two quotations from *Democracy in America* by Alexis de Tocqueville. But if one searches for distinct traces of American influence such as those Charles Ives displayed in his *New England Pieces,* one will be disappointed; for *The Rock* is no more American than was the *Fantaisies symphoniques.* None the less it is a fine work, concise and evolved symphonically from developing motifs. No material is recapitulated and the listener is aware only of continuous growth, moving section by section, to a powerful hymn of thanksgiving, impressive and confident.

The same assurance distinguishes *The Parables*, a symphonic fantasy written for Charles Munch in Rome in the summer of 1957 and completed in Switzerland the following spring. *The Parables* have little Biblical significance and even less connection with the parabolic moralities of Su Tungpo, the fifth-century Chinese philosopher, in which Martinů had shown considerable interest during the war. *The Parables* have their origin in the writings of Antoine de Saint-Exupéry, the French philosopher whose *La Citadelle* had become a source of strength to the composer during the war. Apart from Georges Neveux, Saint-Exupéry was the author whose work Martinů most admired. The two artists had met in New York and established a rapport and friendship which was founded on love for the beauty of simple things, for nature, truth and human relations. In *The Parables* Martinů endeavoured to create in music the emotional state which the reader experiences after studying Saint-Exupéry's work.

The Parable of a Sculpture

And the sculptor fixed the likeness of a face in clay and as you walked by his work you glanced at the face and passed on your way. And then it happened. You were not quite the same. Slightly changed, but changed, turned and inclined in a new direction, only for a while, perhaps, but still for a while. Man thus experienced an indefatigable impulse. The sculptor lightly fingered the clay, placed it in your path and you were changed with the same indefinable impulse. And it would not be otherwise if a hundred thousand years had intervened between his gesture and your passing.

The first *Parable* is the musical analogue of Saint-Exupéry's thoughts on time and experience and is a serene and hauntingly beautiful fantasia which mirrors the philosopher's attempts to abolish the past and transcend the future. Martinů's reflective ideas are worked in great depth, the invention being sustained, the orchestral presentation refined. The second movement continues the theme of transcending time, though here it is the present which is overwhelmed by the future.

The Parable of a Garden

And when I am in a garden which, with its fragrance, is my own domain, I sit on a bench and contemplate. The leaves are falling and the flowers are fading. I sense both death and a new life but no sadness. I am all vigilance as on the high seas, impatient, for it is not a question of reaching any destination. Being on my way cheers me. We go, my garden and I, from the flower to the fruit and from the fruit to the seed towards the flowering of the years to come.

In this *Parable* Martinů returns to the mysterious world of the *Fantaisies symphoniques* with another set of variations; but instead of producing a number of exotic tissues which blossom into clusters of melismatic flowers, he is concerned with reflecting Saint-Exupéry's thoughts about the seasons where autumn and winter are not pictures of decay, but the promise of spring to come. And the restrained musical vein, much subtler than it sounds, skilfully carries the variations which expand naturally into pure lyricism.

When considering a motto for the third *Parable* it was not to *La Citadelle* that Martinů turned, but to Georges Neveux's *Le Voyage de Thesée,* and the 'Parable of a Labyrinth' is prefaced by several lines of dialogue from that play :

Thesée	Who are you?
Man	The Town Crier. I announce marriages and deaths and you are already in the Labyrinth.
Thesée	Who are you?
Woman	I am Ariadne. Who are you?
Thesée	Behold the man who has vanquished the Minotaur! Behold him vanquished by a woman!

The final *Parable* displays to the full Martinů's capacity for building an impressive symphonic structure from minute fragments which are in a constant process of regeneration and are drawn into an organic whole leaving the listener mystified by its unified impression. The music is never still. The textures are rich, the timbres highly contrasted not least in the percussion section. With *The Parables* Martinů produced a triptych of great originality in which he succeeded in capturing the thought of the visionary philosopher who had supplied the initial impulse. Had not Martinů wished to record his debt to Saint-Exupéry he might well have styled this work 'Symphony', for it continues the symphonic line of thought with such force and technical aplomb that it must be regarded as developing out of the *Fantaisies symphoniques*. In this way, it is possible to see *The Parables* as the conclusion of a series of orchestral works which confirm that Martinů was one of the great Czech symphonists of his day, and possibly the only one of any significance after Dvořák, Fibich and Suk.

Martinů's deep admiration for *Le Voyage de Thesée* manifested itself in the chamber opera *Ariadne*, but his inspiration was not solely Neveux's play. Whilst holidaying in Switzerland in the summer of 1958, the composer chanced to hear a broadcast recital of operatic arias sung by Maria Callas; and stirred by her artistry he felt impelled to write something specially for her. The result was the title part in

Ariadne. While the basis of Neveux's four Acts is the classical Greek myth, Martinů selected only scenes from the second and third Acts which deal with the love of Theseus for Ariadne. Martinů begins his chamber opera with the arrival of Theseus and the six youths who have come to Knossos as tribute to King Minos, their fate being to be devoured by the Minotaur who inhabits the Labyrinth. Theseus meets Ariadne and falls in love with her but his companions complain. The bravest of them sets out to fight the Minotaur but is killed. Full of remorse Theseus must decide between love and duty. He chooses to challenge the Minotaur but on coming face to face with the monster sees only his own reflection. He questions the Minotaur as to who is the real Theseus. The Minotaur replies that the beast is, whereupon Theseus, panic-stricken, slays the monster and hastily sails from Crete, leaving Ariadne to lament her desertion and end the opera.

Ever since the Mantuan audience in 1608 was moved to tears by her plight, Ariadne abandoned on Naxos has been a favourite heroine of composers and playwrights. But finely thought out as it is, Neveux's play did not fire Martinů to write another *Juliette*. He could hardly expect the vision to return twice, and instead of transforming *Ariadne* into a Surrealist experience he looked back to possibly what is the most affecting *Ariadne* of all time, Jiří Benda's of 1775. By scaling his score into units of Baroque sinfonias which alternate with period tableaux, Martinů was reverently bowing in Benda's direction and paying less attention to Richard Strauss's pastiche and Roussel's ballet on the same theme. Furthermore, Martinů's Baroque plan is matched by formalised designs within each sinfonia and aria. Thus, the first sinfonia is in binary form, the second is a scherzo with independent trio and the third a fantasia over a drone. Moreover, Martinů underlines his feeling for the seventeenth century by repeating the first sinfonia after the third tableau. While the design of *Ariadne* belongs to an earlier age, the musical language is of the 1950s with lines of development within each tableau based on material of considerable substance. Basically lyrical, the music is a happy combination of majestic power and gossamer delicacy, and again displays Martinů's ability to create finely-judged sonorities reflecting specific dramatic points in the action. In the second tableau, for the confrontation of Theseus and the Minotaur, high wood-winds challenge lower strings, and gaze at one another across a void like Theseus and the monster. In designing his opera for Callas, Martinů attempted to make the rôle of Ariadne as attractive as possible, and of all his heroines she is the most lyrically and firmly drawn. This is not to suggest that the vocal part is undemanding. On the contrary: few, if any, of Martinů's characters are more taxing to sing. The vocal lines abound in florid coloratura and cover a tessitura of more than two octaves including a top E flat *in alt*. While the first two tableaux are really extended duets for Ariadne and Theseus, it is in the aria which comprises the bulk of the third that Martinů reaches the height of his musical expression. Here the deserted Ariadne sings a poignant threnody in the form of a rondo with ornate *bel canto* episodes in the style of a cabaletta. If Benda's melodrama holds a special place in musical history and in early Bohemian music drama, Martinů's version is no less affecting and has proved to be a distinguished addition to the forty or more settings of the myth. It certainly deserves to be better known.

Ariadne was written by way of relaxation between more demanding work on the *Fantasia Concertante* for piano and orchestra which is also known as the Fifth Piano Concerto. As he reverted to a conventional three-movement pattern where everything falls logically into place, Martinů's title is misleading. The form is hardly that of a fantasia and the solo writing, though concertante in spirit, belongs more to the style of the virtuoso piano concerto. In a way it is unfortunate that the musical world expects a composer's new work to be progressively greater and more distinguished than his previous work; for in spite of considerable merits the *Fantasia Concertante* is not the most significant of Martinů's series and does not achieve the synthesis of style or structure to be found in the remarkable *Incantation*. While the Concerto does not break any new ground, the solo writing is brilliant and engaging. The first movement continues where the mellow-sounding *Frescoes* stopped; the Andante seems to pay homage to Bartók's Third Concerto by alternating a simple chorale-like melody with highly contrasted solo passages, while the rondo finale shows Martinů's technique as a craftsman to best advantage with impressive keyboard writing and an overall effect of great strength.

The *Fantasia Concertante* was followed by something more seminal, the three-movement Harpsichord Sonata, and then by a set of orchestral pieces called *Estampes*, written for Robert Witney and the Louisville Symphony Orchestra. Martinů's return to a French title for the orchestral work is significant, for *Estampe,* meaning print or engraving, suggests the composer had something visual in mind; but in spite of this explicit title there is nothing in the score which suggests musical pictorialism. Even so, the music has a surprisingly French timbre, with an elegance of phrase and delicacy of sound which show a return to the Impressionistic idiom of an earlier age. Certainly the reappearance of the piano in the orchestra after an absence of six years emphasises this in the hazily-textured outer movements which frame the pastoral

Andante. It is unfortunate for Martinů that the cor anglais melody here recalls the negro-inspired theme in Dvořák's *New World* Symphony, but the allusion soon passes as oboes and clarinets respond with a version of the *ranz des vaches,* a type of old Swiss melody used to call the cows in when the herd is scattered. Skilful and exhilarating as the *Estampes* may be, the score is not particularly remarkable and what remains is the impression that something greater might have been possible.

Possible, yes; but unlikely when one realises that *Estampes,* the *Fantasia Concertante,* the Harpsichord Sonata, *The Parables, The Rock, Brigand Songs* and two of the chamber cantatas were all completed in between work on *The Greek Passion,* the vast four-act opera on which Martinů had been occupied since 20 February 1956. Within two weeks of handing the Fourth Piano Concerto (*Incantation*) to the Fromm Music Foundation who had commissioned it, Martinů began his first and only tragic opera, and for the next four years his entire life centred around this score. The genesis of *The Greek Passion* dates from 1953 when Martinů was working on *Mirandolina.* With this the composer had fulfilled his obligation to the Guggenheim Foundation, but clearly *Mirandolina* had not satisfied his own desire to write a music drama, and afterwards he impulsively considered adapting Dostoyevsky's *The Devils* for the stage. Realising, perhaps, that the task of compression was too great and that of the composers who had attempted to transform the great Russian classics into opera only Janáček, in *From the House of the Dead,* had succeeded in matching the power and quality of its literary source, he decided against it. Anyway, *Memoirs from the House of the Dead* (1860-2), which formed the basis of Janáček's text, was not a novel but a series of recollections and even Martinů could see that *The Devils* was something quite different.

By the summer of 1954 the composer was no nearer finding a plot, but a chance reading of Nikos Kazantzakis's *Zorba the Greek* filled him with such enthusiasm that he introduced himself to the novelist then living in nearby Antibes. But enthusiasm was hardly sufficient to turn *Zorba,* with its masterly descriptions, into a two-hour operatic experience. Working on the false asumption that the audience would be thoroughly familiar with Kazantzakis's story Martinů selected episodes without bothering too much about continuity or explanation. However, the author could see that *Zorba* lacked the stuff from which operas are made even if the composer could not, and suggested instead one of his other novels, *Christ Recrucified,* previously dramatised for the stage by Renée Saurel and adapted for the screen by Jules Dassin under the title *Celui qui doit mourir.* With this Martinů was on firmer ground. Here was the framework within which he preferred to work – a play within a play – and with it the engagement of Greek novelist and Czech composer was sealed.

By basing his libretto on Kazantzakis's novel Martinů was renouncing his earlier operatic excursions into fantasy, and exchanging Surrealism for reality. The values examined, the characters portrayed, the motives and sentiments considered link Kazantzakis's novel with the greatest European literature, and the years devoted to this operatic narrative brought the composer back to the mainstream of thought and culture. But what was it that brought Greek and Czech together? At first sight few connections between novelist and musician seem apparent, and on closer examination the two artists share even fewer points of contact in tradition or heritage. Martinů's mid-European upbringing and cosmopolitan outlook nourished in Prague, Paris and New York have little in common with the Cretan culture of Kazantzakis, whose metropolitan thought nurtured at the crossroads of Asia and Europe embraced political history, comparative religion and philosophy. However, in *Christ Recrucified* the two artists found a meeting point; but how far Martinů was wise in giving his opera a new name is doubtful since Kazantzakis's title is a valuable pointer to the various levels of thought which develop side by side in the narrative. In the first place *Christ Recrucified* is the story of a village community which proposes to produce a Passion Play. The villagers are to re-enact the Crucifixion, but as the narrative develops the actors identify themselves more and more with the gospel characters they are to portray. Katerina (Mary Magdalene) abandons prostitution for a life of unselfish love. Panait (Judas) is obsessed with the power of gain and stabs his master (Manolios) in the back. Michelis, Kostandis and Yannakos (the Apostles John, James and Peter) waver in their loyalty but end by sharing Manolios's banishment. Manolios (the Christ) who renounces wealth and comfort and seeks to turn his fellow villagers from narrow selfishness to generous service for a group of strangers, is denounced by the religious authorities (Grigoris) and is finally assassinated. The action takes place in and around the village of Lycovrissi during the Turkish occupation of Greece. Grigoris, Priest of Lycovrissi and natural leader of the people, comes face to face with Priest Fotis and his refugees. In spite of his holy office Grigoris refuses help and incites his people to drive out the strangers. There must be no priest in Lycovrissi but himself: there must be no expenditure but on the needs of his own parish. Thus Christ is recrucified by his own people.

Only the severest pruning could reduce Kazantzakis's novel to reasonable length and between August 1954 and January 1956 Martinů, working as his own librettist from the English translation by Jonathan Griffin, brought the original four-hundred page book down to forty typed sheets. These drastic cuts naturally involved the disappearance of many important features including those describing Grigoris's home life with his daughter Mariori, and others which show Kemal Ataturk, the stern Turkish Dictator, in his household. The many vivid scenes of cruelty and vice that had to disappear with him led to a valuable concentration on the main issues, but he also omitted the episodes in which Manolios is accused of Bolshevik sympathies and of spreading Muscovite influence in the Priest Fotis's refugee camp on Mount Sarakina. In Martinů's adaptation it was inevitable that a great deal of historical background would be excluded, but it was unfortunate that the relationships between Manolios and his lover Lenio and between Katerina and Manolios should have been so understated. That it was difficult for Martinů to create a smooth line of development is without question, and in the event he had little option but to accept a series of disjointed episodes in which characters move jerkily from situation to situation with little or no reference to what motivates their actions.

None the less, this provided a working basis for composition and in New York during the spring of 1956 Martinů began researching into the liturgical music of the Greek Orthodox Church. Before leaving the South of France Kazantzakis had given him a list of friends upon whom he could call for help and during his stay in New York Martinů regularly attended services in Greek Churches to become acquainted with the idiom and assimiliate the characteristics of the Greek music. Hymns were notated in pocket books and chants were worked into his sketches. Clearly the composer was going out of his way to give his score authenticity and by the middle of July when he returned to Switzerland the first two Acts were in draft. Martinů had worked with unusual speed for with Rafael Kubelík as Musical Director at Covent Garden there was talk of *The Greek Passion* being premièred at the Royal Opera House in London. Moving to Rome, Martinů had the sketch of Act III on paper by November 1956 and two months later the opera was complete – all, that is, except the final scene. But following the first performance of *The Frescoes* in Salzburg in August Kubelík's interest in the *Passion* began to wane and he decided not to go ahead with the Covent Garden production. This was a disappointment for Martinů, but at least it gave him time to reconsider the score. The task of compression had not been easy and clearly the text was not all it might have been, but the opportunity for an immediate revision was cut short by Herbert von Karajan's request to consider the score for production at the Vienna Staatsoper. Discussions between composer and conductor began during the 1957 Lucerne Music Festival, when it was agreed that Martinů would tidy up the text, have it translated into German and rework certain parts of the score. Without knowing it Martinů had virtually agreed to rewrite the libretto completely. Furthermore, he felt morally obliged to preserve as much of Kazantzakis's original dialogue as possible, and this made his task especially hard. With the author's death the year before there was now no one to whom Martinů could turn for help. The only course open to him was to improvise a number of recitatives and dialogues himself, but while these bound the narrative together they did nothing to facilitate the cumbersome changes of scene the drama involved. Martinů was therefore forced to resort to orchestral interludes. The result, in the second Act, was especially clumsy and feeling the need to compress even more the composer devised a series of dream-like visions for Manolios in Act III. If these do not quite have the dramatic effect of those in *The Plays of Mary,* at least the working method is the same, looking back as it does to the dream fantasies Smetana had incorporated in *The Devil's Wall,* seventy-six years before.

The delays, second thoughts and revisions which dogged *The Greek Passion* remind one of the creative process of another epic, *Boris Godunov,* but Martinů's text was not in the same class as Mussorgsky's. Nevertheless, it was workable and in February 1958 the composer took up the score again. But as Martinů was unable to promise a completion date it was not surprising that Karajan's interest cooled. *The Greek Passion* was becoming a liability. However, in anticipation of an Austrian première, Universal Edition had agreed to print the score in Vienna and the Directors were as anxious as the composer to find a platform for the new work. Having promoted the opera for several months, they opened negotiations with the Zurich Opera and after several meetings it was agreed that *The Greek Passion* should take the following form. Act I, set in the square at Lycovrissi, introduces the villagers being chosen for the various characters in the Passion Play, the refugees seeking shelter and being rejected by Grigoris. Act II shows the gradual influence of the Passion story on the people taking part with the resulting rift in the village community. Here and there a parishioner rejects the selfish policy of the Priest Grigoris and helps the destitute refugees on Mount Sarakina. In Act III Manolios begins to identify himself with Christ and after a series of dreams refuses to marry Lenio. Instead he becomes leader of a group who plan to aid the refugees. The Act closes with Grigoris plotting to destroy the influence of Manolios. Act IV, subtitled 'The Wedding', celebrates the marriage

35. *and* 36. Two scenes from the Prague National Theatre production of *Juliette*, 1938.

37. Martinů in New York.

38. Martinů with Koussevitzky.

of Nikolios, the shepherd boy, with Lenio. Grigoris makes this an occasion to banish all those who reject his authority in the interest of the refugees. The priest, in clear opposition to Manolios, orders the assassination of his opponent and Panait deals the fatal blow. As Katerina, the converted Mary, sings a final litany the refugees carry away the body of their dead champion.

Despite failing health Martinů worked unflaggingly on the score during the winter of 1958. It was not an easy task and he might well have echoed Tolstoy's maxim 'The pleasure was negligible, the remorse immense' as he completed the last pages on 15 January 1959. For months he had been torn with doubts concerning the final scene, being uncertain whether to place the confession of Manolios before or after the rite of excommunication, and whether he should follow the death of Manolios with an aria for Katerina or with a Requiem sung on the Church steps. His preference was to end with a dramatic scena for Katerina, but under pressure from the Directors of Universal Edition, anxious to save the opera from what they considered might be a weak finale, the composer was persuaded to rethink the conclusion. By trying to make the best of both schemes Martinů finally decided to give Katerina a short retreat followed by a Kyrie in the form of a choral march; but quite apart from telescoping the action this really robs the opera of its impact. Bound up with the problem of the last scene were the composer's doubts about the style of some of his music, which though Czech in warmth and feeling incorporates features of Italian *verismo* alongside Greek folk music.

The Greek Passion is a deeply religious work which contains some of the most powerful pages Martinů ever wrote. Admittedly the pace fluctuates as the action moves from scene to scene, and Acts II and III do not have the flow that distinguishes the outer ones; even so, there is no denying the great humanity and unquestioned sincerity of Martinů's expression. The continuous web of sound which distinguished *Juliette* is found here in lesser measure. Possibly as a result of the episodic libretto, the music is conceived in smaller units and paralleled by casual sounding invention or abrupt, summary cadences. This is not to suggest that Martinů follows a pattern of formal arias. There is nothing here which corresponds to an acceptance of set forms except the Scherzo and Trio prefacing Act IV. Even Martinů's use of the Greek chant 'Lord, save Thy people' and his final Kyrie are woven into the score in much the same way that Bohemian and Moravian folk idiom had been utilised in the Symphonies. It is simply that germinal development is less evident in this opera and that Martinů does not always succeed in fusing his sections together. However, each act has a certain unity which is due largely to the composer's impressive handling of huge choral forces in dramatic situations.

At an early meeting in 1954, author and composer had agreed that *The Greek Passion* should be an opera in which the chorus would play a significant part in the action. Later Kazantzakis expressed the hope that the *Passion* would be as much for massed choirs as for soloists and in the event Martinů rose to the occasion, the outer acts being not far short of dramatic oratorio. For the first time in his operatic career he allowed the chorus to assume an important place in the drama, matching the conflict between Grigoris and Manolios with corresponding clashes between the choirs representing the Lycovrissians and the fugitives. Particularly impressive is their antagonism in Act I, where Grigoris attempts to drive out Fotis and his tribe on the grounds that they bring cholera to Lycovrissi; and remarkable, too, are the scenes in Act IV where Fotis and his followers arrive in the town square to mourn the dying Manolios. Here Martinů produces eight-part polyphony of commanding grandeur, massive and powerful and not far removed from the spirit of the Proper of the Mass. The writing for double chorus is balanced and varied as chords and counterpoint are juxtaposed antiphonally with considerable skill and effect. Without doubt these are Martinů's finest operatic moments.

The middle Acts depend less upon fine choral passages than the outer ones and it is here that the principal characters emerge more forcefully. However, it is not upon leading motifs that Martinů depends for musical identification, and while Grigoris and Fotis are given symbolic themes the other figures in the drama are associated with a series of simple cadences. Thus, Kostandis and Yannakos, two of the Apostles, are portrayed by a half-close; Michelis, the third Apostle, is suggested with a plagal cadence; while Manolios is symbolised by a perfect cadence. Aptly, Katerina is given an imperfect cadence. However naïve this system of identification seems, it does lead to some subtle transformations. In Act III Katerina's cadence is transformed into the themes of Grigoris and Fotis at the moment when she finally renounces her desire for Manolios. Later, in Act IV the Apostles' half-close and plagal cadences are made perfect as Michelis, Kostandis and Yannakos in turn defend the banished Manolios. But while these characters are invested with recognisable cadences, Martinů does not always succeed in showing the fascinating way in which Katerina, Panait and Yannakos gradually assume the rôles of Mary, Judas and Peter, which guide their actions and lead to Manolios's destruction.

Martinů's other characters are not so fully drawn. They rise briefly to the surface without explanation but are suggested by recognisable musical features or by distinctive instrumentation. Thus the music of Panait, the unwilling Judas, is accompanied by seconds and ninths; Lenio, Manolios's betrothed, is given a characteristic rising glissando, and Nikolios, the shepherd boy, is depicted by a poignant cor anglais phrase which may well have been coloured by that in the third Act of *Tristan*. The only wholly evil person in the opera is Ladas, the village elder, and he is significantly given a non-singing rôle. Curiously two scenes in which he is the prime mover, the bribery of Yannakos in Act II and his plans with the scheming Grigoris to excommunicate Manolios in Act III, are spoken throughout. And one wonders whether it was the composer's feeling for the stage or just a sense of desperation that forced him to leave these incidents in dialogue. These passages apart, there is much to admire in *The Greek Passion,* not least of all the way Martinů marshalls his orchestral forces. Here he continues to speak with the fluency which distinguished *The Frescoes* and *The Parables,* but as might have been expected it is the dream sequences in Act III where his instrumentation is at its most imaginative. The use of string glissandos, the flutter-tonguing of the flutes, and the combination of viola, clarinet (in the chalumeau region) and piano relate this scene directly to *Incantation*.

In *The Greek Passion* Martinů's sense of music-theatre is seen at its most persuasive. There is scarcely a moment when the drama does not emerge with vigour, power and nobility. Here he is as experienced in handling dramatic situation as was Prokofiev in *War and Peace*; but one cannot help wondering if Martinů had not bitten off just a little more than he could chew. Like Tolstoy's *War and Peace,* Kazantzakis's epic almost defies musical treatment and Martinů is only marginally more successful in creating a series of beautiful frescoes and subtly etched vignettes than was Prokofiev in his opera. While Martinů skilfully illustrates and comments on Kazantzakis's social drama, he never convincingly achieves a purely musical distillation of scene, emotion or character. Possibly this is because his score lacks the real essence of the author's literary sense without which the music, for all its dressing *à la grècque,* can scarcely hint at the true colour and vitality of the original novel.

The Greek Passion was to be Martinů's last opera and his last major work; for although he still had limitless enthusiasm and was anxious to commit his ideas to paper, his health was deteriorating. In July 1958, his term of office at the American Academy in Rome came to an end. He had no wish to continue and even less desire to see North America again. Instead he decided to return to the small villa on Mont Boron, above Nice, where he had known much happiness between 1953 and

1956. Sadly, he was not allowed many months there; for in the autumn a French doctor diagnosed that the composer was suffering from what he believed to be a troublesome stomach ulcer and urged him to consult a specialist. Returning to Switzerland, where Paul and Maja Sacher put a suite of rooms at his disposal on the Schonenberg Estate near Pratteln, Martinů began to feel more at ease. The reception was friendly, the attention close. He knew and loved this corner of Europe and in the dark days of 1939 had come here to rest and write the *Double Concerto*. Now, almost twenty years later, he had returned in search of health, and on 7 November he underwent an operation, the result of which showed him to be suffering from acute stomach cancer. There could be no cure. However, the nature of the complaint was concealed from Martinů who, during December, recovered his strength as best he could. These were sad days for the composer. Apart from his difficulties with the *Greek Passion* he was deeply grieved to learn of the death of his brother František, who had been buried in Polička after a long illness. One by one the lights of home were going out. His thoughts were more and more in the Vysočina and in a fever of activity he began posting to his aged sister in Polička parcels of reviews, critiques of his music, his honorary diplomas, his awards and a pile of letters from distinguished colleagues, all in an attempt to draw himself nearer home. Martinů had always carried in his wallet a picture postcard of the Polička Tower and had kept a small pocket knife with which, as a lad, he had cut sticks for the Easter brooms. Both knife and postcard had accompanied him everywhere and now became his most cherished possessions. Somehow they bound him to his home in the simplest, most direct way. And in order to strengthen the bond with those in Polička he subscribed to *Jitřinka*, the local newspaper, which had recorded his triumphs as a boy more than sixty years before.

I am reading *Jitřinka* (*The Morning Star*) with more attention than I ever did the *New York Times*! The paper is a link between us. I follow every item with interest and when they are building a road I want to read where it is and how long it will take to complete. Please know I am with the people of Polička even though I am miles away. How I enjoy reading the many names which I have known since boyhood and which are still connected with me despite the frontiers that separate us.

After the Christmas festivities which the Sachers made rich and warm, Martinů's condition improved sufficiently for him to travel to Wiesbaden where a new production of *Juliette* had been mounted. For the composer this was a joyful event. Twenty years had passed since the première in Prague and though the German presentation treated the opera as a tragedy and not as a dream fantasy, nothing could shift the opera from the special place it held in Martinů's affection. It was still his finest work and the one that meant most to him. Back in Switzerland it was the vocal score of *Juliette* he kept at hand, for now he felt the need to translate the text into French. Cheered by the opportunity of hearing his opera again he responded with new compositions, nothing ambitious, but a set of songs for children's choir. 'About a Cock', 'The Little Blacksmith' and 'Children's Riddles' have a cheeky, urchin-like quality, although they were written on Clara Schumann's piano, put at his disposal by his hosts.

For all the care and attention the Sachers lavished on the ailing Martinů, little could be done to relieve him from pain. The energetic composer who had loved walking had become a gaunt, ashen-faced invalid who now climbed stairs with agonising effort and had lost all desire for the meals he had once enjoyed with a gourmet's relish. He was too weak to travel to Berlin for the première of the *Fantasia Concertante* at the end of January, yet he refused to let sickness interrupt his work. On 9 January he began to compose a three-movement Nonet intended to mark the thirty-fifth anniversary of the founding of the Czech Nonet. Ironically it was exactly thirty-five years since Martinů had sketched his first Nonet (for flute, oboe, clarinet, bassoon, horn, violin, viola, cello and piano) and what he now produced (for the same combination except that the piano is replaced by double bass) is a tribute to the distance he had travelled in technique. This is the music of home, with mellow echoes of folk dance in the outer movements, and a central Andante which is a rich quarry of melody, strangely at variance with his own sad condition. The Nonet was followed by a less spontaneous chamber work, *Kammermusik No. 1* for clarinet, violin, viola, cello, harp and piano which Martinů sub-titled 'Les Fêtes nocturnes'. This three-movement essay in night music returns to the atmospheric moods and colours of *Incantation* where harp and piano played a similarly important rôle, but here the musical substance is not so rich or inspired. Possibly there are too many false premises in the score, and there is a heaviness which has to be accepted before the music can be appreciated. Disappointing, too, are a couple of pieces for two cellos, written towards the end of March; but the *Variations on a Slovakian Folk Song*, 'Kde bych já věděla' ('If I had known') for solo cello and piano and *Ptačí hody (Festival of Birds)*, a setting of part of the fifteenth-century Třebiň manuscript, show the composer in better form. Here Martinů was renewing his case for the expression of solid homely virtues. But the news he received from home was especially sorrowful; and with the death of his sister at the end of March the last light had gone out in Polička. Martinů mourned her in a set of *Madrigals* for mixed voices which he dedicated to the faithful family friend Maruška Pražanová. In these Czech-sounding choruses Martinů turned four of Erben's Moravian folk poems into a highly personal farewell to life – a leave-taking which in the third chorus, comes close to a requiem anticipating the composer's own death : 'My years pass like the hours, and when life comes to an end lay a stone at my head.'

Feeling that a change of surroundings would help him, Martinů asked to convalesce in Nice and at the beginning of April travelled south to the warm Mediterranean where he began to collect ideas for a cantata to be called *The Prophecy of Isaiah*. Before he could sketch this, however, symptoms of his complaint returned and he was forced to leave the Riviera for Switzerland where he was admitted to the Canton Hospital at Liestal. Though seriously ill, Martinů hated the confines in which he found himself and, realising that the chances of recovery were slight, he begged to be allowed to go back to Schonenberg. His wishes were respected and with medical care provided at the Sachers' expense Martinů worked on the mountain estate which reminded him so much of the Moravian Highlands near Polička. Here he resumed *The Prophecy of Isaiah,* composing in feverish haste and filling his manuscript with almost as many scratchings-out as notes. The words of the Cantata are taken from Isaiah Chapters xxv and xxi, and significantly Martinů chose to work in English. While the score does not break any new ground and remains in the style of the earlier chamber cantatas, this is music of deep nostalgia; and though it was not to be expected that the idiom which exactly matched the subtle naïvety of Bureš's Czech poems would suit the sombre significance of Isaiah, there is a feeling that the composer had never spoken quite like this before. The instrumentation, for piano, trumpet, viola and timpani, is strong and confident, while the choral parts, for male voices, are aflame with feeling, especially in the second movement, a lament where unity is preserved by keeping the dimensions to those of a personal but ardent prayer. The Cantata has undoubted merits, and it is to be regretted that Martinů was not spared to complete the sketch of *The Burden of Moab* (the words are taken from Isaiah xvi) which may well have formed the third and final movement. There remain only one and a half pages, notated in a tired hand, for male voices and piano.

The cancer that was sapping him caused Martinů new pains each day, and despite his will to live he was growing too weak to hold a pen for long periods. Nevertheless he struggled to complete the *Vigilia,* his first and only composition for organ, but after eighty-one bars of fluid monothematic development on a theme that rings with echoes of the four-note motif from Dvořák's *Requiem,* he was obliged to put the manuscript to one side. Possibly the composer contemplated writing several *Vigiliae* or a single work in more than one movement. However, only the opening of a second *Vigilia* was committed to paper and for a children's chorus dedicated to the pupils in the music school which bears his name in Polička he could write no more than the title *Znělka* (*Whirlpool*) and a few notes. He was never to compose again. And the *Vigilia,* completed and edited by the Czech organist Bedřich Janáček, stands in its austere grace as a testament to the fundamental simplicity and honesty of its composer.

During his adult life Martinů had neglected the faith in which he had been raised, and there is little evidence in his work of any interest in religion. Yet with *The Prophecy of Isaiah* and the *Vigilia* he began to manifest a deep interest in spiritual things and now devoted many hours to serious conversation with the local priest. One result of this awakened interest was a desire to consecrate his marriage, and on 16 August 1959 he received the blessing of the church on a union begun twenty-eight years before.

Martinů's condition was grave, but he still kept the score of *Juliette* at his bedside, summoning all his forces to work on the French version. In between he saw the many friends who came to visit him, and none were more welcome than those from Czechoslovakia. At last he could speak his native tongue again and talk about Prague with those who knew the city as he had known it in his teens. With the pianist Josef Páleníček he outlined his hopes and ambitions to meet Walt Disney, Charlie Chaplin and Aldous Huxley. From Karel Šebanek, his old publisher from Hudební matice days, he was keen to know how *Mirandolina* had been received, how Radok's Lanterna Magica had treated *The Opening of the Wells* and when the National Theatre would revive *Juliette*. But with Miloslav Bureš he talked simply about home. Not all his questions were rooted in the old life. He urged Bureš to send him books by Havlíček and Neruda and to find in his sister's estate the collection of Nursery Rhymes by Erben which his mother had given him sixty-three years before, and which he now wanted to set to music. He was keen to hear about the newly-opened theatre at Český Krumlov, because it boasted a large revolving stage, and he begged to have a copy of Jirásek's *Lucerna* which he hoped to adapt as an opera. Most of all he looked forward to receiving new poems from Bureš himself with which to continue the cycle of chamber cantatas begun four years before. Together they agreed on *Pochodování světla* (*Marching Light*), a subject inspired by the customs of the glass blowers

whose workshops at Milovy and Rybeň near Polička had fascinated
Martinů as a child and whose work had been preserved in the Polička
museum. Another cantata was to be based on the legend of Lukaš's
singing linden tree in neighbouring Telecí, but this was never to be
fulfilled. Martinů's mind was filled with numerous other schemes of
composition, most of which survive only in the recording of casual
conversations. By contrast, one cannot help thinking of Sibelius. For ten
years before his death the world waited for an Eighth Symphony, yet
no sketch was found among his papers. Had Martinů lived to Sibelius's
age, it is unlikely that his flow of ideas would have shown any abate-
ment.

By August Martinů had weakened considerably. Nothing could ease
his suffering and he was readmitted to the hospital at Liestal. There was
no hope of recovery. At 7.30 in the evening of 28 August, Martinů
died. The blue eyes, generous and sincere, were closed; the mouth,
witty and kind, was shut; the voice, soft and full of humanity, was silent.
Yet the name Bohuslav Martinů survives because he was both creator
and orator and because he spent his life furthering the cause of Czech
music.

After years of wandering, estrangement, homesickness and nostalgia,
a death abroad was perhaps the most fitting conclusion for a life of
music spent abroad. Each man must go back to the earth from which
he derives, but it was not in Czech earth that Martinů's body was laid
on 1 September 1959. He lies among the Swiss mountains, but perhaps
not for ever. There is talk of taking his remains back to the tower in
Polička, the tower where sixty-nine years before Lucie Křiklavová
had forecast that a great man had been born.

9 The Music of Martinů Considered

It is a well-known paradox that a composer's reputation is devalued by his death and that in the years immediately following, his fame, popularity and reputation are at their lowest. For Martinů the process began during his lifetime, when there were always more than ordinary divergences of opinion concerning the quality of his work. It is not hard to see why. With a catalogue of nearly four hundred scores he must surely have been one of the most prolific composers of his day; yet in some ways this vast output has been the cause of some of the criticism. Sometimes to be prolific is to be facile, and this can lead to self-indulgence. That Martinů's output is uneven and that he was one of the least critical composers of the century cannot be disputed. How else could he have produced such a collection of works? He composed at an incredible rate, and the score of the Concerto for Flute, Violin and Orchestra, completed in ten days, is the rule rather than the exception. Where others created, considered and withdrew a work they felt to be less than good, Martinů produced, published and carried on composing. He was like a bad parent who had no time for his children once they had been brought into the world. For him the process of gestation and parturition was all that mattered. What happened subsequently to his off-spring was none of his concern. He was strangely indifferent to performance and even more so to applause. He hardly ever revised a score (the Cello Concerto No. 1, *Špaliček*, *Sinfonietta Giocosa* and *The Greek Passion* are rare exceptions) and he suppressed nothing. His reputation, therefore, is bound to depend on works, good, bad and indifferent, picked up by chance here and there; for to Martinů composition was as natural and as necessary as breathing. He was a craftsman and a professional who could turn his hand to songs, instrumental pieces, chamber and choral works, symphonies, operas and ballets and was as much at home writing for the concert hall as when turning out scores for the film, radio or television studios. In this century perhaps only Richard Strauss, Prokofiev, Milhaud, Vaughan Williams and Britten can claim to have moved with equal naturalness in all these media; but despite his very considerable achievement Martinů has been one of the slowest to be recognised.

In the first place, his importance is due almost entirely to the intrinsic value of his scores and not to any influence he had had on other composers. He was not a great innovator or conscious theorist like Schoenberg, nor did he attach himself to a great leader as did Berg or Webern. He never occupied the centre of the stage as did Stravinsky. He formed no new school, had few pupils and kept his working methods basically his own. In fact it is his almost permanent isolation which is the most conspicuous feature of his life. He seems to have been fated to stand alone. Even his birthplace, the Polička tower, heralded the solitude he was to know as a student in Prague, as a struggling artist in Paris and as an exile in the United States. Yet despite this sense of isolation, Martinů's outlook was the most cosmopolitan of all Czech composers, and alongside Smetana, Dvořák and Janáček his music has won the greatest possible success and recognition for Czech musical culture outside Czechoslovakia. Within the Republic his music holds a special place. He is regarded as the natural successor to Janáček, and alongside Janáček's operas Martinů's dramatic works form an essential part of the repertoire at the National Theatres in Prague and Brno. But for all this, he is still, in a sense, an unknown composer in the West. It is not that people are unaware of the factors which governed his life. On the contrary: that Martinů grew up in the Nationalistic movement of Czechoslovakia, found academic training irksome, joined the neo-classicists in Paris, discovered his Nationalism in the years before the Second World War and fled to North America where he suffered the pangs of nostalgia for his native land are well known and in 1967 features and influences of his work are appreciated in lesser detail and formed the basis of a B.B.C. television film biography. But the formative it is hard to decide what place Martinů holds in twentieth-century music and which of his scores warrant attention.

On 4 August 1942 Radio Station W.A.B.C. (New York) broadcast a short interview between Martinů and Robert Bager which has proved to have considerable historical value since it underlines the forces that had contributed to the composer's style.

In my music I have been influenced by many things but most of all by the national music of Czechoslovakia, by the music of Debussy and by the English Madrigals. These I heard before 1914 [sic] when the English Singers were in Prague. I was attracted to the freedom of polyphony which I found very different from that of Bach. I recognised something of Bohemian folk music in these madrigals. In Debussy I was attracted to the colours of the orchestra and to the spirit of the music. I have in mind especially the *Nocturnes*. Rhythmic vitality plays an important part in Czech music, so I compose with vital rhythms. Sometimes I use Czech folk songs as themes, but more often I create thematic material coloured by the style and spirit of Czech folk idiom. These I think are the elements which have motivated my music most.

Of the influences Martinů acknowledges the first is undoubtedly the most pervasive. The Bohemian-Moravian highlands were and are a rich quarry for indigenous folk music. Polička is only twelve miles south of Litomyšl, Smetana's birthplace, and fifty miles north of Kaliště, Mahler's hometown. In the Vysočina, Martinů had taken in music with his mother's milk. Grandfather Stodola had taught him folk tunes and Černovský, a folk musician, had shown him how to play the violin. Clearly Martinů had assimilated Moravian folk music unconsciously and to him it was as natural as the Moravian dialect. It was a mode of expression he was to use all his life. The *Songs on One and Two Pages* and operas *The Voice of the Forest* and *Comedy on the Bridge* are rich in folk idiom and racy in feeling. *Kytice, The Opening of the Wells* and *Romance of the Dandelions* became vehicles for expressing the homely tunes of his boyhood; and even large-scale orchestral works like the Fourth Symphony are not without their debt to the rhythms and melodies of the Vysočina.

The debt to Debussy which Martinů mentions is to be found in his exploration of Impressionistic sonorities. Like Debussy, Martinů possessed a flair for instrumental colour, and a keen sensitivity to timbre formed part of a nervous system that was highly strung. He was no purist and enjoyed extending the normal symphony orchestra to include piano, accordion, percussion of all kinds and the wordless voice. As early as 1912 *Niponari* had revealed the influence of the Impressionists and ten years later the ballet *Istar* might well have been taken for the work of a French composer. Although there was some reaction after this Martinů never entirely relinquished his feeling for timbre and *The Frescoes, The Parables* and *Ariadne* written in the 1950s show his skill in orchestration to be as keen as it had been in the 1930s. However, the work in which the debt to Debussy is most obvious is *Juliette*. In Act II, Michel's music seems to have been coloured by that for Golaud in *Pelléas et Mélisande* and later, when the Vendor of Memories produces his collection of old photographs, Martinů seems to echo the side-stepping chords which distinguish Arkel's music in *Pelléas*. Here, chords are not merely steps in a statement but sounds intrinsically interesting and beautiful. To Martinů sonority was more a subject of study than good abstract material or structures and it is not surprising with such an outlook that he became an experimenter in orchestral timbre. While the principal influence in the matter of orchestration was undoubtedly the Impressionist school, his fascination for percussion instruments led him in *The Strangler* to employ the so called 'Mexican' battery (though here as in *The Parables* he was disappointed that the end result still sounded like Debussy rather than

Boulez). More important, his feeling for sonority persuaded him to adopt the concerto grosso style where the balancing and contrasting of large and small forces enabled him to produce many delicate and unusual effects.

Martinů's reference to madrigals sung by the English Singers is interesting but misleading. If he did actually hear sixteenth-century English works in 1914 he successfully managed to resist any direct influence for the next fifteen years. Polyphony appears in his music in a marked way only after 1928 and the first occasion on which he used the title 'Madrigal' occurs in connection with the four-movement Wind Trio written in December 1937. (The first vocal pieces to bear the name *České madrigaly* date from July 1939.) Almost certainly the date 1914 given in his interview was a slip on Martinů's part, for he was notoriously inaccurate when attempting to recall details of his own life and work. Moreover, the English Singers did not appear in Prague before 1922, from which it can be assumed that any influence the great polyphonists had on the composer was indirect. Martinů probably assimilated the spirit of their music rather than the form. During the 1930s scores such as the *Cinq pièces brèves* show that he was beginning to think as much in polyphonic combinations of melodic lines as in harmony and this is seen elsewhere in his work though not, curiously enough, in the choral pieces. At no time in the Thirties did he attempt to write polyphonic music in an antiquarian style. He accepted it only as an element of his normal thought, but in 'Tam s tej strany dunaja', the first of four *Czech Madrigals* written a few months before his death in 1959, Martinů produced something approaching genuine madrigal form.

It is interesting that the composer omitted to mention in his interview the part Roussel had played in his experience. Roussel's influence cannot be overlooked, for it was his symphonies and ballets which became the motive force behind Martinů's visit to Paris in 1923. It was Roussel who was partly responsible for the composer's break with Impressionism and it was he who guided Martinů to follow a style at once neo-classical and nearer his own, as the *Serenade* (1930) and *Partita* for string orchestra (1931) show. From the late Twenties onward bi-tonal and polytonal harmonies became characteristic features of his music and the linear thinking in which Martinů began to indulge after 1928 may well have been taken from Roussel's working method. But for all this there is rather a touching contrast between the frugality of Roussel's output and the prodigality of his pupil's.

Alongside the music of Roussel, that of Stravinsky was to colour Martinů's outlook considerably, and it was noticeably the percussive elements in *Petrushka* and the barbaric insistence on rhythm in the *Rite of Spring* which can be detected in *Half-time* and *La Bagarre*. Martinů's interest in rhythm also led him to explore jazz and popular dance forms in the *Jazz Suite* and *Le Jazz*, a paraphrase of Paul Whiteman's 'Sweet Music'. The phase quickly passed and was followed by a period when the composer turned to the style of the eighteenth-century concerto grosso as a vehicle for expressing modern ideas. More than once Martinů had to declare that he was a 'concerto grosso type' and the Concerto for String Quartet with Orchestra (1931) and the Concertinos for Piano Trio and Orchestra (Nos. 1 and 2) led to purely orchestral works conceived in the same form, culminating in the *Concerto Grosso* of 1937 where the instrumental figuration is modelled on the music of Corelli, Vivaldi and Bach. The Baroque influence of these composers was to stay with Martinů in his use of arpeggiated figures for many years, and though during the period 1948-51 he was to become passionately interested in the music of Haydn, as the *Sinfonia Concertante* and Piano Trio No. 2 show, he never completely relinquished concerto grosso techniques.

Passing as he did from one phase to another, Martinů was for long little more than a child of his time. Living in Paris when the city was the focal point of great cosmopolitan activity, he became an explorer trying to find a valid means of self-expression. The compositions of 1924 to 1934 show him accepting and rejecting first one trend then another. His progress is spasmodic and there is no continuous form of development. His expression changes direction in rapid succession and only from 1934 did he emerge with a more consistent style that was recognisably his own. From the welter of influences, Martinů at forty-four began to find himself. The years 1935 to 1940 show him in full command of his powers and in the United States he established himself and reached maturity with the Symphonies, Concertos and the remarkable *Fantaisies symphoniques*. After 1947, possibly as a result of his accident, his production of worthwhile compositions was erratic and only during the last seven years of his life did he regain a certain consistency.

If these are the formative influences behind the man, how did they manifest themselves in his music? Almost certainly the most characteristic feature of any Martinů score is its rhythmic flexibility, and invariably he chose to work with simple duple and triple patterns because they offered greater scope for syncopation – itself a natural and inevitable part of Bohemian-Moravian folk idiom. But to say this is to suggest that Martinů's music is bound by the barline, and nothing could be further from the truth. Often barline and time signature are little more than an aid to reading and in some works, such as the *Fantasia and Toccata* for solo piano, Martinů dispenses with them for certain passages. Elsewhere he seems to delight in the spontaneity that can be achieved from the use of additive and constantly changing time signatures. A rhythmic legacy was obviously inherited from jazz, as the Sextet for piano and wind instruments (1929) and *Esquisses* for piano solo (1931) show, and other features were taken over from Stravinsky; but it was the toccata elements which contributed most to his music's drive and excitement, and these do much to overcome the shortcomings in structure and tonality that appear from time to time. The folk music of the Vysočina also added considerably to Martinů's rhythmic vocabulary and is certainly responsible for phrase groups of three-, five- and seven-bar lengths, for repeated cadential figures and for the *halekačky* mountain call, put to such good effect in the second Act of *Theatre Beyond the Gate,* in the 'cowgirls' movement of *Kytice* and in *The Opening of the Wells.*

Harmonically Martinů's music belongs to the Romantic school. He never adopted serial techniques, liked to think of his work as basically diatonic and seemed most at home when writing in the key of B flat major or minor. Though he used chromatic alteration and bi-tonal and polytonal combinations as much as anybody else, as the abrasively dissonant *Fantasia* for two pianos of 1929 shows, he invariably began and ended each movement, as Hindemith was to do, with a concord. The Second Symphony opens and closes in the key of D and the Third begins on E flat and ends in E; and in a score such as the *Fantaisies symphoniques* the relationship of keys a perfect fourth apart becomes apparent (the movements being in F, B flat and E flat). But what Martinů does within this framework is often very personal. He makes use of the whole tone scale but more often reverts to the Lydian and Mixolydian modes, and in the opening movement of the Sixth String Quartet there is a suggestion of the Phrygian mode. His preference for a form of progressive tonality has been mentioned in connection with the Symphonies (the initial movement of the Second begins in D minor and closes in B flat), but this technique was extended to other works such as the Third Cello Sonata and the Third Violin Sonata, whose opening movements are recognisably in B flat, while the point to which they progress can be seen to be C. To bind these wandering poles of tonality together Martinů would resort to static bases and ostinatos as a steadying device. The pedal, sometimes in the form of a slow trill or drone originating from the *dudy,* the bagpipe of Moravian folk music, is another link with the music of home and was often the only means by which his fragmentary textures could be sustained, as the opening of the Fifth Symphony reveals, where B natural and B flat pedals pull against each other. However, his harmonic vocabulary could often have a disarming simplicity, especially when he chose to move in progressions of parallel thirds and sixths. This was certainly a feature he inherited from Moravian folk song along with a series of second inversion triads and an organum-like succession of bare fourths and fifths. In common with many of his contemporaries, he would alter chords by striking appoggiaturas with the other notes instead of preceding them, thus producing ninths and sevenths which do not resolve and have no apparent grammatical connection. But of all his harmonic marks of style, the 'Moravian cadence' found in Janáček's *Taras Bulba* and particularly associated with the opera *Juliette* is the most distinguished and the most readily recognisable.

As a melodist Martinů lacks the long shapely tunes of Richard Strauss, Poulenc or Prokofiev. The melodic element in Martinů's scores is, however, just as important even if it is fragmentary and subordinate to considerations of rhythm and texture. His melodic idiom invariably displays certain recognisable marks of style, some of them – scalic passages, triadic tunes and the melismatic hovering between the tonic and the third degree of the scale (sometimes major, sometimes minor) – stemming from Moravian folk idiom. Other features can be more specifically detailed. A descending three-note pattern (a minor third followed by a major second) is paralleled by Skřivánek's folk-song aria in Smetana's *The Secret;* the symbolic use of the familiar Czech chorale 'St. Wenceslas' can be found in *Czech Rhapsody, La Rhapsodie,* Symphony No. 1, the *Fantaisies symphoniques,* and *Memorial to Lidice;* a four-note pattern similar to the leading motif of Dvořák's *Requiem* can be traced to the Third Symphony, the Third Piano Concerto, the Violin Concerto, the *Fantaisies symphoniques* and the *Fantasia and Toccata* for solo piano; plain-chant will be found in the *Field Mass* and Greek liturgical chants in *The Greek Passion.*

But this list of some of Martinů's melodic features omits all hint of the real importance of the melodic element in his work. More than Richard Strauss, Prokofiev or Bartók, Martinů evolved and perfected a technique of germinal development which invites comparison with that of Sibelius. The great tunes of early classical composers can often be separated from their context and can be successfully presented with different instrumentation, different significance and even different harmonisation. With Martinů the tune is not a separate element. The three notes which generally form the motif grow, change, acquire force as the movement pushes forward until they are seen to be the very elements out of which the whole musical structure has developed. This achievement of musical unity through continuously developing motifs may well be Martinů's greatest contribution to the art of composition. It was this

145

system which occupied his mind more frequently than any other and about two thirds of his entire production shows him adopting this working method. Far more than Sibelius, Roussel, Janáček or Bartók, Martinů has made this technique his own and it holds a place in his life's work quite apart from individual pieces.

Consideration of the influence of Czech folk idiom, Debussy, the music of the eighteenth century and so on in forming Martinů's musical mind does not give a complete account of the process. Although he was first and last a composer, he was subject to various important non-musical influences. He was an omnivorous reader. He knew and loved the works of Czech and Russian authors and used them for the basis of *Comedy on the Bridge*, *The Marriage* and *What Men Live By*. Goldoni's *La Locandiera* inspired *Mirandolina* and Kazantzakis's *Christ Recrucified* was the source of *The Greek Passion*. His willingness to join forces with literary members of the Surrealist circle led him to collaborate with Georges Ribemont-Dessaignes in *The Tears of the Knife* and *The Three Wishes* and with Georges Neveux in *Juliette* and *Ariadne*. The works of Goethe, Heine, Poe, Bureš and others inspired early songs and late cantatas, and ancient oriental literature supplied the subject of *The Epic of Gilgamesh*. But in spite of this wide field of literary influences it is surprising that Martinů, unlike Milhaud, Stravinsky or Poulenc, found no inspiration in the work of Cocteau, Apollinaire or Claudel. Of his contemporaries, it was only the philosophy of Antoine de Saint-Exupéry that moved him to compose *The Parables*, while the poetry of Walt Whitman and W. H. Auden which prompted Vaughan Williams, Delius and Stravinsky to give their best left no impression on Martinů. The cinema, however, fascinated him and his alertness to modern trends and techniques led him to experiment with film episodes in *The Three Wishes*. He gained practical experience in writing for the cinema between 1922 and 1935, when he produced the scores to five documentary films and incidental music to Pirandello's *Six Characters In Search Of An Author* and André Gide's *Oedipus*. In the Thirties he began to explore the possibilities of radio in *Voice of the Forest*, *Comedy on the Bridge* and *Kytice,* and in the Fifties attempted (sometimes unsuccessfully) to come to grips with the techniques of television opera in *What Men Live By* and *The Marriage*.

Clearly Martinů was a man of so lively and receptive a mind that he could quickly assimilate every new trend. Instinctively in the Twenties he had responded to the accumulated culture and tradition of Paris, but though he made himself familiar with the intellectual fashions of the day he did not succumb to all of them. With the exception of neo-classicism, jazz and the music of Roussel and Stravinsky, Martinů

39. Martinů's original sketch for the *Concerto da Camera* for violin and orchestra.

40. Martinů in 1948.

remained unconvinced by much that he found around him. His meagre knowledge of French and his natural shyness made it difficult for him to make friends easily. He formed no important association with painters or sculptors and seemed to concern himself little with the aesthetics of contemporary art. The work of Picasso and of Braque left no impression on him and he later displayed a stronger affinity with the work of Piero della Francesca than with Cubism and Fauvism. The only artists with whom Martinů made contact at this time were Jan Zrzavý, František Tichý and Jáno Bednář, and by contrast one cannot but think of Stravinsky whose circle of acquaintances included most of the significant painters and theatrical designers of the day. Even in the world of the theatre, Martinů was influenced less than other composers: he never made contact with Diaghilev, let alone wrote for him.

Looking back over Martinů's life, it is possible to see the Second World War as one of the most formative forces on his mind and therefore on his art. In company with Bartók and Hindemith he was obliged to leave war-scarred Europe and re-establish himself on alien soil as best he could. For many years he hung uncertainly between the old world and the new. After the war he could never reconcile himself to the Communist regime, yet he never made roots in North America. However much he incorporated Moravian and Bohemian folk idiom in all that he wrote and whatever his nostalgia for his native land, he could never bring himself to return. He joined the large, distinguished and rather pathetic body of American citizens whose gratitude to their hosts could never compensate for the loss of their patrimony. The parallel with Bartók is immediate. But whereas Bartók on the surface never allowed political feeling to influence his music, Martinů, on some half-a-dozen occasions at least, found inspiration in political events. The *Czech Rhapsody* celebrates the founding of the First Republic in 1918; the *Double Concerto* (1938) is the composer's protest against the Nazi invasion of Czechoslovakia; the *Field Mass* is a testament and tribute to the Czech volunteers; the *Memorial to Lidice* was prompted by war-time atrocities in his homeland; the Third Piano Concerto was coloured by the death of Jan Masaryk in 1948; and *The Greek Passion* attracted him less for Kazantzakis's literary merits, great though they are, than for its treatment of the subject of an oppressed people.

It is not unreasonable to expect the work of such uprooted artists as Martinů, Bartók and Hindemith to reflect the contemporary and political events in which they themselves were deeply involved; yet Bartók seemed to inhabit a private region where world-shattering and world-shaping events never raised an echo. He deliberately shut out the political scene when he composed and concentrated on pure musical content. In

Mathis der Maler Hindemith did indeed express indirectly his resentment at the treatment of the artist in Nazi society, but otherwise appeared to join Bartók in keeping art and political feeling in separate compartments. More than either Bartók or Hindemith, Martinů used his music to express the pity, horror and resentment provoked by contemporary events. Tragedy is as much a factor in his art as it is in that of Kafka. And while Kafka from his Berlin suburb dreamt of an America no one knew, Martinů, from the real America, remembered a Bohemia which no longer existed. Nevertheless at all times he remained wholly Czech. He never yielded to the influence of his foreign environment; he looked to Czech folk music and drama as part of his heritage, and resisted every pressure to become French or American in feeling. And if passages in the Violin Concerto of 1943 suggest the scores of Aaron Copland this is coincidental; for his musical outlook, like that of Martinů, was coloured by years of study in Paris where he, too, made acquaintance with the welter and chaos of the Twenties.

The variety of interests which influenced Martinů might suggest that he was a dilettante. Nothing could be further from the truth. He was before everything else a musician, and compositions of widely differing value poured endlessly from his pen. While admitting that much of his vast output can claim no permanent place in the musical repertoire because of weaknesses in either form or content or both, it is possible to regard some twenty or so pieces at least as having significant value or lasting originality. Each of the following scores is of sufficient calibre to justify its standing alongside Bartók, Hindemith or Prokofiev and is a work which only Martinů could have produced.

> Symphonies Nos. 1, 2, 3, 4, 5
> *Fantaisies symphoniques*
> *The Parables*
> *The Frescoes*
> *Concerto Grosso*
> *Double Concerto*
> Piano Concerto No. 4 (*Incantation*)
> Concerto for Two Pianos
> Violin Concertos Nos. 1, 2
> *Concerto da Camera* (for violin and strings)
> *Juliette*
> *Ariadne*
> *The Greek Passion*
> String Quartet No. 5

> Piano Quartet No. 1
> *Fantasia and Toccata* for solo piano
> *The Epic of Gilgamesh*
> *Field Mass*
> *Kytice*
> *The Opening of the Wells*
> *The Romance of the Dandelions*

As a symphonist Martinů must be counted among the six or eight contemporary composers who have enriched this field. None of his symphonies is directly programmatic as are Shostakovitch's Seventh (*Leningrad*), Eleventh (*1905*) and Twelfth (*The Year 1917*). Nevertheless, external influence is sometimes evident as it is in the Third Symphony of Honegger, the Eighth of Shostakovitch, and in the Fourth, Fifth and Sixth of Vaughan Williams. This trio of symphonies records the reaction of a great and sensitive man to the contemporary scene, now facing the horror of external events, now retreating into the sanctuary of the resolved mind. The parallel in Martinů's work is to be found in the First, Third and Sixth Symphonies. But comparison with Shostakovitch and Vaughan Williams gives no hint of the originality of structure in the composer's symphonic works. Roussel's Third Symphony has won attention for its use of a four-note motif as a means of unifying the four movements, but the device is not organic. Sibelius's use of developing motifs as exemplified in his symphonies displays a much more organic use of the system; but it was left to Martinů to continue and further the work of Sibelius in motif development and extend the process of progressive tonality within movements as exploited by Mahler and Nielsen.

The six symphonies and a number of his orchestral scores indicate how far apart from Schoenberg, Berg and Webern Martinů stands. It is possible to compare Martinů's *Half-time* with Honegger's *Rugby*, while what Honegger seems to be able to evoke in terms of brakes and cam-shafts in *Pacific, 231* is paralleled in Martinů's propeller noises in *La Bagarre*. In both groups of works the composers attempted to create music of an exteriorised nature; both composers wrote music of abundant energy and motoric rhythms, using linear techniques. In the *Serenade, Partita, Inventions* and *Ricercari,* however, Martinů was looking back to the eighteenth century and establishing a point of contact with Roussel and Conrad Beck who were revitalising old forms in a contemporary idiom. But where Beck, under the influence of Bach, developed a severe, unsmiling way of writing, Martinů managed to combine the linear thinking of Bach with the Gallic wit of his mentor. Yet although

Martinů was using early forms for the *Inventions* and *Ricercari* there was no suggestion of pastiche. He turned to them because he saw in them an anticipation of his own technique.

He adopted the style of the concerto grosso in his *Double Concerto* and *Concerto Grosso* for the same reason. From the early years of this century composers have been attracted to the concerto grosso form. Elgar in his *Introduction and Allegro* and Vaughan Williams in his *Tallis Fantasia* had used it, adhering more closely to traditional form than ever Martinů did, while Bloch in his *Concerto Grosso* (1924) and Tippett in his *Double Concerto* maintained eighteenth-century custom by repeating whole sections almost unaltered. Stravinsky's excursion into the territory in 1938 has interesting similarities and dissimilarities with Martinů's. *Dumbarton Oaks* is pastiche plain and simple, derived from the idiom of Bach's *Brandenburg Concertos*. Here Stravinsky is using a development similar to Bach's, as also did Martinů. Richard Strauss's *Metamorphosen* also provides a link with Martinů, though in an altogether different way. Looking back over the changes that had occurred in Europe during his lifetime, notably the tragedy of Germany's defeat and ruin, and her cultural tradition (as manifest in his beloved Munich Opera House) broken beyond recall, Strauss found the material for his thoughts in a fragment from the Funeral March in Beethoven's Third Symphony and a phrase from the second Act of Wagner's *Tristan und Isolde*. Martinů put his two major excursions into the form to similar use. But his feelings were of course quite different. He expressed his feelings about the Munich crisis in the *Concerto Grosso*, and about the Nazi invasion of Czechoslovakia in the *Double Concerto*, with a strongly personal emotion of a kind usually associated with Mahler rather than Martinů.

Martinů's achievement in the solo concerto is less easy to estimate. A score like the Harpsichord Concerto of 1935, which nicely combines solo harpsichord with obbligato piano and thus anticipates Frank Martin's *Petite symphonie concertante* by ten years, is dazzling and superficially attractive, but does not otherwise represent the significant Martinů. Three concertos, however, stand out as having lasting qualities. The Concerto for Two Pianos challenges comparison with Bartók's Sonata for Two Pianos and Percussion (rescored by the composer for two pianos and orchestra). While Bartók regards his solo instruments more percussively than does Martinů, and the remarkable pianistic effects are more contrapuntal and barbaric than anything Martinů produces, the Concerto is no less demanding and no less satisfying. It is a brilliant, extravert work which wears well, not because of its rhythmic vitality or its masterly solo writing, but because of its musical personality, its urgency and, above all because of its sense of excitement. The Violin Concerto of 1943 is another fine score and in some respects it looks back to Proko-fiev's Second Violin Concerto which appeared five years earlier. Both works are lyrical in feeling, brilliantly written for the soloist and nostalgic in their use of folk idiom. *Incantation*, the Piano Concerto No. 4, is entirely unconventional. Here Martinů is at his most masterly and both movements show him exploiting every form of piano writing except the purely lyrical. In some respects it is an experimental work, but the technical and idiomatic aspects of new sonorities, such as those in the first movement cadenza where piano and harp are combined, are any-thing but merely experimental – this is where Martinů is saying some-thing completely new and important.

The first fifty years of this century have seen the field of chamber music enriched by some of the finest work of contemporary composers, and one has only to consider the place the string quartet and works for piano and strings have in the catalogues of Bartók, Schoenberg, Berg and Webern to realise, by comparison, how unimportant these media were for Martinů. Though he produced over sixty works in this field few bring him into serious competition with his contemporaries. In certain scores the interest seems to flag as he becomes more intent on pleasing the performer than the listener. Technically Martinů's chamber music is eminently playable, and delightfully arranged for the various combinations, and in this respect it stands close to Honegger's. But while it fulfils most of the essentials of good chamber music it often falls short of a standard set by Hindemith or Prokofiev and few, if any, of Martinů's chamber pieces invite comparison with Beethoven – a privi-lege reserved almost exclusively for Bartók. Nevertheless, Martinů was a passionate believer in chamber music, and next to opera it was the form of expression in which he most enjoyed working.

I am always more myself in pure chamber music. I cannot express what pleasure it gives me when I start work and begin to handle four instru-mental parts. In a quartet one feels at home. Outside it may be raining and darkness is falling but these four voices take no heed. They are independent, free to do what they like, free to create a unity, a new har-monious note.

While Martinů obviously enjoyed writing for chamber groups he seldom seems to have regarded this music as a vehicle for his most significant thoughts. This is not to suggest that he treated the form casually. Far from it. But rather less than one tenth of his chamber compositions are of vital and permanent interest, and many scores rattle on mechanically like twentieth-century Telemann. However, the Second

Cello and Third Violin Sonatas are vigorous and powerful; the *Madri-gals* for violin and viola have all the brilliance of the duos of Wieni-awski while containing far richer thought; the Quartet for piano and strings recalls the turbulence and drama of the composer's experiences in the harrowing war years; the Quartet for oboe, violin, cello and piano has a graceful, stylised charm, and the Nonet, written within months of the composer's death, has all the freshness of youth, pre-sented with the happiest choice of instrumentation. Of the String Quartets, the Third pays homage to Debussy, the Fourth to Honegger. The Fifth and Sixth bear comparison with Bartók's Third and Sixth in their remarkable harmonic pungency and force of intellect; whereas the Sixth is impressive because of its spontaneity and vivid personal idiom, the Fifth is remarkable for the occasions when lyricism breaks through the abrasive textures to reveal an intensity of beauty only rarely felt in Bartók's Third.

If Bartók's chamber pieces are among the best of our time, his con-tribution to dramatic music is somewhat less remarkable. The reverse is true of Martinů and a review of his stage work gives a variety of interesting parallels with the outstanding contemporary productions of the opera house. The earliest opera, *The Soldier and the Dancer*, a satirical piece in the style of Offenbach, was to that extent fifty years behind the times when it appeared in 1926; but with its experiments in mimicry, the introduction of jazz, anticipating Weill's *Mahagonny*, and Křenek's *Jonny spielt auf*, it is typical of the Twenties. The pattern set by *The Soldier and the Dancer* was not to be repeated. *The Tears of the Knife*, an experimental work remarkable for the eccentric nature of its plot, marks Martinů's sympathy for the Parisian *avant-garde* theatre. It is possible to draw a parallel between *The Tears of the Knife* and Hindemith's *Neues vom Tage*: in both operas the element of burlesque is paramount, but in Martinů's score there is a sense of the macabre which is not to be found anywhere in the Hindemith. *The Three Wishes* is a special work which epitomises those qualities fashionable in the music of *Les Six* during the 1920s and looks back to the fantasy world Prokofiev inhabited in *The Love of Three Oranges*. But most important is the way Martinů and his librettist, Ribemont-Dessaignes, combined stage and film techniques in a manner that anticipated Milhaud's *Christopher Columbus* and Honegger's *Jeanne d'Arc au bûcher*. Miracle plays and folk dramas of Czechoslovakia were to motivate *The Plays of Mary,* while Surrealist fantasy led to *Juliette*. The dream world, the disassociated figures and images of Neveux's play bring to mind Tippett's *Midsummer Marriage* nearly twenty years later. Despite its deliberate remoteness from reality, Martinů's opera evokes in an audience profound emotions of pity and fear, of sympathy and resentment in the way that Berg does in *Wozzeck* and Britten in *Peter Grimes*. But mention of these composers in no way implies that their working methods or operatic techniques are shared by Martinů who invariably, and not always wisely, insisted on being his own librettist. *Juliette* shows his sense of the theatre at its most expert. His handling of dramatic situations is sure even though his prime concern is to create a feeling of the stage rather than of reality. *Juliette* is his most significant opera and by comparison the works created for radio and television (*Voice of the Forest, Comedy on the Bridge, What Men Live By* and *The Marriage*) solve none of the problems which the two different media impose. In *Mirandolina,* however, he produced his most successful comedy which can be happily paralleled with Prokofiev's *Betrothal in a Monastery,* and in *Ariadne* he made an eighteenth-century gesture in twentieth-century dress. With *The Greek Passion* Martinů achieved a standard of operatic writing which is the equal of *Juliette,* though so different from it. *The Greek Passion* is his only tragic opera and though, like Prokofiev's *War and Peace,* its unwieldy, episodic nature militates against true operatic form, Martinů's understanding of dramatic situation is impressive and much of the music is beautiful, compelling and sometimes visionary. Clearly the composer was here engaged on a work of high seriousness in which his deepest convictions were involved.

Martinů's career as an operatic composer is similar to that of Prokofiev or Hindemith. The early works are satirical and identify him with the *avant-garde.* In the 1930s Martinů's conception of opera changed and he became more dependent upon its visual qualities. Where Prokofiev abandoned the style of *The Love of Three Oranges* for *The Fiery Angel* and *War and Peace,* where Hindemith grew out of the pastiche of *Mörder, Hoffnung der Frauen* and *Das Nusch-Nuschi* towards the more earnest *Cardillac* and the philosophical *Mathis der Maler,* so Martinů similarly rejected Surrealism for fantasy and far more significant work. At their best his operas display a seriousness of purpose which is the equal of Hindemith's, an understanding of stage techniques no less accomplished than Britten's and an ability to create characters as forceful as those of Prokofiev.

In the field of ballet Martinů's achievement was less even. This is strange, for ballet, with its opportunities for fantasy, might have been expected to attract a composer who so often preferred the world of imagination to that of fact. Apart from *The Strangler,* his ballets date from the formative years; thus he emerges under the influence of Debussy in *Istar* and emulates the satirical Poulenc of *Les Biches,* the Satie of *Parade* and the Prokofiev of *Chout* in *Revolt* and *Kitchen*

Revue, though he never assimilated jazz to the extent that Stravinsky did in *L'Histoire du soldat* or Milhaud in *La Création du monde.* However interesting Martinů's early ballets are, the only work to leave a deep impression is *Špaliček. Anastasia* and *Echoing of Trumpets,* which have been created as ballets by Kenneth Macmillan and Antony Tudor from the *Fantaisies symphoniques* and *Memorial to Lidice* since the composer's death hardly count. However, with *Špaliček* the affinity between Prokofiev and Martinů stops; for *Cinderella* and *Romeo and Juliet* maintain the tradition of Russian classical ballet with an objectivity, restrained lyricism and pathos rarely to be found in *Špaliček.* This can be accounted for by the fact that Martinů saw *Špaliček* as a vehicle for transporting Moravian folk songs and dances from the village green to the theatre stage. The composer's indebtedness to Stravinsky's sung ballets is obvious but another, and in some ways more important, point of contact is with Szymanowski's ballet-pantomime *Harnasie.* Each work celebrates in its own way something of the folk dances and customs of the composer's youthful environment. And as the Tatra-Polish folk element is pervasive in Szymanowski, so Bohemian-Moravian folk idiom is decisive in Martinů. The attitude of both men toward folk music is similar: they both succeed in capturing the very essence of their national characters without direct quotation of folk song. For Martinů the ballet stage was a happy place for experiment and here his taste for attaching new ideas to old had unlimited scope. The similarity to Stravinsky is again immediate, but Martinů's achievement was smaller. For all his interest and aptitude, he did not find himself in this genre, and even in the realm of choral music he made few significant contributions to the accepted categories.

Martinů, it would appear, always felt choral music to be closer to the soil than to heaven, and perhaps this explains why his output contains no church music and only one score with a religious purpose. Bloch, Stravinsky, Poulenc, Blacher, Rubbra, Kodály, Vaughan Williams, and Janáček, regardless of their absorbing preoccupation with other work, all produced at least one Mass or Service; but in spite of his upbringing in the Church and his return to it at the end of his life, Martinů's nearest approach to a liturgical work is the *Field Mass,* which anticipates in a remarkable way Britten's *War Requiem. The Epic of Gilgamesh* is Martinů's sole contribution to large-scale oratorio, and important though it is, it shows that the composer felt less at ease when working with many voices in a concerted form or when interpreting the mind of tradition. He was at home in the simplest situation, in the intimacy of the Polička streets, in the friendly atmosphere of the surrounding countryside. For this reason *Kytice* and the four chamber cantatas which treat in nostalgic mood the folk customs and legends of the Bohemian-Moravian highlands are among his most original contributions to choral music. There appears to be no parallel to these scores in the music of his contemporaries; for whereas a folk tune, or folk-tune influence, is noticeable in the works of Bartók, Prokofiev, Kodály and Vaughan Williams, in Martinů's cantatas there seems to be no distinction between this and the original idiom, since he speaks with the fluency of an unselfconscious Moravian who had absorbed the essence of folk idiom into his very being.

Naturally enough the rhythms and patterns of Moravian folk dance form an important part of *The Opening of the Wells,* the *Brigand Songs* and the charming *Petrklíč* cycle, and folk dance is also the foundation of the bulk of Martinů's piano music. Here again a point of contact with Szymanowski can be established; but where Szymanowski's Opus 50 pieces made a marriage of Tatra themes and Mazurka rhythms, Martinů turned to Moravian folk melody and to the small dance forms which Smetana had treated years before. In spite of scores such as the *Fantasia and Toccata,* Martinů was a composer of piano miniatures and though he was not a pianist like Prokofiev, he had the same feeling for the piano, the same appreciation for the layout of the keyboard. However, Martinů did not adopt in any extreme measure the view that the piano was necessarily to be treated solely as a percussion instrument. He made little use of keyboard counterpoint, unlike Hindemith in *Ludus Tonalis,* Bartók in *Mikrokosmos* or Shostakovich in his *Preludes and Fugues;* nor does his work bear any comparison with the large-scale sonatas of Skryabin. Martinů's single excursion into the realm of the piano sonata does not entitle him to any comparison with Prokofiev, though, like Prokofiev's, Martinů's piano music is technically in the tradition of the early twentieth-century in that he uses the full sonorities of the instrument and does not treat the piano in a quasi-eighteenth-century style. Martinů's natural feeling for Czech dance forms enabled him to write the twentieth-century equivalent of the salon pieces Smetana and Fibich had produced in the previous century. However, the *Czech Dances* for two pianos are the exception. The three movements are not far short of the pattern of the two-piano sonatas established by Poulenc, a score with which Martinů's *Dances* can favourably be compared.

From this brief review of Martinů's work and the comparison with his contemporaries, it seems that he is perhaps nearest to Prokofiev; and by a strange coincidence their careers had certain similarities. Both composers grew up in the Nationalist movements of their countries; both found academic training irksome; both joined the neo-classic, *avant-garde* movement in Paris; both rediscovered their Nationalism in the years before the Second World War; both succeeded in fusing national and cosmopolitan elements as a result of long periods of residence in France. But whereas Prokofiev returned to Russia in 1933, conformed to the party line and accepted official praise and rebuke, Martinů, the victim of war, remained a refugee in a land which gave him shelter and fame but where he suffered the pangs of nostalgic regret. Despite this difference, both men were devoted, dedicated and prolific – if a little uneven. Nevertheless both men served their art in striving after and achieving new modes of expression and in contributing much to the contemporary scene.

If ever there was a dedicated artist, it was surely Bohuslav Martinů. He was indifferent to wealth and social position, and no consideration of financial gain ever turned him from composition. He was a deep thinker who began in the religious tradition of Europe and returned to it at the last, having meanwhile explored many intellectual pursuits and accepted none of them. Had Martinů not been a musician he might well have been a man of letters. He was rational, well-read and an entirely personal artist. Yet his cosmopolitanism and his variety of interests never allowed him to forget his native land. His years of residence in France, North America, Italy and Switzerland affected him in various ways, but both man and music remained totally Czech to the very end.

10 Catalogue of Works

Martinů's vast output and curiously indifferent attitude to compositions once they had been completed makes it difficult to catalogue his works. He himself enumerated few of his own pieces and never resorted to a table or systematic list of opus numbers. He was notoriously careless when recalling details of his own scores, was often unaware of the whereabouts of manuscripts and invariably had to be reminded that he had even written certain works. The complexity of Martinů's life's course, taking him from Prague to Paris, to North America and back to Italy and Switzerland, makes impossible the task of bringing all his manuscripts together. However, two main sources exist: the Martinů Museum in Polička, Czechoslovakia, and the private collection of the composer's widow in Vieux-Moulin, France. The former contains well over a hundred youthful efforts and much else besides, while Madame Martinů's library houses a substantial collection of works from the middle period and later years. The remaining two hundred or so scores can be traced to museums and private collections in Prague, Brno, Paris, Switzerland and throughout the United States.

To make a summary of all Martinů's scores is obviously a daunting task. Fortunately much important catalogue work has been done by the composer's friend and first biographer Miloš Šafránek and more recently by the Czech musicologist Jaroslav Mihule. Over the last few years I have been fortunate in having access to the Archives in Polička and to Madame Martinů's library and the following catalogues are the result of my findings in Czechoslovakia and France. I would like to express my thanks to Charlotte Martinů and to the curators of the Polička Museum for making so much material available to me and to mention Harry Halbreich's comprehensive table of the composer's works (1968) which has provided a useful check list.

1. LIST OF WORKS IN ORDER OF COMPOSITION

1902	*Tři jezdci* (*The Three Riders*), string quartet	Polička
1907	*Posvícení* (*Candlemass* or *Village Wake*), suite for flute and strings	Polička
1909	*Elegy*, for violin and piano	Polička
	Dumka, for piano	Polička
1910	*Five Waltzes*, for piano: *Andante*; *Valse Mignone* (*sic*); *Tempo di Valse*; *Tempo di Valse*; *Tempo di Valse*	Prague, 14 January–1 April
	Než se naděješ (*Before You Know*), song; text: J. Cěrvenka	Prague, 20 March
	V přírodě (*In Nature*), song; text: V. Hálek	Prague, 20 March
	Pastel, song; text: B. Kaminský	Prague, 20 March
	Utonulá (*The Drowned Maiden*), song; text: J. Sládek	Prague
	Až buděme staří (*When We Are Old*), song; text: A. Klášterský	Prague
	Dělníci moře (*Les Travailleurs de la mer*), sketch for a symphonic poem	Polička, 18–20 April
	Romance for violin and piano	Smiřice
	Concerto for violin and piano	Polička
	Two small songs in folk idiom: (a) *Pověra* (*Superstition*); text: J. Manin (b) *Dívčí píseň* (*Maiden's Song*); text: J. Sládek	Prague, 25–26 April
	Smrt Tintagilova (*The Death of Tintaliles*), symphonic poem to a Maeterlinck puppet play	Prague, 8–21 June
	Smuteční pochod (*Funeral March*), for piano	Prague
	Anděl smrti (*The Angel of Death*), symphonic poem	Prague, 6–13 July
	Nocturne, song; text: A. Klášterský	Prague
	Spící (*The Sleeper*), song; text: E. A. Poe	Polička, 21 July
	Idyle, for piano	Polička
	Two songs: (a) *Proč zoubky tvé tak smály se?* (*Why Have you Laughed at Me?*), text: V. Houdek (b) *Kde jsme to byla?* (*Where Have I Been?*), text: R. Jesenká	Želiv, 5–6 August

Dívčí sny (Maiden's Dream), song; Prague
text : R. Huch

Zpěv a hudba (Song and Music), Prague
song; text : unknown

Ballade, for piano Prague, 10 October

Sousedská, for piano Prague, 14 October

Zimní noc (A Winter's Night), song; Prague
text : A. Heyduk

Líbej, milá, líbej (Kiss Me, Beloved), Prague, 17 October
song; text : J. Manin

Pohádka o zlatovlásce (Tales of the Prague, 12 October–
Golden Fleece), for piano 11 November
(a) *Fairy tale* (b) *Pastorale* (c)
Dumka (d) *Barcarolle* (e) *Valse*

Náladová kresba (Picture of a Mood), Polička, 25 December
song; text : V. Klen

V noci (In the Night), song; text : Prague, 14 January
R. Mayer

Dvě písně (Two Songs) : Polička, 10 February
(a) *Dívčí píseň (A Maiden's Song)*,
(b) *Až přijde den (When Day
Comes)*; text : J. Sládek

Cradle Song, for violin and piano Polička

Adagio for violin and piano Polička

Tři písničky (Three Little Songs) : Prague, 11–26 May
(a) *Má matička (Mother Bear)*, text :
J. Sládek
(b) *Pravý počet (The Correct Number)*, text : E. Mužík
(c) *Chybili jsme ráno (We Roamed
in the Morning)*, text : J. Manin

Piano quintet Polička, 6 June–1 August

Chanson triste, for piano Polička, October

Jašková zpěvánka (Jašek's Song), Prague
text : K. Tetmajer

Song (without title), text : E. Mužík Prague

Umírá duše (Starving Soul), sketch for Prague
a song; text : unknown

První láska (First Love), song; text :
E. Mužík

Slzy (Tears), song; text : J. Sládek Polička, 24 December

1912 Z *pohádek Andersenových (Seven* Polička, 1–7 January
*piano pieces on Hans Andersen's
Fairy Tales)* :
(a) *Ballade* (b) *Barcarolle* (c) *Novelette* (d) *Polonaise* (e) *Valse Mignone*

(*sic*) (f) *Intermezzo* (g) *Legende*	
Konec všemu (*All is Ended*), song; text : E. Mužík	Prague, 14 January
Mrtvá Láska (*Dead Love*), song; text: E. Mužík	Prague, 20 January
First movement of a symphony (sketch)	Prague
Píseň beze slov (*Song Without Words*), for piano	Prague
Nocturne, for piano	Prague
Ty píšeš mi (*You Write to Me*), song; text : A. Heyduk	Prague, March
Ráno raníčko, pleju obilíčko (*Early in the Morning I Sort the Grain*), song; text : unknown	Prague, 10 March
Lucie, song; text : A. de Musset	Prague
Dětství (*From Childhood*), song; text : D. von Liliencron	Prague, 13 March
Padlo jíní na pole (*Hoar-Frost in the Field*), song; text : H. Heine	Prague, 18 March
Vdejte mne, matičko (*Marry Me, Mother*), song; text : K. Tetmajer	Prague, 20 March
Růže (*The Rose*), song; text: E. Mužík	Prague
To všechno už jen zbylo (*Only This Remains*), song; text : J. Sládek	Prague
Ballade, for piano, 'The Last Chords of Chopin'	Prague
Noc každou tebe drahá zřím (*I See You Every Night, My Love*), song; text : H. Heine	Prague
Offertorium, for soprano and organ	Polička
Ave Maria, for soprano and organ	Polička
String Quartet (lost)	Polička
Andante, for orchestra (sketch)	Polička
Fantaisie, for violin and piano	Polička, July
Two Nocturnes, for string quartet (lost)	Polička
Andante, for string quartet	Polička
Ballade, for piano, 'Under Miss Vilma's Umbrella'	Polička
Mluv ke mně dál! (*Speak On!*), song; text : K. Tetmajer	Polička, 22 August
Opuštěná milá (*The Jilted Maiden*), song; text : L. Grossmanová-Brodská	Polička, 23 August
Niponari, seven songs with orchestra	Polička, August

to Japanese poetry

Kdysi (*Once Upon a Time*), song; text: L. Grossmanová-Brodská	Polička, 3 September
O mrtvých očích (*Dead Eyes*), song; text: V. Martínek	Polička, 17 September
Ohnivý muž (*The Fiery Man*), song; text: V. Hlavsa	Polička
Píseň prvního listopadu (*Song for the First of November*); text: V. Hlavsa	Polička
Tři panny za světlé noci (*Three Maidens on a Bright Night*), song; text: V. Hlavsa	Polička
Stará píseň (*Old Song*), text: V. de l'Isle-Adam	Polička
Komárova svatba (*Gnat's Wedding*), song to a Czech folk poem	Polička
Svítaj, Bože! (*Let There Be Light, O God!*), song to a Slovakian folk poem	Polička
V zahradě na hradě (*In the Castle Garden*), song to a Czech folk poem	Polička
Labutě (*The Swan*), song; text: J. Wojkovic	Polička
Mám staré párky rád (*I Love Old Parks*), song; text: J. Borecký	Polička
Písnička o Haničce (*Song of Hanička*); text: Kalhus	Polička
Štěstí to dost (*Enough Happiness*), song; text: D. von Liliencron	Prague, 11 December

1913	*Le Soir*, for voice and harp; melodrama to a text by Albert Samain	Prague
	La Libellule (*The Dragonfly*), for voice, violin, harp and piano; melodrama to a text by Henri d'Orange	Prague
	Danseuses de Java, for voice, viola, harp and piano; melodrama to a text by Arthur Symonds	Prague
	Prelude on the theme of *The Marseillaise*, for piano	Prague
	Prelude in F minor, for piano	Prague
	Matičko má, hocha mám (*Mother Mine, I Have a Friend*), song to Spanish words; text: unknown	Prague
	Three songs to French words; text	

unknown :
  (a) *Le Sapin de Noël* (b) *Le Petit
Oiseau* (c) *Le Soir*

	Noc (Night), meloplastic dance scene in one act	Polička
	Composition for orchestra (untitled)	Polička
1914	Nocturne No. 1 in F sharp minor, for orchestra	Polička
	Loutky III (Puppets), four pieces for piano : (a) *Pierrot's Serenade* (b) *The Sentimental Puppet* (c) *Colombine* (d) *Puppet Dance*	Polička
	Tance se závoji (Dances with a Veil) meloplastic dance scene (lost)	Prague
	Four Little Goethe Songs : (a) *Šťastná jízda (Good Journey)* (b) *Písnička skřítků (Elfenson)* (c) *Štěstí lásky (Lucky in Love)* (d) lost	Prague
1915	Nocturne for piano	Polička, June
	Nocturne for orchestra; *Růže noci (Rose in the Night)*	Polička
	Ballade for orchestra; *Villa na moři (Villa by the Sea)*	Polička
	Tři lyrické skladby (Three Lyric Pieces), for piano	Polička, November
	Jarní píseň (Spring Song), for piano	Prague?
1916	*Ruyana, 'A Sea Fantasy'*, for piano	Borová, February
	Five Polkas, for piano	Polička and Borová, June
	Stín (The Shadow), ballet in one act	Polička
1917	String quartet in E flat minor, fourth movement incomplete	Polička
	Burlesque for piano	Polička
	Sníh (Snow); three pieces for piano : (a) *Vločky sněhu (Snow Flakes)* (b) *Večer (Evening)* (c) *Na saních (Sledging)*	Polička, March
	Večer (Evening), song; text : G. Moore	Polička, 26 March
	Valse caprice, for piano	Polička
	Nálada (Mood Picture), for piano	Polička
	Furiant, for piano	Polička
	Šest prostých písní (Six Simple Songs), texts : unknown	Polička
	Ovčákova píseň nedělní (A Shepherd's Sunday Song); text : Uhland	Polička

41. *and* 42. Scenes from the Prague Smetana Theatre production of
Martinů's opera *Mirandolina*.

43. Martinů with Rudolf Firkušný in 1946.

44. Martinů with Miloslav Bureš in 1956.

	Koleda (*Carols*); sung ballet in four acts (lost)	Polička
1918	*Letní svita* (*Summer Suite*) six lyric pieces for piano	Polička, January
	Ukolébavky (*Cradle Songs*); texts: Falke, Liliencron, Raabe	Polička
	Three songs: (a) *Nejkrásnější smrt* (*Sweet Death*) (b) *Dlouhé putování* (*A Long Pilgrimage*) (c) *Uzdraven* (*The Recovery*); texts: Hafis	
	Loutky II (*Puppets*), five pieces for piano: (a) *Puppet Theatre* (b) *Harlequin* (c) *Colombine Remembers* (d) *The Sick Puppet* (e) *Colombine Sings*	
	String quartet No. 1	Polička
	Česká rapsódie (*Czech Rhapsody*), cantata	Polička, May–June
	Kouzelné noci (*Magic Nights*), three songs with orchestral accompaniment; texts: Li-Tai-Po and Tschang-Jo-Su	Polička, November
1919	Sonata for violin and piano in C major	Polička, 3 January– 2 February
	Two choruses, for male voices, on Czech folk poetry: (a) *O měsíci* (*Moonshine*) (b) *Žena tanečnice* (*The Dancer*)	Prague
	Kočičí foxtrott (*Kitten's Foxtrot*), for piano	Polička
	Malá taneční svita (*Small Dance Suite*), for large orchestra	Polička, September
1920	*Sen u minulosti* (*Dream of the Past*), composition for orchestra	Prague
	Jaro v zahradě (*Spring in the Garden*), four pieces for piano	Prague
	Three Slovakian Folk Songs, harmonised by Martinů	Prague
	Motýli a rajky (*The Butterflies and the Birds of Paradise*), three pieces for piano	Prague
1921	*Večer na pobřeží* (*Evening on the Sea-shore*), three pieces for piano	Luhačovice
	Three songs for the cabaret 'Červená Sedma'	Prague

M

	Istar, ballet in three acts	Polička/Prague
	First orchestral suite from *Istar*, arranged by F. Bartoš	
	Second orchestral suite from *Istar*, arranged by F. Bartoš	
1922	*Modrá hodina* (*The Blue Hour*), composition for orchestra	Prague
	Improvizace na jaře (*Improvisations in the Spring*), for piano	Prague
	Kdo je na světě nejmocnější? (*Who Is the Most Powerful in the World?*)	Prague
	Ballet Suite from *Who Is the Most Powerful in the World?*, arranged by F. Dyk	
	Slovácké tance a obyčeje (*National Dances and Customs of Slovakia*), music for a documentary film	Prague
	Three songs; texts, K. Toman:	Prague
	(a) *Po cestách zavátých* (*On Snowswept Paths*)	
	(b) *Ty, jenž sídlíš v nebesích* (*Thou, Who Dwellest in Heaven*)	
	(c) *Můj bratr dooral* (*My Brother has Finished Ploughing*)	
1923	String trio No. 1	Paris, 17 December
	Loutky I (*Puppets*), five pieces for piano:	Polička/Paris
	(a) *Colombine's Dance* (b) *The New Puppet* (c) *The Shy Puppet* (d) *Fairytale* (e) *Puppet's Dance*	
1924	Scherzo for piano	Paris, 10 February
	Bajky (*Fables*), five pieces for piano:	Paris
	(a) *On the Farm* (b) *The Humorous Rabbit* (c) *Monkeys* (d) *Fairytale* (e) *Angry Bear*	
	Quartet for clarinet, horn, cello and side drum in C major	Paris, April
	Prelude for piano	Paris, May
	Composition for piano (without title)	Paris
	Half-time, rondo for large orchestra	Polička, summer
	Concertino, for cello, wind, piano and percussion in C minor	Paris, autumn
	Nonet No. 1 (incomplete), for flute, oboe, clarinet, bassoon, horn, violin, viola, cello and piano	Paris

1925   *Instruktivní duo pro nervózní*   Paris, 20 February
      (*Instructive Duo for Nervous Players*)
      Dětské písničky (*Children's Songs*) :   Paris
      Volume I for the Osuský Children
      Volume II for the Children of
      Fernand Couget
      Čínské písně (*Chinese Songs*)   Paris
      Film en miniature, six pieces for   Paris
      piano :
      (a) *Tango* (b) *Scherzo* (c) *Cradle Song* (d) *Valse* (e) *Chanson* (f) *Carillon*
      Concerto for piano and orchestra   Polička, August–October
      No. 1
      String quartet No. 2
      Vzpoura (*Revolt*), ballet-sketch in one   Paris/Prague, 1 November
      act

1926   Sonata for violin and piano   Paris, February
      The Butterfly that Stamped, ballet in   Paris, 9 March
      one act
      Orchestral suite from *The Butterfly*   Paris, 9 March
      that Stamped
      Three Czech Dances, for piano   Paris
      (a) *Obkročák* (b) *Dupák* (c) *Polka*
      La Bagarre (*Tumult*), for large   Paris
      orchestra
      Habanera, for piano   Paris

1927   Duet for violin and cello (No. 1) :   Paris
      (a) Prelude (b) Rondo
      Pro tanec (*For Dancing*), for piano   Paris
      Le Raid merveilleux, mechanical   Paris, March
      ballet
      Trois esquisses de danses modernes :   Paris, April
      (a) Blues (b) Tango (c) Charleston
      La Revue de cuisine, jazz suite and   Paris, Easter
      ballet in one act
      Voják a tanečnice (*The Soldier and*   Polička/Paris, July–June
      the Dancer), opera in three acts
      On tourne! (*Shoot!*) ballet in one   Polička, August
      act for marionettes with film
      episodes
      String quintet   Polička, 27 September–
            5 October
      Black Bottom, for piano   Polička, 9 October

	Three impromptus for violin and piano	Paris
	Le Noël, three pieces for piano	Paris, December
1928	*Le Jazz*, piece for orchestra with vocal refrain	Paris, January
	Les Larmes du couteau (*The Tears of the Knife*), opera in one act	Paris, 15–24 March
	Four pieces for piano	Paris, Easter
	La Rhapsodie (*Allegro symphonique*), for orchestra	Paris, 14 May
	Jazz-Suite for small orchestra: (a) Prelude (b) Blues (c) Boston (d) Finale	Paris, June
	Concertino for piano (left hand) and orchestra	Paris
1929	Sextet for wind and piano	Paris, 28 January–4 February
	Scherzo for flute and piano, arranged from third movement of Sextet above	
	Le Départ (*The Departure*), symphonic interlude from *The Three Wishes*	Paris, 15 May
	Les Trois Souhaits (*The Three Wishes*), opera-film in three acts	Paris, 28 May
	Blues, for piano	Paris
	La Danse, for piano	Polička, July
	Prélude, for piano, to inaugurate the new Polička Theatre	Polička, August
	Six Characters in Search of an Author, improvisations for piano for Pirandello's play	Polička, 29 August
	La Fantaisie, for two pianos	Polička/Paris, August–September
	Eight preludes for piano (a) *In the Form of a Blues* (b) *In the Form of a Scherzo* (c) *In the Form of an Andante* (d) *In the Form of a Dance* (e) *In the Form of a Caprice* (f) *In the Form of a Largo* (g) *In the Form of a Study* (h) *In the Form of a Foxtrot*	Paris
	Prelude in the Form of a Scherzo, arranged for orchestra	Paris
	Sonata for violin and piano No. 1	Paris, November

	String quartet No. 3	Paris, 10 December
	Cinq pièces brèves, for violin and piano	Paris, December
	Three Children's Christmas Carols	Paris, December
1930	*Avec un doigt*, for piano (three hands)	Paris, 16 January
	Échec au roi (Check to the King), ballet in one act	Paris, 10 January–17 February
	Wind quintet	Paris
	Vocalise-Étude, song without words, for voice and piano	Paris
	Ariette-Vocalise, arranged for violin and piano	Paris
	Ariette-Vocalise, rearranged for cello and piano	Paris
	Nocturnes, four studies for cello and piano	Paris
	Pastorales, six studies for cello and piano	Paris
	Études faciles, nine pieces for two violins	Paris
	Suite miniature, seven pieces for cello and piano	
	Piano trio No. 1 (*Cinq pièces brèves*)	Paris, 20–30 May
	La Semaine de bonté (Week of Kindness), incomplete opera in three acts	Paris
	Borová, seven Czech dances for piano	Polička/Paris
	Borová, first Czech dance arranged for orchestra	Polička/Paris
	Cello concerto No. 1	Polička/Paris, August–October
	Three Apollinaire Songs: (a) *White Snow* (b) *The Farewell* (c) *Comedians*	Paris
	Sonatina for two violins and piano	Paris
	Serenade for chamber orchestra	Paris, November
	Les Rondes, six dances for oboe, clarinet, bassoon, trumpet, two violins and piano	Paris, 23 November
1931	*Seven Arabesques*, for cello and piano	Paris
	Seven Arabesques, arranged for violin and piano	Paris
	Rhythmic Studies, seven pieces for violin and piano	Paris
	Esquisses, six pieces for piano (Set 1)	Paris
	Esquisses, six pieces for piano (Set 2)	Paris

	Four piano pieces	Paris
	Jeux, six piano pieces	Paris
	Concerto for string quartet and orchestra	Paris
	Sonata for violin and piano No. 2	Paris
	Staročeská říkadla (*Old Czech Nursery Rhymes*), six pieces for female voices	Paris
	Three children's songs	Polička
	Festive Overture for a Sokol Festival, overture for orchestra	Paris, October
	Partita (*Suite No. 1*), for string orchestra	Paris, December
1932	Sonata for two violins and piano	Paris, January
	Špaliček, ballet in three acts	Paris, 20 January 1931– 11 February 1932
	Orchestral suite from *Špaliček*, No. 1	Paris, 20 January 1931– 11 February 1932
	Orchestral suite from *Špaliček*, No. 2	Paris, 20 January 1931– 11 February 1932
	Waltz and Polka from *Špaliček*, for piano	Paris, 20 January 1931– 11 February 1932
	Divertimento (Serenade No. 4) for small orchestra	Paris, 29 February
	Serenade No. 2, for violin and viola	Paris, March
	Serenade No. 1, for clarinet, horn, three violins and viola	Paris, 25 March
	Serenade No. 3, for oboe, clarinet, four violins and cello	Paris, 1 April
	Sinfonia Concertante No. 1, for two orchestras	Paris, Spring
	Esquisses de danses, five pieces for piano	Paris
	Four piano pieces for children	Polička
	Piece for piano (without title)	Paris
	Melo, music for a film	Paris
	String sextet	Paris, 20–27 May
	Sextet, arranged for string orchestra	U.S.A., 1951
	Four songs and nursery rhymes for children	Paris, 1 June
	Two songs on Negro folk texts	Paris
	Les Ritournelles, six pieces for piano	Paris
	Two Ballades, for contralto and piano	Paris, December
1933	Piano quintet No. 1	Paris, March

	Velikonoční (Easter), song; text: K. J. Erben	Paris, April
	Concertino for piano trio with string orchestra No. 1	Paris, Easter
	Concertino for piano trio with string orchestra No. 2	Paris, 20–31 August
	Concerto for violin and orchestra No. 1	Paris, June 1932–February 1933 and September–December 1933
	Marijka nevěrnice (Unfaithful Marijka), music for a feature film	Prague, December
1934	Inventions for orchestra	Paris, January
	Four Songs of Mary, for mixed chorus	Paris, 14 January
	Hry o Marii (The Plays of Mary), opera in four parts	Paris, May 1933– 10 July 1934
	Piano concerto No. 2	Paris, July–October
	String trio No. 2	Paris
1935	*Střevníček (The Dance Shoe)*, music to a documentary film	Prague, March
	Město živé vody: Mariánské Lázně, music to a documentary film	Prague, March
	Listek do památníku (Album Leaf), for piano	Prague, March
	Skladba pro male Evy (Composition for Little Eva), for piano	Paris
	Hlas lesa (The Voice of the Forest), radio opera in one act	Paris, April–May
	Two pieces for harpsichord	Paris, June
	The Judgement of Paris, ballet in one act	Paris, July
	Concerto for harpsichord and small orchestra	Paris, 11 September
	Veselohra na mostě (Comedy on the Bridge), radio opera in one act	Paris, 10 December
	Small suite from *Comedy on the Bridge*	Paris
1936	*Oedipus*, incidental music to Gide's play	Prague, January
	Small suite from *Oedipus*	Prague, January
	Dumka No. 1 for piano	Paris
	Dumka No. 2 for piano	Paris
	Divadlo za bránou (Theatre Beyond the Gate), opera/ballet in three acts	Paris, 18 June 1935– 30 April 1936
	Commedia dell'Arte, orchestral suite	Paris

	from *Theatre Beyond the Gate*	
	Concerto for flute, violin and orchestra	Paris, October
	Juliette, opera in three acts	Paris, 17 May 1936–
		24 January 1937
1937	Sonata for flute, violin and piano	Paris, New Year
	Alexander bis, opera buffa in one act	Paris, 8 March
	String quartet No. 4	Paris, April–May
	Fourths and Octaves, small piano pieces	Paris
	Le Train hanté, for piano	Paris
	Koleda milostna, song to a Czech folk poem	Paris
	Kytice (Bouquet), cantata for soloists, choir and orchestra	Paris
	Intermezzo, four pieces for violin and piano	Paris
	Sonatina for violin and piano	Paris
	Concerto Grosso for chamber orchestra	Paris, 3 November
	Duo Concertante for two violins and orchestra	Nice, November–December
	Trio for flute, violin and bassoon	Nice, December
	Les Madrigaux, four pieces for oboe, clarinet and bassoon	Nice, December
1938	*Tre Ricercari,* for chamber orchestra	Paris, January–February
	String quartet No. 5	Paris, April–May
	Concertino for piano and orchestra	
	Fenêtre sur le jardin, four piano pieces	Vieux-Moulin, August
	Double Concerto for two string orchestras, piano and timpani	Vieux-Moulin, August, Pratteln, 29 September
1939	*Pohádky (Fairytales),* for piano	Paris, January
	Vim hajíček (I Know of a Little Wood), song to a Czech folk poem	Paris, January
	Promenades, for flute, violin and harpsichord	Paris, February
	Bergerettes, five pieces for violin, cello and piano	Paris, 20 February
	Suite Concertante, for violin and orchestra	Paris 1939–New York 1945
	Sonata for cello and piano No. 1	Paris, 12 May
	Eight Czech Madrigals, for mixed chorus	Vieux-Moulin, July
	Polní mše (Field Mass), cantata for male voices, wind, brass and percussion	Paris, November–December
1940	*Vojenský pochod (Military March),*	Paris, January

<table>
<tr><td></td><td>for military band</td><td></td></tr>
</table>

	Fantaisie and Toccata, for piano	Aix-en-Provence, August–September
	Sinfonietta Giocosa, for piano and small orchestra	Aix-en-Provence, September–November
	Sonata da Camera, for cello and small orchestra	Aix-en-Provence, November–December
1941	Mazurka for piano	New York, April
	Concerto da Camera, for violin and small orchestra	Edgartown, Massachusetts, July–August
	Dumka No. 3, for piano	Jamaica, Long Island, September
	Sonata for cello and piano No. 2	Jamaica, Long Island, November–December
1942	Piano quartet	Jamaica, Long Island, 21 April
	Nový Špalíček, eight songs to Czech folk poetry	Jamaica, Long Island, June
	Symphony No. 1	Jamaica, Long Island, May–September
	Variations on a theme of Rossini, for cello and piano	New York, October
	Madrigal-Sonata, for flute, violin and piano	New York, November
1943	Concerto for two pianos and orchestra	New York, 3 January–23 February
	Concerto for violin and orchestra (No. 2)	New York, 23 February–26 April
	Seven Songs on One Page, to Czech folk poetry	New York
	Symphony No. 2	Darien, Connecticut, 29 May–24 July
	Památník Lidicím (Memorial to Lidice), for orchestra	Darien, Connecticut, 3 August
	Five Madrigal Stanzas, for violin and piano	New York, November
1944	Piano quintet No. 2	New York, 15 February–14 April
	Symphony No. 3	Ridgefield, Connecticut, 2 May–14 June
	Trio for flute, cello and piano	Ridgefield, Connecticut, 23 June–31 July
	Fantaisie, for theremin, oboe, string quartet and piano	Ridgefield, Connecticut, September
	Seven Songs on Two Pages, to Czech folk poetry	New York, October

	Sonata for violin and piano No. 3	New York, November–December
1945	Cello concerto No. 2	New York, 20 December 1944–26 February 1945
	Symphony No. 4	New York/Cape Cod, 1 April–14 June
	Sonata for flute and piano	Cape Cod, 15 June–3 July
	Czech Rhapsody, for violin and piano	Cape Cod, 5–19 July
	Études and Polkas, sixteen pieces for piano	Cape Cod, 27 July–28 August
	Thunderbolt P-47, scherzo for orchestra	Cape Cod, 1–15 September
1946	Symphony No. 5	New York, February–May
	Toccata e Due Canzoni, for chamber orchestra	New York/Tanglewood, 15 May–3 October
	String quartet No. 6	New York, October–December
1947	*Three Madrigals*, duets for violin and viola	New York, 17 February–19 July
	String quartet No. 7 (*Concerto da Camera*)	New York, June
	Quartet for oboe, violin, cello and piano	New York, 15 September–21 October
1948	Piano concerto No. 3	New York, 10 December 1947–10 March 1948
	The Strangler, ballet for three dancers	New York, 16 May
	The Fifth Day of the Fifth Moon, for piano	New York, 20 May
	Les Bouquinistes du Quai Malaquais, for piano	New York, 24 May
	Fanfares for a Sokol Festival	New York, 5 June
	Five Madrigals, for mixed choir	New York, 15 June
1949	*Sinfonia Concertante*, for violin, cello, oboe, bassoon and small orchestra	New York, 15 January–5 May
	Morceau facile, bagatelle for piano	New York, March
	Three Czech Dances, for two pianos	New York, 5 March–11 April
	Mazurka-Nocturne for oboe, two violins and cello	New York, August
	Barcarolle for piano	New York, 10 December
1950	Piano trio No. 2	New York, 10–22 February
	Sinfonietta La Jolla, for piano and small orchestra	New York, January–March
	Concerto for two violins and orchestra (No. 2)	New York, 1 May–10 June

	Intermezzo for orchestra	New York, September
	Duo for violin and viola (No. 2)	New York, 13 October
1951	Piano trio No. 3	New York, 21 April–15 May
	Improvisation for piano	New York, summer
	Serenade for two clarinets, violin, viola and cello	New York, 18 October–11 November
	Stowe-Pastorals, for five recorders, clarinet, two violins and cello	New York, 5–25 November
1952	*What Men Live By*, television opera in one act	New York, 20 December 1951–11 February 1952
	Rhapsody Concerto, for viola and orchestra	New York, 15 March–18 April
	Three songs for women's voices, unaccompanied, on Czech folk poetry	New York
	Three songs for women's voices, with violin, on Czech folk poetry	New York
	Sonata for cello and piano No. 3	Vieux-Moulin, 10 September–5 October
	The Marriage, television opera in two acts	New York, 5 October–30 November
1953	Concerto for violin, piano and orchestra	New York, 1 December–10 March
	Fantaisies symphoniques (Symphony No. 6)	New York, 1951–Paris, 26 May, 1953
	Plainte contre l'inconnu (*Accusation Against the Unknown*), unfinished opera	Nice, summer
	Overture for orchestra	Nice, 10–15 November
1954	*Mirandolina*, opera in three acts	Nice, 15 December
	Saltarello from *Mirandolina*, orchestral interlude	Nice, 30 June
	Hymn to St. James, cantata	Nice, 18 July
	Petrklíč (*The Primrose*), five vocal duets with instrumental accompaniments	Nice, 1–5 August
	Mount of Three Lights, cantata	Nice, 20–25 November
	Sonata for piano	Nice, 26 November–17 December
1955	*The Epic of Gilgamesh*, oratorio	Nice, 23 December 1954–16 February, 1955
	The Frescoes of Piero della Francesca, three pieces for orchestra	Nice, 20 February–13 April
	Concerto for oboe and small orchestra	Nice, April–May
	Otvírání studánek (*The Opening of the Wells*), chamber cantata	Nice, July

	Sonata for viola and piano	New York, 22 November–16 December
1956	Sonatina for clarinet and piano	New York, 20 January
	Sonatina for trumpet and piano	New York, 2 February
	Piano concerto No. 4 (*Incantation*)	New York, 22 December 1955–6 February 1956
	Impromptu for two pianos	Basle, June
	Legenda z dýmu bramborové nati (*Legend of the Smoke from Potato Fires*), chamber cantata	Rome, 5–14 October
1957	*Zbojnické písně* (*Brigand Songs*), for male voices	Rome, 8–20 January
	Vzpominky (*In Memoriam*), for piano	Rome, 12 March
	The Rock, symphonic prelude for orchestra	Rome, March-April
	Romance z pampelišek (*Romance of the Dandelions*), chamber cantata	Rome, 12–18 May
	Divertimento, for two recorders	Rome, 20–24 March
	Piano concerto No. 5 (*Fantasia Concertante*)	Pratteln, 2 September 1957–3 January 1958
	The Parables, for orchestra	Rome, 15 June–1 July
1958	Sonata for harpsichord	Pratteln, March
	Estampes, for orchestra	Pratteln, 15 March–2 April
	Ariadne, chamber opera in one act	Pratteln, 13 May–15 June
	Duet for violin and cello (No. 2)	Pratteln, 28 June–1 July
	The Greek Passion, opera in four acts	Nice/New York/Rome/Pratteln, 20 February 1956–15 January 1959
1959	*Písničky pro dětské sbor* (*Three Songs for Children's Choir*)	Pratteln, January
	Nonet, for flute, oboe, clarinet, bassoon, horn, violin, viola, cello and double bass	Pratteln, 9 January–1 February
	Mikeš z hor (*Mikeš from the Mountains*), chamber cantata	Pratteln, 2–13 February
	Kammermusik No. 1, for clarinet, violin, cello, harp and piano	Pratteln, 14 February–3 March
	Piece for two cellos	Pratteln, March
	Variations on a Slovakian Folk Song, for cello and piano	Pratteln, 12 March
	Ptačí hody (*Festival of the Birds*), for children's choir and trumpet	Pratteln, 19 March
	Madrigals, five pieces for mixed chorus (unaccompanied)	Pratteln, 14–20 March
	Two Impromptus for harpsichord	Pratteln, 21 March

Vigilia, incomplete composition for organ	Pratteln, April–May
The Prophecy of Isaiah, cantata	Nice, April–May
The Burden of Moab, incomplete chorus sketch	Pratteln, 16 July
Znělka (The Whirlpool), for children's choir	Pratteln, 16 July

2. LIST OF WORKS IN CATEGORIES

OPERAS

1926–7   *Voják a tanečnice (The Soldier and the Dancer)*, lib. J. L. Budín

1928   *Les Larmes du couteau (The Tears of the Knife)*, lib. G. Ribemont-Dessaignes

1929   *Les Trois Souhaits (The Three Wishes)*, lib. G. Ribemont-Dessaignes

      Semaine de bonté (Week of Kindness), lib. G. Ribemont-Dessaignes (incomplete)

1933–4   *Hry o Marii (The Plays of Mary)*, lib. B. Martinů and H. Ghéon

1935   *Hlas lesa (The Voice of the Forest)*, radio opera, lib. V. Nezval

      Veselohra na mostě (Comedy on the Bridge), radio opera, lib. B. Martinů after Klicpera

1936   *Divadlo za bránou (Suburban Theatre or Theatre Beyond the Gate)*, lib. B. Martinů

1937   *Alexander bis*, lib. A. Wurmser

1936–7   *Juliette or The Key to Dreams*, lib. B. Martinů after Neveux

1952   *What Men Live By*, television opera, lib. B. Martinů after Tolstoy

      The Marriage, television opera, lib. B. Martinů after Gogol

1953   *Accusation Against the Unknown*, lib. B. Martinů after Neveux (incomplete)

1954   *Mirandolina (La Locandiera)*, lib. B. Martinů after Goldoni

1958   *Ariadne*, lib. B. Martinů after Neveux

1956–9   *The Greek Passion*, lib. B. Martinů after Kazantzakis

BALLETS

1912–14   *Tance se závoji (Dances with a Veil)*

1913–14   *Noc (Night)*, lib. A. Kohout

1914   *Stín (The Shadow)*, lib. A. Kohout

1917   *Koleda*, lib. B. Martinů

1918–22   *Istar*, lib. J. Zeyer

1922   *Kdo je na světě nejmocnější? (Who Is the Most Powerful in the World?)*, lib. B. Martinů

1925   *Vzpoura (Revolt)*, lib. B. Martinů
1926   *The Butterfly that Stamped*, lib. B. Martinů after Kipling
1927   *Le Raid merveilleux*, lib. B. Martinů
         La Revue de cuisine (Kitchen Revue), lib J. Kröschlová
         On Tourne! (Shoot!), lib. B. Martinů
1930   *Échec au roi (Check to the King)*, lib. A. Coeuroy
1931–2   *Špalíček*, lib. B. Martinů after fairy tales and nursery rhymes
1935   *The Judgement of Paris*, lib. Boris Kochno
1948   *The Strangler*, lib. Robert Fitzgerald

WORKS FOR LARGE ORCHESTRA

1910   *Les Travailleurs de la mer*, symphonic sketch
         La Mort de Tintagiles, overture
         Anděl smrti (Angel of Death), symphonic poem
1913–14 Composition for orchestra
1914–15 *Nocturne* for orchestra
1915   *Nocturne – Růže noci (Roses in the Night)*, symphonic dance
         Ballade – Villa by the Sea, symphonic dance
1919   *Malátá neční svita (Small Dance Suite)*
1922   *Modrá hodina (The Blue Hour)*, three symphonic pieces:
              (a) Vanishing Midnight
              (b) Grove of Satyrs
              (c) Shadows
1924   *Half-time*, Rondo for orchestra
1926   *La Bagarre (Tumult)*
1928   *Le Jazz*
         La Rhapsodie (Allegro Symphonique)
1931   *Festive Overture for a Sokol Festival*
1934   *Inventions*
1940   *Military March*
1942   Symphony No. 1
1943   Symphony No. 2
         Memorial to Lidice
1944   Symphony No. 3
1945   Symphony No. 4
         Thunderbolt P-47, Scherzo for orchestra
1946   Symphony No. 5
1950   *Intermezzo*
1953   Overture
1951–3   *Fantaisies symphoniques* (Symphony No. 6)
1955   *The Frescoes of Piero della Francesca*
1957   *The Rock* (symphonic prelude)
1957–8   *The Parables*
1958   *Estampes*

WORKS FOR SMALL ORCHESTRA

1907	*Posviceni* (*Candlemass* or *Village Wake*) for flute and strings
1928	*Jazz Suite*
1930	*Serenade* for chamber orchestra
1931	*Partita* (*Suite No. 1*) for string orchestra

CONCERTED WORKS

1932	*Sinfonia Concertante* for two orchestras
1937	*Concerto Grosso*
1938	*Tre Ricercari*
	Double Concerto for two string orchestras, piano and timpany
1946	*Toccata e Due Canzoni*
1947	*Concerto da camera* (arrangement of seventh string quartet)

CONCERTED WORKS WITH KEYBOARD

1925	Concerto No. 1 for piano and chamber orchestra
1926	Concertino for piano (left hand) and chamber orchestra
1934	Concerto No. 2 for piano and orchestra
1935	Concerto for harpsichord and chamber orchestra
1938	Concertino for piano and orchestra
1940	*Sinfonietta Giocosa* for piano and small orchestra
1943	Concerto for two pianos and orchestra
1948	Concerto No. 3 for piano and orchestra
1950	*Sinfonietta La Jolla*
1955–6	Concerto No. 4 (*Incantation*)
1957	Concerto No. 5 (*Fantasia Concertante*)

CONCERTED WORKS WITH VIOLIN

1933	Concerto for violin and orchestra (No. 1)
1937	*Suite Concertante* for violin and orchestra
	Concerto for two violins and orchestra (No. 1)
1941	*Concerto da camera* for violin, piano, percussion and strings
1943	Concerto for violin and orchestra (No. 2)
1950	Concerto for two violins and orchestra (No. 2)
1953	Concerto for violin, piano and orchestra

CONCERTED WORKS WITH VIOLA

1952	*Rhapsody Concerto* for viola and orchestra

CONCERTED WORKS WITH CELLO

1924   Concertino for cello and chamber ensemble
1930   Cello concerto No. 1 (revised 1955)
1940   *Sonata da camera* for cello and chamber orchestra
1944–5 Cello concerto No. 2

OTHER CONCERTED WORKS

1931   Concerto for string quartet and orchestra
1932   *Divertimento* for violin, viola, oboe, piano and strings
1933   Concertino for piano trio and strings No. 1
        Concertino for piano trio and strings No. 2
1936   Concerto for flute, violin and chamber orchestra
1949   *Sinfonia Concertante* for violin, cello, oboe, bassoon and chamber
        orchestra
1955   Oboe concerto

CHAMBER MUSIC

DUOS
1927   Duo for violin and cello
1930   *Études faciles* for two violins
1947   *Three Madrigals* for violin and viola
1950   Duets for violin and viola
1957   *Divertimento* for two recorders
1958   Duet for violin and cello in D major
1959   Piece for two cellos

TRIOS
1923   String trio No. 1
1930   Piano trio No. 1 (*Cinq pièces brèves*)
        Sonatina for two violins and piano
1932   Sonata for two violins and piano
        Serenade for two violins and viola
1934   String trio No. 2
1937   Sonata for flute, violin and piano
        Trio for flute, violin and bassoon
        Les Madrigaux for oboe, clarinet and bassoon
1939   *Promenades* for flute, violin and harpsichord
        Bergerettes for violin, cello and piano
1942   *Madrigal-Sonata* for flute, violin and piano
1944   Trio for flute, cello and piano
1950   Piano trio No. 2
1951   Piano trio No. 3

45. Scene from the Prague National Theatre production of Martinů's last opera, *The Greek Passion*.

46. Charlotte and Bohuslav Martinů with Maja Sacher in 1959.

47. Bust of Martinů by Irene Cordreano-King.

QUARTETS
1902   *The Three Riders* for string quartet
1912   String quartet
        Two Nocturnes for string quartet
        Andante for string quartet
1917   String quartet in E flat minor
1918   String quartet No. 1
1924   Quartet for clarinet, horn, cello and side drum
1925   String quartet No. 2
1929   String quartet No. 3
1937   String quartet No. 4
1938   String quartet No. 5
1942   Piano quartet
1946   String quartet No. 6
1947   String quartet No. 7 (*Concerto da Camera*)
        Quartet for oboe, violin, cello and piano
1949   *Mazurka-Nocturne* for oboe, two violins and cello

QUINTETS
1911   Piano quintet
1927   String quintet
1930   Wind quintet
1933   Piano quintet No. 1
1944   Piano quintet No. 2
1951   *Serenade* for violin, viola, cello and two clarinets

SEXTETS
1929   Sextet for flute, oboe, clarinet, two bassoons and piano
1932   *Serenade No. 1* for clarinet, horn, three violins and viola
        String sextet
1959   *Kammermusik No. 1* for clarinet, violin and viola, cello, harp and
        piano

SEPTETS
1930   *Les Rondes,* six pieces for oboe, clarinet, bassoon, trumpet, two
        violins and piano
1932   *Serenade No. III* for oboe, clarinet, four violins and cello
1944   *Fantaisie* for theremin, oboe, string quartet and piano

NONETS
1924–5 Nonet for flute, oboe, clarinet, bassoon, horn, violin, viola, cello
        and piano (incomplete)
1951   *Stowe-Pastorals* for five recorders, clarinet, two violins and cello
1959   Nonet for flute, oboe, clarinet, bassoon, horn, violin, viola, cello
        and double bass

N

Martinů

COMPOSITIONS FOR SOLO INSTRUMENTS WITH PIANO

VIOLIN AND PIANO
1909 *Elegy*
1910 *Romance*
Concerto
1911 *Berceuse*
Adagio
1912 *Fantaisie*
1919 Sonata in C
1926 Sonata in D minor
1927 *Impromptu*
Sonata No. 1
1929 *Cinq pièces brèves*
1931 *Sept études rhythmiques*
Sonata No. 2
1937 *Four Intermezzi*
Sonatina
1943 *Five Madrigal Stanzas*
1944 Sonata No. 3
1945 *Czech Rhapsody*

CELLO AND PIANO
1930 *Four Nocturnes*
Six Pastorales
Suite Miniature (seven pieces)
1931 *Seven Arabesques*
1939 Sonata No. 1
1941 Sonata No. 2
1942 *Variations on a Theme of Rossini*
1952 Sonata No. 3
1959 *Variations on a Slovakian Theme*

VIOLA AND PIANO
1955 Sonata

FLUTE AND PIANO
1945 Sonata

CLARINET AND PIANO
1956 Sonatina

TRUMPET AND PIANO
1956 Sonatina

PIANO COMPOSITIONS

1909	*Dumka*
1910	Five Waltzes
	Smuteční pochod (Funeral March)
	Idyle
	Ballade and Sousedská
	Pohádka o zlatovlásce (Tales of the Golden Fleece)
1911	*Chanson Triste*
1912	*Z pohádek Andersenových (Seven Pieces on Hans Andersen's Fairytales)*
	Píseň beze slov (Song Without Words)
	Nocturne
	Ballade 'The Last Chords of Chopin'
	Ballade 'Under Miss Vilma's Umbrella'
1913	*Prelude on the Theme of The Marseillaise*
	Prelude in F minor
1914	*Loutky III (Puppets)*
1915	*Nocturne*
	Tři lyrické skladby (Three Lyric Pieces)
	Jarni píseň (Spring Song)
1916	*Ruyana – 'A Sea Fantasy'*
	Five Polkas
1917	*Burlesque*
	Sníh (Snow)
	Valse Caprice
	Nálada (Mood Picture)
	Furiant
1918	*Letní svita (Summer Suite)*
	Loutky II (Puppets)
1919	*Kočičí foxtrott (Kitten's Foxtrot)*
1920	*Jaro v zahradě (Spring in the Garden)*
	Motýli a rajky (The Butterflies and the Birds of Paradise)
1921	*Večer na pobřeží (Evening on the Sea-shore)*
1922	*Improvizace na jaře (Improvisations in the Spring)*
1924	*Loutky I (Puppets)*
	Bajky (Fables)
	Scherzo
	Prelude
	Composition without title
1925	*Instruktivní duo pro nervózní (Instructive Duo for Nervous Players)*
	Film en miniature (six pieces)
1926	*Three Czech Dances*
	Habanera

1927	*Pro tanec (For Dancing)*
	Trois Esquisses de Danse Modernes
	Black Bottom
	Le Noël
1928	Four Pieces
1929	*Blues*
	La Danse
	Prelude to inaugurate the Polička Theatre
	Eight Preludes
1930	*Avec un Doit*
	Borová, seven Czech dances
1931	*Esquisses*, Six pieces (Set I)
	Esquisses, Six pieces (Set II)
	Four pieces
	Jeux, six pieces
1931–2	Waltz and Polka from *Špaliček*
1932	*Esquisses de Danses*
	Four children's pieces
	Piece without title
	Les Ritournelles
1935	*Lístek do památniku (Album Leaf)*
	Skladba pro male Evy (Composition for Little Eva)
1936	*Dumka* (No. 1)
	Dumka (No. 2)
1937	*Fourths and Octaves*
	Le Train hanté
1938	*Fenêtre sur le jardin*
1939	*Pohádky (Fairytale)*
1940	*Fantasie and Toccata*
1941	*Dumka* (No. 3)
	Mazurka
1945	*Études and Polkas* (sixteen pieces)
1948	*The Fifth Day of the Fifth Moon*
	Les Bouqinistes du Quai Malaquais
1949	*Morceau facile*
	Barcarolle
1951	*Improvisiation*
1954	Sonata
1957	*Vzpominky (In Memoriam)*

COMPOSITIONS FOR TWO PIANOS

1929	*La Fantaisie*
1949	*Three Czech Dances*
1956	*Impromptu*

COMPOSITIONS FOR HARPSICHORD

1935   Two pieces
1958   Sonata
1959   Two Impromptus

COMPOSITION FOR ORGAN

1959   *Vigilia*, unfinished, but completed by B. Janáček

SONGS FOR VOICE AND PIANO

1910   *Než se naděješ (Before you Know)*
V přírodě (In Nature)
Pastel
Utonulá (The Drowned Maiden)
Až budeme staří (When We Are Old)
Pověra (Superstition)
Dívčí píseň (Maiden's Song)
Nocturne
Spící (The Sleeper)
Proč zoubky tvé tak smály se? (Why Have You Laughed at Me?)
Kde jsem to byla? (Where Have I Been?)
Zpěv a hudba (Song and Music)
Dívčí sny (Maiden's Dream)
Zimní noc (Winter's Night)
Líbej, milá, líbej (Kiss me, Beloved)
Náladová kresba (Mood Picture)
1911   *V noci (In the Night)*
Dívčí píseň (A Maiden's Song)
Až přijde den (When Day Comes)
Má matička (Mother Dear)
Pravý počet (The Correct Number)
Chybili jsme ráno (We Roamed in the Morning)
Jaškova zpěvánka (Jašek's Song)
Píseň (Song)
Umírá duše (Starving Soul)
První láska (First Love)
Slzy (Tears)
1912   *Konec všemu (All is Ended)*
Mrtvá láska (Dead Love)
Ty píšeš mi (You Write to Me)
Ráno raníčko, pleju obiličko (Early in the Morning I Sort the Grain)
Lucie

Dětství (From Childhood)
Padlo jíní na pole (Hoar Frost in the Field)
Vdejte mne, matičko (Marry Me, Mother)
Růže (The Rose)
To všechno už jen zbylo (Only This Remains)
Noc každou tebe drahá zřím (I See You Every Night, My Love)
Mluv ke mně dál! (Speak On!)
Opuštěná milá (The Jilted Maiden)
Kdysi (Once Upon a Time)
O mrtvých očích (Dead Eyes)
Ohnivý muž (The Fiery Man)
Píseň prvního listopadu (Song for the First of November)
Tři panny za světlé noci (Three Maidens on a Bright Night)
Stará píseň (Old Song)
Komárova svatba (Gnat's Wedding)
Svítaj, Bože (Let There be Light, O God!)
V zahradě na hradě (In the Castle Garden)
Labutě (The Swan)
Mám staré párky rád (I Love Old Parks)
Písnička o haničce (Song of Hanička)
Štěstí to dost (Enough Happiness)

1913	*Matičko má, hocha mám (Mother Mine, I Have a Friend)*
	Le Sapin de Noël
	Le Petit Oiseau
	Le Soir
1915	*Šťastná jízda (Good Journey)*
	Písnička skřítků (Elfen Song)
	Štěstí lásky (Lucky in Love)
1917	*Večer (Evening)*
	Šest prostých písní (Six Simple Songs)
	Ovčákova píseň nedělní (A Shepherd's Sunday Song)
1918	*Ukolébavky (Eight Cradle Songs)*
	Nejkrásnější smrt (Sweet Death)
	Dlouhé putování (A Long Pilgrimage)
	Uzdraven (The Recovery)
1920	Three Slovakian folk songs
1921	Three songs from the Cabaret 'Červena sedma'
1922	*Po cestách zavátých (On Snow-swept Paths)*
	Ty, jenž sídlíš v nebesích (Thou Who Dwellest in Heaven)
	Můj bratr dooral (My Brother Has Finished Ploughing)
1925	*Děstké písničky (Children's Songs)*
	Čínské písné (Chinese Songs)
1930	*Vocalise-Étude*
	Three Apollinaire songs
1931	Three Children's songs
1932	Four songs and nursery rhymes for children

Two songs on Negro folk texts
Two Ballades for contralto and piano
1933   *Velikonoční (Easter)*
1937   *Koleda milostná (Carol)*
1939   *Vim hajiček (I Know of a Little Wood)*
1942   *Nový Špaliček* (Eight Songs)
1943   *Seven Songs on One Page*
1944   *Seven Songs on Two Pages*

SONGS FOR VOICE AND ORCHESTRA

1912   *Niponari,* seven songs for female voice and small orchestra to
        Japanese lyrics
1918   *Magic Nights,* three songs with large orchestra to Chinese poems
        by Li-Tai-Po and Tschang-Jo-Su

MELODRAMAS

1913   *Le Soir,* for voice and harp, to words by Albert Samain
        La Libellule, for voice, violin, harp and piano, to words by Henri
        d'Orange
        Danseuses de Java, for voice, viola, harp and piano, to words by
        Arthur Symonds

UNACCOMPANIED CHORAL MUSIC

1919   Two choruses for male voices on folk poetry
1931   Old Czech nursery rhymes (six pieces for female voices)
1934   Four Songs of Mary (for mixed choir)
1939   Eight Czech Madrigals (for mixed choir)
1948   Five Czech Madrigals (for mixed choir)
1952   Three choruses for women's voices on folk poetry
1957   *The Brigand Songs* for male voices on Slovakian folk poetry
        Romance of the Dandelions (for mixed voices), cantata to words
        by Miloslav Bureš
1959   Three choruses for children's voices
        Four Madrigals for mixed choir on Moravian folk poetry
        The Whirlpool, incomplete sketch for children's voices

CHORAL MUSIC WITH INSTRUMENTAL ACCOMPANIMENT

1952   *The Birth of Our Lord* ⎫
        The Ascension   ⎬ for women's voices and violin
        The Way to Paradise ⎭
1954   *Hymn to St. Jacob,* text by Jaroslav Daněk : cantata for mixed

choir, soloists, strings, horn and organ

Petrklíč, five duets on Moravian folk poetry for women's voices, with violin and piano

Mount of Three Lights, cantata to words by W. E. Morton, for soloists, speaker, male voices and organ

1955   *Opening of the Wells*, chamber cantata to words by Miloslav Bureš, for soloists, speaker, women's choir, strings and piano

1956   *Legend of the Smoke from Potato Fires*, chamber cantata to words by Miloslav Bureš, for soloists, mixed choir, woodwind, horn, accordion and piano

1959   *Mikeš of the Mountains*, chamber cantata to words by Miloslav Bureš, for soloists, mixed choir, strings and piano

Festival of Birds, text from Třebíň manuscript, for children's voices and trumpet

Prophecy of Isaiah, two-part cantata to words from the Bible, for soloists, male voices, viola, trumpet, piano and timpany

The Burden of Moab, incomplete sketch to words from the Bible, for male voices and piano

CANTATAS AND ORATORIOS WITH ORCHESTRA

1918   *Czech Rhapsody*, text by Alois Jirásek, for baritone soloist, mixed choir, orchestra and organ

1937   *Kytice (Bouquet of Flowers)*, five-part cantata on Czech folk poetry, for soloists, chorus and orchestra

1939   Three extracts from the opera *Juliette*, for soloists, chorus and orchestra

Field Mass, cantata to words by Jiří Mucha and extracts from the Psalms, for baritone soloist, male voices, woodwind, brass, harmonium and percussion

1954–5   *The Epic of Gilgamesh*, three-part oratorio on the Babylonian legend, for soloists, speaker, chorus and orchestra

FILM AND INCIDENTAL MUSIC

1922   *Slovácké tance a obyčeje (National Dances and Customs of Slovakia)*, music for a documentary film

1929   *Six Characters in Search of an Author*, improvisations for Pirandello's play

1932   *Melo*, Music for a film

1933   *Marijka nevěrnice (Unfaithful Marijka)*, music for a feature film

1935   *Střevíček (The Dance Shoe)*, music for a documentary film

Město živé vody: Mariánské Lázně, music for a documentary film

1936   *Oedipus*, incidental music to André Gide's play

Appendix

Martinů's First Violin Concerto

This book was in its final stages of production when a manuscript score of Martinů's long-lost Violin Concerto No. 1 came to light. Since the concerto is of considerable musical substance, this appendix has been added to make this study of the composer's work as complete as possible.

The concerto was written at the request of the American-Russian violinist Samuel Dushkin sometime during the winter of 1932, but with preparations for the ballet Špaliček at the Prague National Theatre occupying his mind, Martinů seems to have lost interest in the concerto early in February 1933. It was only after the Špaliček premiere on September 19th that he took up the piece again, but even then his heart was not in it, for the score remained on his desk until the end of December. At this time Martinů seems to have been more than usually careless in preserving his manuscript, for Dushkin never received it; moreover, its whereabouts is mentioned in no letter nor is it found in any work-list. When Miloš Šafránek was preparing for publication a catalogue of the composer's works in 1944, Martinů remembered the concerto as 'incomplete and lost'. Šafránek still believed this to be the case when he produced his 'authorised' monograph in 1964, but surprisingly the concerto exists, and in a totally complete form. After the War the full score mysteriously found its way to North America where it came into the private collection of Hans Moldenhauer in Spokane, Washington. In 1973 the Czech violinist, Josef Suk, acquired a copy and prepared to give the first performance with the Chicago Symphony during the 1974 season. Owing to an orchestral dispute in Chicago the concerto was premiered by the Czech Philharmonic in Prague, since when Suk has championed it with Charles Mackerras to whom I am greatly indebted for making the score available to me. The British première is promised for February 1975.

The First Violin Concerto is a 23-minute, three-movement work of real worth. Though intended for Dushkin, the manuscript bears no dedication, nor is there a date when Martinů actually completed the 122-page score. There can be no question of the work's authenticity, for the first page contains an autograph next to the French title. Written shortly after Martinů's marriage, the concerto is richly lyrical and almost certainly reflects the composer's newly-found emotional security. Unusually for Martinů, the solo part contains a number of bowing marks, scratchings-out and revisions which suggest that he was taking especial pains to ensure that it would be as attractive to the soloist as possible.

The opening movement (Allegro Moderato is the tempo suggested by Suk since Martinů omitted to provide an indication himself) is energetic and vital. The invention is more rhythmic than melodic with engaging syncopations that hover around E (sometimes major, sometimes minor). A rhapsodic middle section flirts with A major, but Martinů is here concerned less with key or form. His main aim is to give his soloist writing of real distinction and this he does. There is no cadenza, but the solo part sparkles with every kind of display and reminds us what a brilliant violinist Martinů himself must have been. The lightly scored Andante is pastoral in feeling and inhabits a world of Moravian folk idiom. Here Martinů looks forward to the lovely Second Violin Concerto of 1943 by providing a continuous dialogue which moves engagingly between solo violin and wind. This leads without break to the finale, a boisterous Allegro where Martinů's feeling for the toccata gives his music a definite forward thrust. Later, he builds up excitement by additive cross rhythms, harsh tonalities and a greater insistence on percussive elements. Possibly too many musical ideas flood in as one theme jumps over the next, but somehow the soloist manages to lead triumphantly back to the opening material and the concerto closes in a blaze of dazzling arpeggios.

Bibliography

Alte und neue Musik, 25 Jahre Basler Kammerorchester, Zurich 1952

Rudolf Bauer, *Das Konzert,* Berlin 1955

Kurt Blaukopf, *Lexicon der Symphonie,* Cologne 1953

Miloslav Bureš, *Martinů a Vysočina,* Havlicku Brod 1960

John Clapham, 'Martinů's Instrumental Style', *Music Review* xxiv, London 1963

Peter Evans, 'Martinů the Symphonist', *Tempo* lv, London 1960

Pierre-Octave Ferroud; 'A Great Musician of Today', *The Chesterian,* London 1937

Manfred Gräter, *Konzertführer – Neue Musik,* Frankfurt 1955

Harry Halbreich, *Martinů – Werkverzeichnis, Dokumentation und Biographie,* Zurich 1968

Vladimír Helfert, *Geschichte der Musik in der Tschechoslovakischen Republik,* Prague 1936

Bohuslav Martinů, 'Albert Roussel', *Revue Musicale* Paris 1937

Bohuslav Martinů, *Domov, Hudba a Svět,* Prague 1966

Charlotte Martinů, *Ma Vie avec Bohuslav Martinů* (to be published)

Jaroslav Mihule, *Symphonie Bohuslava Martinů,* Prague 1959

Jaroslav Mihule, *Bohuslav Martinů v obrazech,* Prague 1964

Jaroslav Mihule, *Bohuslav Martinů,* Prague 1966

Jaroslav Mihule, *Martinů,* Prague 1972

Paul Nettl, *The Book of Modern Composers,* New York 1943

Rudolf Pečman, *Stage Works of Martinů,* Prague 1967

Miloš Šafránek, 'Bohuslav Martinů', *Music Quarterly* 3, xxix 1943

Miloš Šafránek, *Martinů – The Man and his Music,* New York 1944/London 1946

Miloš Šafránek, *Martinů – Life and Works,* Prague/London 1963

Miloš Šafránek, 'Martinů und das musikalische Theater', *Musica* No. 12, Kassel 1959

Zdeněk Zouhar, *Martinů – sborník, vzpominek a studie,* Brno 1957

Index

Index

Vojan, Eduard, 11
Von Karajan, Herbert, 129–30
Voragaine, Jacobus de, *Legenda Aurea*, 57

Wagner, Richard, *Fliegende Holländer, Der*, 12; *Lohengrin*, 12; *Tannhäuser*, 12; *Tristan und Isolde*, 133, 150
Walton, William, *Belshazzar's Feast*, 112
Webern, Anton, 140, 149, 151
Weill, Kurt, *Dreigroschenoper, Der*, 46; *Lindberghflug, Der*, 37; *Mahagonny*, 152; *Royal Palace*, 45
Weingartner, Felix, 23
Whiteman, Paul, 42, 143

Whitman, Walt, 146
Wiener, Jean, 32
Wieniawski, Tadeusz, 9, 152
Witney, Robert, 120
Wolf-Ferrari, Ermano, *Jewels of the Madonna*, 15; *Susanna's Secret*, 15
Wurmser, André, 103

Zemánek, Vilém, 23
Zeyer, Julius, 26, 57, 58; *Old Tale*, 43
Zich, Otakar, *Malířský nápad*, 15
Žižka, Jan, 2
Zouhar, Zdenek, x
Zrzavý, Jan, 33, 51, 147
Zuna, Milan, 9, 10